U0129847

英语专业八级
人文知识与改错特训

金利 编著

西安交通大学出版社
XI'AN JIAOTONG UNIVERSITY PRESS

图书在版编目(CIP)数据

英语专业八级人文知识与改错特训 / 金利编著. —
西安：西安交通大学出版社，2013.7
ISBN 978-7-5605-5238-5

Ⅰ. ①英… Ⅱ. ①金… Ⅲ. ①大学英语水平考试—自
学参考资料 Ⅳ. ①H310.42

中国版本图书馆 CIP 数据核字（2013）第 092602 号

书　　名	英语专业八级人文知识与改错特训	
编　　著	金　利	
责任编辑	黄科丰	
封面设计	贾臻臻	
出版发行	西安交通大学出版社	
地　　址	西安市兴庆南路 10 号（邮编：710049）	
电　　话	(010)62605588　62605019（发行部）	
	(029)82668315（总编室）	
读者信箱	bj62605588@163.com	
印　　刷	北京鑫海达印刷有限公司	
字　　数	325 千	
开　　本	880mm×1230mm　1/32	
印　　张	9.5	
版　　次	2013 年 7 月第 1 版　2013 年 7 月第 1 次印刷	
书　　号	ISBN 978-7-5605-5238-5/H · 1493	
定　　价	18.80 元	

新东方图书策划委员会

前　言

2004年2月，教育部高等学校外语专业教学指导委员会英语考试大纲修订组根据英语专业学生的整体水平和社会发展对大学英语专业学生的要求，颁布了新的专业八级考试大纲和新的考试样题，并已于2005年正式实施。新大纲里增加了一种全新的客观题型：人文知识。该题型采用选择题形式，要求考生从每题的四个选项中选出一个最佳答案，共10题。其测试范围包括英语国家概况、英语文学知识以及英语语言学知识，旨在测试考生对英语国家人文知识的掌握情况。改错考题虽然一直在英语专业八级考试中出现，但在新的考试大纲中，该部分在试卷中的顺序有所变动，由第二部分调整为第四部分；同时改错文章的长度也有所变化，由200词左右调整为250词左右。题目数量、答题时间、分值和比重不变。

为了帮助考生尽快了解新大纲、熟悉新题型，编者根据多年来对英语专业八级考试的研究，精心策划、编写了本书。全书分两个部分，第一部分是人文知识，第二部分是改错。全书紧扣考试大纲，深入剖析专八人文知识考题和改错考题的特点、难点，以全新的视角、全新的理念带考生体验全新的专八备考模式：

真题自测知识探底，专八大纲全面解读

本书在两个部分的第一章都安排了真题自测，供考生进行自我测试。考生可以在了解考题的基础上，知晓自己的水平，以便更好、更有针对性地使用本书。真题点评部分，编者对题目和考点进行了细致的分析与解读，以使考生对真题有更加深刻的了解。

本书从大纲着眼，从测试要求、测试形式、测试目的和测试内容的角度对大纲进行了解读，以使考生更加清晰地了解考试大纲，让考生得以及早准备、从容备战。

考点分类逐个击破，知识技巧悉心点拨

本书按照考纲人文知识的测试范围将这一部分分成英语国家概况、英语文学知识和英语语言学知识三章分别讲解，对人文知识考点进行科学分类、系统归纳、逐个击破。在改错部分，本书分别从改错的文章题材、体裁、考点等方面进行了深入剖析，用

表格的形式展现，用大量的数据说明。充分列举真题实例加深考生对各考点的理解，在剖析每个考点后为考生提供了相关考点的知识链接，以夯实基础知识为主，以掌握应试技巧为辅。

历年真题即讲即练，全真模拟强化提高

本书在两个部分都为考生准备了历年真题专项训练和全真模拟集训。历年真题专项训练可以使考生在学习了相关知识、了解了相关技巧后，能够马上通过真题练习进行巩固和加深。在全真模拟集训部分，编者为考生精心编写了人文知识400题和改错40篇，这些模拟题难度适中，力求达到真题水准。所有真题和模拟试题都配有详实、准确的点评与解析，为考生逐一解疑释惑。

人文知识和改错在专八考试中所占比重不大——都是10%，但是这两部分内容仍然不可忽视。因此，利用有限的时间和精力，抓住人文知识和改错要点，争取这两个部分少丢分、甚至不丢分，才是确保专八考试顺利通过的王道。本书就是一本助力专八考试，能让考生在较短时间取得较好复习效果的一本书，希望考生能用好本书。

本书得以顺利完成，要特别感谢汇智博纳工作室的金利、蒋志华老师以及何静、张继龙、李岩岩、白敏、梅晓燕、杨金宝、李素素等老师。他们对英语教学和研究的热爱和投入才使得本书能在第一时间与考生见面。

最后预祝即将参加专八考试的各位考生马到成功！

编　者

目　录

第一部分　人文知识

第二部分 改错

第一部分 人文知识

PART III GENERAL KNOWLEDGE (10 MIN)

There are ten multiple-choice questions in this section. Mark the best answer to each question on ANSWER SHEET TWO.

31. The full official name of Australia is
    A. The Republic of Australia. B. The Union of Australia.
    C. The Federation of Australia. D. The Commonwealth of Australia.
32. Canada is well known for all the following EXCEPT
    A. its mineral resources. B. its heavy industries.
    C. its forest resources. D. its fertile and arable land.
33. In the United States community colleges offer
    A. two-year programmes. B. four-year programmes.
    C. postgraduate studies. D. B.A. or B.S. degrees.
34. In _____, referenda in Scotland and Wales set up a Scottish parliament and a Wales assembly.
    A. 2000 B. 1946
    C. 1990 D. 1997
35. Which of the following clusters of words is an example of alliteration?
    A. A weak seat. B. Knock and kick.
    C. Safe and sound. D. Coat and boat.
36. Who wrote *Mrs. Warren's Profession*?
    A. George Bernard Shaw. B. William Butler Yeats.
    C. John Galsworthy. D. T. S. Eliot.
37. *Sister Carrie* by Theodore Dreiser is a(n)
    A. autobiography. B. short story.
    C. poem. D. novel.
38. Which of the following italicized parts is an inflectional morpheme?
    A. *Un*lock. B. Govern*ment*.
    C. Go*es*. D. *Off*-stage.

39. _____ is a language phenomenon in which words sound like what they refer to.

    A. Collocation   B. Onomatopoeia

    C. Denotation   D. Assimilation

40. The sentence "Close your book and listen to me carefully!" performs a(n) _____ function.

    A. interrogative   B. informative

    C. performative   D. directive

答案速查

31~35	DBADC	36~40	ADCBD

① 整体介绍

本部分共设有10题。前4题考查的是英语国家概况，中间3题考查的是英美文学知识，最后3题考查的是英语语言学知识。

➥ 考查英语国家概况的4题中，第31题考查澳大利亚的全称，第32题考查加拿大的资源和产业，第33题考查美国的社区大学，第34题考查苏格兰和威尔士在哪一年进行人民投票选举成立地方议会。

➥ 考查英美文学知识的3题中，第35题考查文学概念的实例分析之头韵法，第36题考查爱尔兰剧作家乔治·萧伯纳(George Bernard Shaw)的文学作品，第37题考查美国现代小说的先驱和代表作家西奥多·德莱塞(Theodore Dreiser)创作的第一部长篇小说《嘉莉妹妹》(Sister Carrie)。

➥ 考查英语语言学知识的3题中，第38题考查语言学概念的实例分析之inflectional morpheme(曲折语素)，第39题考查拟声法(onomatopoeia)这一语言学概念，最后一题考查语言学概念的实例分析之语用学当中语言的基本功能。

② 试题点评

31. [答案]D [考点]澳大利亚政治。

[精析]澳大利亚的全称是澳大利亚联邦(The Commonwealth of Australia)。澳大利亚名义上的国家元首是英王或者英女王，英王或女王任命总督为其代表，总督实际上不干预政府的运作。澳大利亚政府为联邦制，包含六个州及两个领地(北领地和首都领地)，各州设有州长，负责州内事务。澳大利亚政府由众议院多数党或党派联盟组成，每届政府任期三年。内阁是政府的最高决策机关。国家的最高行政领导人是总理。

32. [答案]B [考点]加拿大的资源和产业。

[精析]加拿大是世界上的第三大产矿国，故排除A；加拿大的森林覆盖率为全国总面积的44%，居世界第二，故其拥有丰富的森林资源，排除C；加拿大农业经济非常发达，肥沃的大平原是世界上最重要的小麦和油菜产地，使得加拿大成为世界上最大的农产品出口国之一，故排除D。和许多第一世界的国家一样，加拿大经济以服务业为主，并不注重发展重工业，故选B。

33. [答案]A [考点]美国教育。

[精析]美国的社区大学(community colleges)指的是在美国的州或市用州民或市民

的税金来运营的两年制短期大学，为希望去插读四年制的大学或职业培训课程后直接就业的学生提供教育。美国社区大学是美国教育体系的重要组成部分，目前约有1200多所。在美国，从两年制大学转入四年制大学时，只要学生的学分足够（一般为90学分），就可以申请进入四年制大学继续读大三、大四，最后毕业。学生的GPA分数较高时，就可以申请全美排名靠前的四年制大学。

34. [答案]**D** [考点]英国政治。

[精析]英国是由英格兰、苏格兰、威尔士和北爱尔兰组成的联合王国，主体是英格兰。英格兰分为43个郡，苏格兰下设32个区(包括3个特别管辖区)，威尔士下设22个区，北爱尔兰下设26个区。自从苏格兰和威尔士1997年进行公民投票选举成立地方议会，下放了管理权以来，苏格兰、威尔士议会及其行政机构全面负责地方事务，中央政府仍控制外交、国防、总体经济和货币政策、就业政策以及社会保障。referenda意为"公民投票"，Scottish parliament意为"苏格兰议会"，Wales assembly意为"威尔士国民议会"。故选D。

35. [答案]**C** [考点]文学概念的实例分析。

[精析]头韵法(alliteration)是指英语中相连的两个或两个以上的单词以相同的辅音或语音开头的修辞方法。这一修辞方法主要是为了增强语言的节奏感和美感。不发音的字母不构成头韵。如选项B，看上去两个开头字母"k"是一样的，但是knock的开头字母"k"不发音，所以不能和kick形成头韵修辞法。这一点需要大家格外注意。本题答案为C。

36. [答案]**A** [考点]文学作家及作品。

[精析]《华伦夫人的职业》(*Mrs. Warren's Profession*)是爱尔兰剧作家乔治·萧伯纳(George Bernard Shaw)的作品，他的其他作品还有《圣女贞德》(*Saint Joan*)和《卖花女》(*Pygmalion*)。威廉·巴特勒·叶芝(William Butler Yeats)是爱尔兰诗人、剧作家。其代表有《塔楼》(*The Tower*)、《盘旋的楼梯》(*The Winding Stair and Other Poems*)和《驶向拜占庭》(*Sailing to Byzantium*)。约翰·高尔斯华绥(John Galsworthy)是英国小说家、剧作家，代表作是长篇小说三部曲《福尔赛世家》(*The Forsyte Saga*)，其中最著名的是第一部《有产业者》(*The Man of Property*)。T. S. 艾略特(Thomas Stearns Eliot)是一位诗人、剧作家，出生于美国，但39岁时加入英国国籍。代表作是长诗《荒原》(*The Waste Land*)和剧本《大教堂谋杀案》(*Murder in the Cathedral*)。

37. [答案]**D** [考点]文学作家的文学作品。

[精析]西奥多·德莱塞(Theodore Dreiser)，美国现代小说的先驱和代表作家。《嘉莉妹妹》(*Sister Carrie*)是德莱塞创作的第一部长篇小说，也是美国文学史上最著

5

名的作品之一。小说讲述了农村姑娘嘉莉来到大城市芝加哥寻找幸福，为摆脱贫困，出卖自己的贞操，先后与推销员和酒店经理同居，后又凭美貌与歌喉成为歌星的故事。

38. ［答案］C ［考点］语言学概念的实例分析。

［精析］inflectional morpheme（曲折语素）在英语中共有八个，分别是：

（1）-'s（possessive）名词所有格，如my father's dog。

（2）-s（plural）名词复数，如two dogs。

（3）-ing（present participle）动词现在分词，如 reading a book。

（4）-s（third person present singular）动词第三人称单数，如goes to school。

（5）-ed（past tense）过去式，如 washed。

（6）-en（past participle）过去分词，如 taken, written。

（7）-er（comparative）比较级，如faster。

（8）-est（superlative）最高级，如fastest。

A项中的un属于前缀，B项中的ment属于后缀，D项中的off属于合成词的一部分，故选C。

39. ［答案］B ［考点］语言学概念。

［精析］拟声法（onomatopoeia）是英语语言学分支——英语修辞学中的一个重要修辞手法，和我们汉语的拟声词有相似之处。拟声法是指用词语模拟客观事物的声音，以增强讲话或文字的实际音感，比如ding-dong（叮咚）、tick（滴答）、howl（嚎叫）等等。根据题干"听起来就像所要讲的意思"，答案应选B。在语言学中，A项 collocation意为"搭配"，C项denotation意为"指示，指代"，D项assimilation意为"语音同化"。

40. ［答案］D ［考点］语言学概念的实例分析。

［精析］本题考查的是语用学当中语言的基本功能。A项interrogative是询问功能，通常这类句子都是疑问句，如：How old are you? B项informative是信息功能，指讲述一件事情或者提供某种信息。C项performative是施为功能，比如法官宣判、会议宣布开始。D项directive是指示功能，指说话人让听者去做某事。大部分的祈使句都具有这个功能，故选D。此外，语言还有其他三种功能：phatic（寒暄功能）、expressive（表达功能）和evocative/emotive（感情功能）。

第三节 TEM-8考试大纲对人文知识的要求

1 测试要求

(a) 能基本了解主要英语国家的地理、历史、现状、文化、传统等。
(b) 能初步具备英语文学知识。
(c) 能初步具备英语语言学知识。
(d) 考试时间10分钟。

2 测试形式

本部分采用选择题形式，要求学生从每题的四个选项中选出一个最佳答案。共10题。题干有空缺型和问答型两种。

3 测试目的

人文知识部分测试学生对主要英语国家社会与文化、英语文学与英语语言学基本知识的掌握程度。

4 测试内容

考查内容主要包括：
(a) 主要英语国家社会与文化知识。
(b) 英语文学知识。
(c) 英语语言学知识。

英语专业八级人文知识测试内容

	2013	2012	2011	2010	2009	2008	2007	2006	2005	2004
英语国家概况	澳大利亚政治	新西兰文化	英国地理	英国政治	新西兰政治	加拿大地理	英国历史	美国历史	加拿大地理	英国地理
	加拿大资源	英国政治	澳大利亚历史	加拿大历史	英国地理	美国政治	加拿大政治	新西兰地理	美国政治	美国文化
	美国教育	美国文化	加拿大文化	澳大利亚历史	美国历史	美国文化	美国历史	澳大利亚地理	美国地理	澳大利亚地理
	英国政治	加拿大地理	美国历史	英国历史	澳大利亚地理	新西兰政治	澳大利亚历史	英国政治	英国政治	美国文化

	2013	2012	2011	2010	2009	2008	2007	2006	2005	2004
英语文学知识	文学概念	作家作品	作家贡献	作家贡献	作家作品	作家作品	作家作品	作家年代	作家作品	作家流派
	作家作品	作家作品	文学概念	作家作品	作家贡献	作家作品	作家流派	作家作品	作家流派	作家作品
	作家作品	文学概念	作家作品	文学概念	作家作品	作家年代	作家作品	文学概念	作家流派	作家作品
英语语言学知识	实例分析	实例分析	基本概念	基本概念	基本概念	基本知识	基本概念	概念区分	基本概念	概念区分
	基本概念	实例分析	实例分析	实例分析	基本概念	实例分析	基本概念	实例分析	基本知识	实例分析
	实例分析	基本概念	基本概念	实例分析	实例分析	实例分析	实例分析	语言学家代表理论	语言学家代表理论	实例分析

　　总结：由上表可以看出，英语国家概况主要考查英国、美国、加拿大、澳大利亚和新西兰等国家的地理、历史、政治和文化现状；在每年的4个国家概况考题中，通常会有一道考查英国概况，一道考查美国概况，其他两道是对加拿大、澳大利亚和新西兰概况的交替考查，考生在复习英语国家概况时要有所侧重。

　　文学知识部分考查最多的是英美国家的作家作品，每年考题中都至少会出现一道，同时，作家所属的流派、在文学方面的贡献、生平及其生活的年代也会交替出现，2006年、2010年、2012年和2013年真题中还考查了基本的文学概念。

　　语言学知识部分主要考查的是语言学的基本概念和语言学实例分析，几乎每年都会分别考查一道，同时还考查语言学基本概念区分和语言学家及其代表理论等语言学基本知识。

第一节 美国概况

美国全称"美利坚合众国"，简称"美国"，英文缩写为U.S.或U.S.A.（可以有缩写符，也可以没有）。美国的绰号是"山姆大叔"。美国本土位于北美洲中央地带，东濒大西洋，西临太平洋，北靠加拿大，南接墨西哥。美国人口超3亿，仅次于中国和印度，居世界第三位。外来移民是美国人口增长的重要因素之一，美国也因民族众多而被称为"大熔炉"（the Great Melting Pot）。美国的国旗通常被称为"星条旗"，国旗上有50颗星，代表美国的50个州；国徽主体为一只胸前带有盾形图案的美国国鸟白头鹰；国歌为《星条旗永不落》（*The Star-Spangled Banner*）。美国首都为华盛顿哥伦比亚特区（Washington D. C.)，是为纪念美国开国元勋乔治·华盛顿和发现美洲新大陆的哥伦布而命名的，它在行政上由联邦政府直辖，不隶属于任何州。

1 地理概况

There are 50 states in the US, including Alaska located on the northwest of Canada and Hawaii in the central pacific. Of all states in America, Alaska is the largest in area and Rhode Island the smallest. But on the mainland, Texas is the largest state of the country. Except Alaska and Hawaii, there are 6 major geographical regions on the mainland of the US.

（1）New England 新英格兰地区

1）States and Capitals 州和首府

Geographical Regions	States Included	Capitals
New England 新英格兰地区	Maine（缅因州）	Augusta（奥古斯塔）
	New Hampshire（新罕布什尔州）	Concord（康科德）
	Vermont（佛蒙特州）	Montpelier（蒙彼利埃）
	Massachusetts（马萨诸塞州）	Boston（波士顿）
	Rhode Island（罗德岛州）	Providence（普罗维登斯）
	Connecticut（康涅狄格州）	Hartford（哈特福德）

2）Key Points 重点总结

① **New England** is the birthplace of America and the chief center of the American War of Independence.

9

② **Harvard** and **Massachusetts Institute of Technology** are located in Boston.

③ **Boston** is also the birthplace of Transcendentalism.

④ **New Englanders** were originally called Yankees.

（2）The Middle Atlantic States 大西洋沿岸中部地区

1）States and Capitals 州和首府

Geographical Regions	States Included	Capitals
The Middle Atlantic States 大西洋沿岸中部地区	New York（纽约州）	Albany（奥尔巴尼）
	Pennsylvania（宾夕法尼亚州）	Harrisburg（哈里斯堡）
	New Jersey（新泽西州）	Trenton（特伦顿）
	Delaware（特拉华州）	Dover（多佛）
	Maryland（马里兰州）	Annapolis（安纳波利斯）
	West Virginia（西弗吉尼亚州）	Charleston（查尔斯顿）

2）Key Points 重点总结

① **Washington D.C.:** It is the capital city of the US. The White House（白宫）and the Capitol（美国国会大厦）are located here.

② **New York:** It is the biggest city of the State of New York and of the US. It is also a famous cosmopolitan city in the world and the Headquarters of the United Nations （联合国总部）is located here.

Five boroughs（行政区）**:** Manhattan（曼哈顿区）, Brooklyn（布鲁克林区）, Queens（皇后区）, the Bronx（布朗克斯区）and Staten Island（斯塔滕岛）.

Famous buildings: Empire State Building（帝国大厦）, Statue of Liberty（自由女神像）.

Famous universities: Columbia University（哥伦比亚大学）and Cornell University（康奈尔大学）are located here.

③ **Gettysburg**（葛底斯堡）**:** It is the place where Abraham Lincoln delivered his famous speech *The Address at Gettysburg*（《葛底斯堡演说》）in Pennsylvania.

④ **Philadelphia**（费城）**:** It is in the Independence Hall（独立大厅）of Philadelphia, Pennsylvania that the *Declaration of Independence*（《独立宣言》）is approved.

（3）The Midwest 中西部地区

1）States and Capitals 州和首府

Geographical Regions	States Included	Capitals
The Midwest 中西部地区	Ohio（俄亥俄州）	Columbus（哥伦布）
	Indiana（印第安纳州）	Indianapolis（印第安纳波利斯）
	Michigan（密歇根州）	Lansing（兰辛）
	Illinois（伊利诺伊州）	Springfield（斯普林菲尔德）
	Wisconsin（威斯康星州）	Madison（麦迪逊）
	Missouri（密苏里州）	Jefferson City（杰斐逊城）
	Iowa（爱荷华州）	Des Moines（得梅因）
	Minnesota（明尼苏达州）	St. Paul（圣保罗）
	Kansas（堪萨斯州）	Topeka（托皮卡）
	Nebraska（内布拉斯加州）	Lincoln（林肯）
	North Dakota（北达科他州）	Bismarck（俾斯麦）
	South Dakota（南达科他州）	Pierre（皮尔）

2）Key Points 重点总结

① The Great Lakes（五大湖）and the Great Plains（中部大平原）are located here.

The Great Lakes: Lake Superior（苏必利尔湖）(the largest fresh water lake in the world), Lake Michigan（密歇根湖）(the only one entirely in the US), Lake Huron（休伦湖）, Lake Erie（伊利湖）and Lake Ontario（安大略湖）.

② **The Midwest** is America's most important agricultural area.

③ **Chicago**, which is in Illinois, is the country's leading center of heavy industry, and it is the biggest industrial center in the Great Lakes district and the world's best collections of modern architecture.

④ **Detroit**, which is the largest city in Michigan, is the automobile capital of the world.

⑤ **The Mississippi River** is also called "Father of Waters"（江河之父）or "Old Man River"（老人河）. The world's great continental river is crossing this area. It is the fourth longest river in the world.

⑥ **The Ohio River**（俄亥俄河）, called the American Ruhr（鲁尔河）, is also located in this region.

（4）The South 南部地区

1）States and Capitals 州和首府

Geographical Regions	States Included	Capitals
The South 南部地区	Virginia（弗吉尼亚州）	Richmond（里士满）
	Kentucky（肯塔基州）	Frankfort（法兰克福）
	North Carolina（北卡罗来纳州）	Raleigh（纳罗利）
	South Carolina（南卡罗来纳州）	Columbia（哥伦比亚）
	Georgia（佐治亚州）	Atlanta（亚特兰大）
	Florida（佛罗里达州）	Tallahassee（塔拉哈西）
	Alabama（亚拉巴马州）	Montgomery（蒙哥马利）
	Mississippi（密西西比州）	Jackson（杰克逊）
	Tennessee（田纳西州）	Nashville（纳什维尔）
	Arkansas（阿肯色州）	Little Rock（小石城）
	Louisiana（路易斯安那州）	Baton Rouge（巴吞鲁日）
	Texas（得克萨斯州）	Austin（奥斯汀）
	Oklahoma（俄克拉何马州）	Oklahoma City（俄克拉何马城）

2）Key Points 重点总结

① **The South** is rich in mineral resources and contains 90% of the American textile industry.

② **Texas** is the largest state on the mainland, and the second largest state of the US.

③ **Huston**, in the southeast of Texas, is the biggest industrial center of oil.

④ **The Appalachian Mountains**（阿巴拉契亚山脉）is crossing this region.

（5）The American West 美国西部

1）States and Capitals 州和首府

Geographical Regions	States Included	Capitals
The American West 美国西部	Montana（蒙大拿州）	Helena（海伦娜）
	Wyoming（怀俄明州）	Cheyenne（夏延）
	Colorado（科罗拉多州）	Denver（丹佛）
	New Mexico（新墨西哥州）	Santa Fe（圣菲）
	Arizona（亚利桑那州）	Phoenix（菲尼克斯）
	Utah（犹他州）	Salt Lake City（盐湖城）
	Nevada（内华达州）	Carson City（卡森城）
	Idaho（爱达荷州）	Boise（博伊西）

2）Key Points 重点总结

① **The Rockies** are crossing the region, and the Rocky Mountains is the backbone of the North America Continent and is known as the Continental Divide（大陆分水岭）.

② **Yellow Stone National Park**（黄石国家公园）is in Wyoming and the Grand Canyon （大峡谷）in Arizona.

③ **Denver, Phoenix** and **Salt Lake City** are respectively the biggest city of their states, and Las Vegas（拉斯维加斯）is the biggest city of the State of Nevada.

④ **The Rio Grand River**（格兰德河）forms a natural boundary between Mexico and the United States.

（6）The Pacific Coast and the New States 太平洋沿岸地区和新州

1）States and Capitals 州和首府

Geographical Regions	States Included	Capitals
The Pacific Coast and the New States 太平洋沿岸地区和新州	California（加利福尼亚州）	Sacramento（萨克拉门托）
	Washington（华盛顿州）	Olympia（奥林匹亚）
	Oregon（俄勒冈州）	Salem（塞勒姆）
	Alaska（阿拉斯加州）	Juneau（朱诺）
	Hawaii（夏威夷州）	Honolulu（火奴鲁鲁）

2）Key Points 重点总结

① **State of California** is called "The Golden State" and has the biggest population, with Los Angeles as its biggest city, which is also the second biggest city of the country, next only to New York. Besides, Los Angeles is also the major center of film and TV production. Universal Studios Hollywood（好莱坞环球影城）and Disneyland（迪斯尼乐园）are located here.

San Francisco is surrounded on three sides by water and the second largest harbor next to Los Angeles in the Pacific Coast.

② **State of Washington** is named after President George Washington, with Seattle （西雅图）as its biggest city.

③ **State of Alaska**, the biggest state in the US, is separated from Russia's Siberia（西伯利亚）in the west by the Bering Strait（白令海峡）, and Eskimos（爱斯基摩人）live here.

④ **Hawaii** is in the Pacific Ocean, and Mauna Loa（莫纳罗亚山）, the world's largest active volcano, is located here.

⑤ **The Colorado River**（科罗拉多河）and the Columbia River（哥伦比亚河）are in the west of the US.

2 人口概况

The USA is the third most populous country in the world after China and India and the most populous states are California, Texas, New York, Florida and Illinois. The first Americans were Indians.

Immigration accounts for a major source of population growth. The first immigrants in the American history came from England and the Netherlands.

3 历史概况

Important Events	Key Points
Discovery of the New World 发现新大陆(1492)	• In 1492, by Christopher Columbus.
The Establishment of English Colonies 殖民地建立时期 (1607~1733)	• Jamestown(詹姆斯敦), Virginia: Founded in 1607, was the first permanent English colony established in America. • 1607~1733, thirteen colonies along the Atlantic coast were established by Britain.
The War of Independence 独立战争时期 (1774~1783)	• On September 5, 1774, the First Continental Congress was convened in Philadelphia. • On April 19, 1775, the battles of Lexington (列克星敦) and Concord (康科德) near Boston marked the beginning of the American War of Independence. • On May 10, 1775, the Second Continental Congress was convened in Philadelphia and the Continental Army led by George Washington was founded. • 1776, the *Declaration of Independence* (《独立宣言》) was drafted by Thomas Jefferson (托马斯·杰斐逊). • Defeating the British at Saratoga, the turning point of the war. • 1783, the *Treaty of Paris* (《巴黎条约》), in which Britain recognized the independence of the USA. • 1789, the Federal Government, George Washington as the first president.

Important Events	Key Points
The Civil War 南北战争时期 （1861~1865）	• In 1861, the American Civil War broke out. • The Union Army defeated the Confederate Army at Gettysburg（葛底斯堡）, which was the turning point of the war. • Confederate resistance ended after Lee（李将军）surrendered to Grant（格兰特）at Appomattox Court House（阿波麦托克斯县府）on April 9, 1865.
Economic Development 经济快速发展时期 （1877~1900）	• Gilded Age（镀金时代）
The Great Depression 经济大萧条时期 （1929~1933）	• Franklin D. Roosevelt's New Deal helped get America out of the Depression.
World War II 二战时期 （1941~1945）	• December 1941, the Japanese bombing of Pearl Harbor. • Teheran Conference（德黑兰会议） • The end of the Depression founded the basis for postwar prosperity.
The Civil Rights Movement 民权运动	• On December 1, 1955, Rosa Parks（罗莎·帕克斯）, a black woman in Alabama, refused to give her seat to a white passenger and she was arrested, which caused the Montgomery Bus Boycott（蒙哥马利公共汽车抵制行动）. • Martin Luther King Jr. was the national leader of the Civil Rights Movement.
The Vietnam War 越南战争时期 （1961~1975）	• There was serious disagreement within the ruling circle. • The image of the United States was discredited.
The Watergate Scandal 水门事件 （1972~1974）	• President Richard Nixon was involved in the Watergate Scandal and he was the first president who resigned during presidency because of scandal in American history.

（1）*The Constitution of the United States* and *Bill of Rights*《美国宪法》和《人权法案》

The Constitution of the United States 《美国宪法》	• The oldest written constitution in the world, drafted in 1787 and put into effect in 1789. • The basic instrument of American government and the supreme law of the land. • An amendment to the Constitution can be initiated by a two-thirds' vote in each house of the Congress. • The Constitution has 7 articles and 27 amendments.
Bill of Rights 《人权法案》	• Refers to the first ten amendments to the Constitution, put forward by James Madison（詹姆斯·麦迪逊）in 1791.

（2）**The Federal System 联邦制**

The Constitution（《美国宪法》）sets up a strong national government, which has two layers of rule. There is central or federal government for the nation and there are also state and local governments. Each layer of government has separate and distinct powers laid down in the Constitution. And the government is divided into three branches: the legislative branch（立法）, the executive branch（行政）and the judicial branch（司法）.

Congress 国会	• In the United States, the power to make laws is given to Congress, which represents the legislative branch of government. • Consists of two houses: the Senate and the House of Representatives. • The Senate is composed of 100 members, 2 from each state. The senatorial term is 6 years, and every 2 years one-third of the Senate stands for re-election. • The membership of the House of Representatives is based on the population of each state and the term is 2 years.
The President 总统	• Represents the executive branch to enforce the law. • The term of the President is 4 years. • The President is the military's commander-in-chief. • President has the power to negotiate foreign treaties, nominate government officials, ambassadors and judges, and grant pardons to national offenders.

The Supreme Court 最高法院	• The Supreme Court is the highest court in the United States and the only judicial branch which explains the Constitution. • The Court consists of a chief justice and eight associate justices who are nominated by the President and confirmed by the Senate. Once appointed, justices have life tenure unless they are removed after impeachment.
Checks and Balances 三权分立	• Each branch of the government has part of the power, and can check the actions of the other branches. Eg: Congress may pass a law, but the President can veto it. The Congress may pass the law again by a two-thirds' vote and the President cannot veto it. But the law may still be cancelled if the Supreme Court decides it goes against the Constitution.

（3）**Political Parties 政党**

Democratic Party 民主党	• Symbol: a donkey（the old one） （驴子作为民主党的党徽已经使用了一个多世纪，现在民主党的党徽换成一个圆圈，中间是一个字母"D"的标志。） • Grew out of "anti-Federalists" and was formally founded in 1828. • Insists on greater federal involvement in the nation's economic issues and less state's rights.
Republic Party 共和党	• Symbol: an elephant • Was founded in 1854. • Doesn't favor federal involvement in the nation's economy and grants more power to the state.

5 文化概况

Education 教育	• Elementary and secondary education covers 12 years for ages 6 through 18 and is often with a pattern of graded schools. • Higher education, which began with the founding of Harvard College in 1636, has three principal functions: teaching, research and public service. • Some well-known universities: Harvard University （哈佛大学）, the most famous and the oldest private university in Massachusetts. Yale University（耶鲁大学）in Connecticut.

Education 教育	Princeton University（普林斯顿大学）in New Jersey. Columbia University（哥伦比亚大学）in the City of New York, belongs to Ivy League（常青藤盟校）. Massachusetts Institute of Technology (MIT)（麻省理工学院）. Stanford University（斯坦福大学）and University of California, Berkeley（加州大学伯克利分校）in California.
Architecture and Music 建筑与音乐	• The skyscraper was the first unique American contribution to architecture; Sears Tower （西尔斯大厦）in Chicago once was the tallest building of the world, and was completed in 1974. • Jazz is considered the US's unique contribution to music.
Sports 体育	• Baseball（棒球）: the most popular sports in America, and it was originated from cricket in Britain and developed in America; the first baseball game was held in 1839 in New York State. • Basketball（篮球）: it was originated in the US.
Mass Media 大众传媒	• Newspapers: *The Wall Street Journal*（《华尔街日报》）, *U.S.A. Today*（《今日美国》）, *The New York Times*（《纽约时报》）, *Los Angeles Times*（《洛杉矶时报》）, *Washington Post*（《华盛顿邮报》） • Magazines: *Reader's Digest*（《读者文摘》）, *TV Guide*（《电视指南》）, *National Geographic*（《国家地理》）, *Time*（《时代》） • News and Cable Networks: CBS（the Columbia Broadcasting System）, NBS（the National Broadcasting System）, ABC（the American Broadcasting Company）, PBS （the Public Broadcasting Service）, CNN（Cable News Network）
Festivals 节日	• Easter（复活节）: one day between 22nd, March and 25th, April. • Memorial Day（阵亡将士纪念日）: the last Monday in May. • Independence Day（独立纪念日）: 4th, July. • Halloween（万圣节）: 31st, October. • Veterans Day（美国老兵纪念日）: the second Monday of November. • Thanksgiving Day（感恩节）: the last Thursday of November. • Christmas（圣诞节）: 25th, December.

第二节 英国概况

英国的全称是"大不列颠及北爱尔兰联合王国"（The United Kingdom of Great Britain and Northern Ireland）。其中"大不列颠"指的是英格兰（England）、苏格兰（Scotland）和威尔士（Wales）。英国位于欧洲大陆西北面，英国本土位于大不列颠群岛，被北海、英吉利海峡、凯尔特海、爱尔兰海和大西洋包围。英国的国旗为"米字旗"，国徽即"英王徽"。英国的首都为伦敦（London），位于英格兰东南部的平原上，是欧洲最大和最具国际特色的城市。

1 地理概况

（1）Geographical Regions 地理分区

The UK is made up of the Great Britain and Northern Ireland, and the Great Britain is divided into three political divisions: England, Scotland and Wales.

Geographical Regions	Key Points
England 英格兰	• London is its capital city and also the capital of the UK. London is situated on the north bank of the River Thames （泰晤士河）, and some important scenery spots in London are St. Paul's Cathedral（圣保罗大教堂）, Big Ben（大本钟）, Whitehall（白厅）, National Gallery（国家艺术画廊）, Westminster Abbey（威斯敏斯特教堂）, Buckingham Palace （白金汉宫）, the Tower of London（伦敦塔）, and the London Eye（伦敦眼）. • The largest, southern part of Great Britain, with Wales to its west and Scotland to its north. • The English are Anglo-Saxons（盎格鲁-撒克逊人）.
Scotland 苏格兰	• Edinburgh is its capital city. • Three natural zones: the highlands in the north（北部高地）, the central lowlands（中部低地）(containing most of the industry and population）, and the southern uplands（南部高地）. • Gaelic language is still heard in the Highlands and the Western Isles. • The Scots are mainly Celts（凯尔特人）.

Geographical Regions	Key Points
Wales 威尔士	• Cardiff（加的夫）is its capital city. • Most of it is mountainous. • The Welsh are Celts.
Northern Ireland 北爱尔兰	• Belfast（贝尔法斯特）is its capital city. • The Irish are Celts.

（2）**Mountains, Rivers and Lakes** 山川、河流、湖泊

Mountains 山川	• The Pennines（奔宁山脉）are the principal mountain chain in England. • Ben Nevis（本尼维斯山）, located in Scotland, is the highest mountain in the Great Britain.
Rivers 河流	• The longest river in Britain is the Severn River（塞文河）. • The most important and second largest river is Thames River. • River Clyde（克莱德河）is the most important river in Scotland.
Lakes 湖泊	• The Lough Neagh（内伊湖）in Northern Ireland is the largest lake in Britain.

2 历史概况

Important Events	Key Points
Early Settlers 早期居民	• The first known settlers of Britain were the Iberians（伊比利亚人）. • The Celts began to arrive in 700 BC after the Iberians and until the Romans.
Roman Occupation 罗马统治时期	• 1st to 5th century. • Julius Caesar（凯撒大帝）came for the first time. • In 43 AD, the Emperor Claudius（克劳迪亚斯大帝）invaded Britain successfully. • Influence on Britain: built many towns, roads, temples and buildings and also brought the new religion, Christianity, to Britain. But had no impact on the language or culture of ordinary Britain people.

Important Events	Key Points
The Anglo-Saxons 盎格鲁-撒克逊人	• In the mid-5th century. • Invasion of Jutes（朱特人）, Saxons（撒克逊人）and Angles（盎格鲁人）. • Contribution: laid the foundation of English state.
The Norman Conquest 诺曼征服	• In 1066, William the Conqueror（征服者威廉）landed in England and built the Norman Empire, and thus the feudal system. • The Norman Conquest of 1066 is the best-known event in English history. • Feudal system（封建制度）was completely established in English.
The Great Charter 《大宪章》	• In 1215, also called *Magna Carta*. • It was a statement of feudal and legal relationship between the crown and the barons, a guarantee of the freedom of the church and a limitation of the power of the king.
The Beginning of Parliament 议会的雏形	• Simon de Montfort（西蒙·德·蒙特福德）summoned in 1265 the great council, the earliest prototype of current British parliament, to meet at Westminster which developed later into the House of Lords（上议院）and the House of Commons（下议院）known as a parliament.
The English Renaissance 英国文艺复兴时期	• Renaissance was the transitional period between the Middle Ages and modern times, covering the years 1300s~1600s. • The Renaissance began in Italy. • The English Renaissance was largely literary, and achieved its finest expression in the so-called Elizabethan drama, and its first exponents（倡导者）were Christopher Marlowe（克里斯托弗·马洛）, Ben Jonson（本·琼森）, and William Shakespeare（威廉·莎士比亚）.
The Industrial Revolution 工业革命时期	• As a result of the industrial revolution, Britain was by 1830 the "workshop of the world".
Colonial Expansion 殖民扩张时期	• English colonial expansion began with the colonization of Newfoundland（纽芬兰）in 1583. By 1900 Britain had built up a big empire, "on which the sun never sets".
Postwar Britain 战后的英国	• One of the most far-reaching consequences of World War II was that it hastened the end of Britain's empire.

21

(1) Constitution 宪法

Britain has no single document of constitution. British constitution is made up of statute law, common law and conventions.

(2) Constitutional Monarchy 君主立宪制

The UK is a constitutional monarchy, and the head of state is a king or a queen. It is governed, in the name of the Sovereign by his or her Majesty's government. Parliament has the authority to make law, and the judiciary determines common law and interprets statutes.

King or Queen 国王或女王	• The king or queen is the head of state（国家元首）. Queen Elizabeth II is the current Queen and Head of the Commonwealth. • The queen or king is only the symbol of the whole nation.
Parliament 议会	• Consists of the Sovereign（君主）, the House of Lords（上议院）and the House of Commons（下议院）. • The House of Lords acts as a non-elected House of revision, complementing but not rivaling the elected House. • The House of Commons consists of 651 members and has the ultimate authority to make law, and with a maximum duration of 5 years.
The Cabinet and Ministry 内阁和内阁部长	• Her Majesty's Government is the body of ministers responsible for the conduct of national affairs. • Cabinet is presided over by the Prime Minister（首相）and Cabinet members hold meetings under the chairmanship of the Prime Minister for a few hours each week to decide Government policies on major issues. • Ministers are responsible collectively to Parliament for all Cabinet decisions.
Justice and Law 司法	• There is no single legal system in the Britain. The sources of laws include: statutes, common laws, equity law and European Community Law（欧共体法）.

(3) Political Parties 政党

There are mainly two parties in the UK: the Conservative Party(保守党) and the Labour Party（工党）. The leader of the majority party, which wins most seats at a General Election （大选）, is appointed Prime Minister（首相）and the party which wins the second largest number of seats becomes the Official Opposition（官方反对党）to help formulate policy, criticize the Government and debate with the government.

④ 文化概况

Education 教育	• Compulsory education extends from 5 to 16 years old. • 2 most famous universities: University of Oxford and University of Cambridge. • University of Oxford was founded in 1167 in the city of London and University of Cambridge was founded in 1209 in the city of Cambridge.
Religion 宗教	• Established churches: the Church of England and the Church of Scotland. • Unestablished churches: the Anglican Churches, the Free Churches and the Roman Catholic Church.
Mass Media 大众传媒	• Broadcasting: the British Broadcasting Corporation（BBC）. • Television: BBC Television Service. • Newspapers: Daily papers: *Daily Express*（《每日快报》）, *Daily Mail*（《每日邮报》）, *Daily Mirror*（《每日镜报》）, *Daily Star*（《每日星报》）, *Financial Times*（《金融时报》）, *The Guardian*（《卫报》）, *The Times*（《泰晤士报》）. Sunday papers（星期日报）: *The Observer*（《观察家报》）（the world's first Sunday newspaper）. • News agency（通讯社）: Reuters（路透社）.
Sports 体育	• Football: the most popular sports in England and in Europe. • Cricket: the most typical English sports; has existed since the 16th century. • Tennis: the modern game originated in England in the 19th century. • Golf: the home of golf is Scotland and it has been played since the 17th century. And the oldest golf club in the world, the Honourable Company（爱丁堡高尔夫球会员荣誉公司）, is located in Scotland.

有关加拿大、澳大利亚、新西兰和爱尔兰四国的概况，在考试中主要涉及的是地理、历史和政治方面的知识，因此本部分只针对这4个国家的地理、历史和政治3方面的重要考点进行介绍。

1 地理概况

（1）Canada 加拿大

Canada is the world's second largest country and it covers 2/5 of the North American continent. Most areas of Canada are sparsely-populated and 60% of its population is concentrated between Quebec City(魁北克市) and the western end of Lake Ontario(安大略湖). The origins of most Canadians are British and French. And the native people, the Eskimos or Inuit and Indians account for only 1.5%. *O Canada*(《哦，加拿大！》) is Canadian national anthem. Totally, Canada consists of 10 provinces and 2 territories, and is divided into 6 geographical regions.

Geographical Regions	Key Points
Atlantic Provinces **大西洋省**	• The Grand Banks（大浅滩）is one of the world's greatest fishing grounds.
St. Lawrence—Great Lakes Provinces **圣劳伦斯—五大湖区**	• The most developed part of Canada, including the St. Lawrence lowlands, and the southern part of Quebec(魁北克省) and Ontario（安大略省）. • Quebec, with a strong French culture, is the largest province in Canada and the country's second largest city—Montreal（蒙特利尔）is located here. • Ottawa（渥太华）is the capital city of Canada and Toronto（多伦多）is the largest city of Canada. They are both in the province of Ontario. • The St. Lawrence River（圣劳伦斯河）is the most important river in Canada.

Geographical Regions	Key Points
the Canadian Shield 加拿大地盾	• It's a region of hills, covering half of Canada. • Mackenzie（马更些河）, the longest river of Canada, Great Bear Lake（大熊湖）, the largest lake of Canada and Great Slave Lake（大奴湖）, the deepest lake of Canada are located in this area.
the Prairie Provinces 大平原地区	• Famous for wheat production.
the Province of British Columbia 不列颠哥伦比亚省	• Vancouver（温哥华）is the largest city in the area and also the third largest city in the country.
Northern Provinces 北部省份	• This area is bare and thinly settled.

（2）Australia 澳大利亚

Australia is the world's 6th largest country and is located in the southern hemisphere. It is a continent with few people for its hot and dry environment. Aboriginals（原住民）are the native people in Australia. Geographically, it is divided into 3 regions: the Great Western Plateau（西部高原）, the Eastern Highlands（东部高地）and the Central Eastern Lowlands（中东部低地）. And politically, it is divided into 6 states and 2 territories.

Political Divisions	Key Points
New South Wales 新南威尔士州	• The First State established by Britain and the oldest state. • Sydney, its capital, is Australia's largest city. • The Great Dividing Range（大分水岭）is Australia's main watershed（分水线）.
Victoria 维多利亚州	• Melbourne（墨尔本）, its capital, is Australia's second largest city.
Queensland 昆士兰州	• The Sunshine State. • Brisbane（布里斯班）, its capital, is the gateway to two of Australia's major tourist playgrounds, the Gold Coast（黄金海岸）and the Great Barrier Reef（大堡礁）. • Lake Eyre（艾尔湖）, the largest lake of Australia is located here.

Political Divisions	Key Points
Western Australia 西澳大利亚州	• It is the biggest state of Australia and its capital, Perth（珀斯），is with a perfect climate.
South Australia 南澳大利亚州	• Adelaide（阿德莱德），its capital, is known for its arts festival. • The longest river, the Murray River（墨累河），is running into Encounter Bay（因康特湾）near Adelaide.
Tasmania 塔斯马尼亚州	• It is an island, the smallest of the Australian states.
Northern Territory 澳北区	• Darwin（达尔文市）is the only city in the state.
Australian Capital Terrltory 澳大利亚首都直辖区	• Canberra（堪培拉）is the capital of Australia.

（3）New Zealand 新西兰

New Zealand is in the Southern Pacific, and it is the first to get the new day for it is on the west of the International Date Line（国际日期变更线）. There are two main islands: North Island and South Island. The capital city of New Zealand is Wellington（惠灵顿），and the largest city is Auckland（奥克兰）. They are both in the North Island.

There are mountains all over New Zealand, and the highest mountain is Mountain Cook（库克山），called the Southern Alps（南阿尔卑斯山）. The largest river in North Island is the Waikato River（怀卡托河）and the Clutha River（克鲁萨河）is the largest river in South Island. The largest lake is Lake Taupo（陶波湖）.

New Zealand has the world's biggest farm. The native people of New Zealand are Maoris（毛利人）.

（4）Ireland 爱尔兰

Ireland is an island in northwest Europe in the North Atlantic with Dublin as its capital. The highest mountain in Ireland is Carrauntoohil（卡朗图厄尔山），the longest river is the Shannon River（香农河）and the largest lake is Lough Corrib（科里布湖）. Irish Gaelic is the first official language of Ireland, and 90% of the Irish believe in Catholic.

2 历史概况

Nations	Key Points
Canada 加拿大	• In 1535, Italian sea captain Jacques Cartier（雅克·卡蒂亚）sailed up the St. Lawrence River. • In 1608, the French explorer Samuel de Champlain（萨缪尔·德·尚普兰）established his habitation in Quebec City, which laid the roots of French Canada. • In 1763, the whole Canada came under the British rule. • In 1931, Canada became a member state of the Commonwealth of Nations（英联邦）. • In 1982, Canada passed the *Constitution Act*（《加拿大宪法法案》）.
Australia 澳大利亚	• In 1770, English navigator James Cook （詹姆斯·库克）exclaimed Australia as British colony, and at first it is a place of imprisoning convicts. • On January 1, 1901, the Commonwealth of Australia（澳大利亚联邦）came into being. • In 1927, Australia moved the capital to Canberra. • In 1931, Australia became an independent country of the Commonwealth of Nations.
New Zealand 新西兰	• In 1856, New Zealand became British self-governing colony. • In 1865, Wellington became the capital. • In 1893, New Zealand became the first country to give women the right to vote. • In 1947, it became absolutely independent.
Ireland 爱尔兰	• In 1921, it got independent from Britain. • In 1949, it separated from the Commonwealth of Nations.

3 政治概况

Nations	Key Points
Canada 加拿大	• A member of the Commonwealth of Nations. • The King or Queen of the UK is the head of Canada, and the queen is represented in Canada by the Governor General（总督）appointed on the recommendation of the Prime Minister. • Parliament: it has legislative powers of Canada and is composed of the Senate（参议院）and the House of Commons（下议院）.

Nations	Key Points
Canada 加拿大	• The Prime Minister and other members of the Cabinet exercise executive power. • Major parties: the Liberal Party（自由党）and the Progressive Conservative Party（进步保守党）, and the Prime Minister is the leader of the majority party in the House of Commons. • Official languages: English and French.
Australia 澳大利亚	• A member of the Commonwealth of Nations. • The King or Queen of the UK is also the head of Australia and is represented by the Governor General（总督）. • Australia has a written Constitution, which came into effect in 1901. • Parliament: the House of Representatives（众议院）and the Senate（参议院）; the election the House of Representatives is held at least every 3 years. • The executive consists of the Prime Minister and other members of the ministry, and the major decision-making body in the government is the Cabinet. • Major parties: the Australian Labor Party（澳大利亚工党）(the eldest and the largest), the Liberal Party of Australia（澳大利亚自由党）, the National Party of Australia（澳大利亚国家党）and the Australian Democrats（澳大利亚民主党）.
New Zealand 新西兰	• The British Monarch（英国君主）is also the head of New Zealand represented by the Governor General. • One chamber of the parliament is the House of Representative, and general election was held every 3 years. • 2 main parties: the National Party（国家党）and the Labor Party（工党）.
Ireland 爱尔兰	• The head of the state is the president with a term of 7 years. • All the legislative powers are vested in the Parliament, which consists of the House of Representatives and the Senate. • Parliament: the House of Representatives and the Senate.

第四节 历年真题测评

Test 1

真题测试

31. The Maori people are natives of
    A. Australia.   B. Canada.
    C. Ireland.   D. New Zealand.

32. The British monarch is the Head of
    A. Parliament.   B. State.
    C. Government.   D. Cabinet.

33. Americans celebrate Independence Day on
    A. July 4th.   B. October 11th.
    C. May 31st.   D. September 6th.

34. Canada is bounded on the north by
    A. the Pacific Ocean.   B. the Atlantic Ocean.
    C. the Arctic Ocean.   D. the Great Lakes.

真题点评

31. ［答案］D ［考点］新西兰人文。

［精析］毛利人(Maori)是新西兰的土著居民，早在1000多年前，他们乘坐独木舟(waka hourua)来到此地繁衍生息。现在，毛利人虽然只占新西兰总人口的14%，但其语言和文化却对新西兰的生活有着重要的影响。澳大利亚的土著人是古利人(Kooris)，40000多年前，定居澳大利亚大陆。加拿大的原著民包括印第安人(Indian)和因纽特人(Inuit)，其中大部分生活在靠近北极的北部地区。爱尔兰人的先民主要是属于克尔特部落群的盖尔人(Gael)，并吸收有伊比利亚人、诺曼人、盎格鲁-撒克逊人。

32. ［答案］B ［考点］英国政治。

［精析］英国君主(The British monarch)是英国及英国海外领地的国家元首(the Head of State)，但"统而不治"。议会(Parliament)是国家的最高权力机构和立法机关，分为上下两院。占有多数席位的政党领袖通过君主任命成为首相(prime minister)。事实上，首相才是国家政治生活中的最高决策者和领导者。内阁

29

（Cabinet）是英国的政府，由首相组建，内阁对议会或首相负责，如果议会通过对内阁不信任案时，整个内阁（包括首相）要么下台，要么内阁提请国家元首宣布解散议会，重新进行议会选举。

33. [答案] A　[考点] 美国人文。

　　[精析] 每年7月4日是美国的独立日，以纪念1776年7月4日大陆会议在费城正式通过《独立宣言》。《独立宣言》庄严宣告美利坚合众国脱离英国而独立。因此通过《独立宣言》的这一天也成为美国的独立日。10月份有哥伦布日，为10月12日或10月的第二个星期一，以纪念哥伦布于1492年首次登上美洲大陆。五月有阵亡将士纪念日，时间原为5月30日，1971年以后，为保证联邦雇员都能享有这一休息日，许多州将它改在五月的最后一个星期一。9月6日是劳工节，确切日期是每年九月的第一个星期一。

34. [答案] C　[考点] 加拿大地理。

　　[精析] 加拿大位于北美洲北部，东临大西洋（the Atlantic Ocean），西濒太平洋（the Pacific Ocean），西北部邻美国阿拉斯加州，东北与格陵兰隔戴维斯海峡遥遥相望，南接美国本土，北靠北冰洋（the Arctic Ocean），故选C。

Test 2

真题测试

31. The northernmost part of Great Britain is
　　A. Northern Ireland.　　　　　　　B. Scotland.
　　C. England.　　　　　　　　　　　D. Wales.

32. It is generally agreed that _____ were the first Europeans to reach Australia's shores.
　　A. the French　　　　　　　　　　B. the Germans
　　C. the British　　　　　　　　　　D. the Dutch

33. Which country is known as the Land of Maple Leaf?
　　A. Canada.　　　　　　　　　　　B. New Zealand.
　　C. Great Britain.　　　　　　　　　D. The United States of America.

34. Who wrote the famous pamphlet, *The Common Sense*, before the American Revolution?
　　A. Thomas Jefferson.　　　　　　　B. Thomas Paine.
　　C. John Adams.　　　　　　　　　D. Benjamin Franklin.

真题点评

31. [答案] B　[考点] 英国地理。

[精析] 大不列颠群岛(Great Britain)是英国本土的重要组成部分，主要包括英格兰(England)、苏格兰(Scotland)和威尔士(Wales)三个部分，其中英格兰在大不列颠群岛的南部和中部地区，威尔士位于西南部，苏格兰则位于北部地区，北爱尔兰(Northern Ireland)在爱尔兰半岛上，不在大不列颠群岛上。

32. [答案] D [考点] 澳大利亚历史。

[精析] 第一个到达澳大利亚海岸的是荷兰人威廉姆·简士（Willem Janszoon），他带领他的船队"杜伊夫根"号(*Duyfken*)于1606年登陆，并命名此地为"新荷兰"，这是首次有记载的外来人在澳大利亚的真正登陆；同年的早些时候，西班牙航海家托勒斯(Luis Vaz de Torres)的船只驶过位于澳大利亚和新几内亚岛(伊里安岛)之间的海峡，但并未到达澳大利亚海岸；之后在1770年，英国航海家库克船长(Captain James Cook)发现澳大利亚东海岸，将其命名为"新南威尔士"，并宣布这片土地属于英国。

33. [答案] A [考点] 加拿大。

[精析] 枫树（maple tree）是加拿大的国树，也是加拿大民族的象征，枫叶(maple leaf)则是加拿大的国花，加拿大国旗上也印有枫叶，加拿大素有"枫叶之国"(Land of Maple Leaf)的美誉。

34. [答案] B [考点] 美国历史。

[精析]《常识》(*The Common Sense*)是英裔美国思想家、作家和政治活动家托马斯·潘恩(Thomas Paine)的作品，该书公开提出美国独立革命的问题，并竭力强调革命之后建立共和政体。《常识》一出，立刻风靡北美大陆，被誉为"美国独立革命的教科书"。托马斯·杰斐逊(Thomas Jefferson)是第三任美国总统，主要贡献是起草了《独立宣言》(*Declaration of Independence*)。约翰·亚当斯(John Adams)是美国第一任副总统，后来又当选为美国第二任总统，同时也是《独立宣言》起草委员会的成员，曾被誉为"美国独立的巨人"，由于他体型较为矮胖，因此也有"圆胖先生"的称号。本杰明·富兰克林(Benjamin Franklin)作为政治家的声誉比不上他作为美国历史上第一位享有国际声誉的科学家、发明家和音乐家的声誉，他参加起草了《独立宣言》和美国宪法，其流传最广的事迹是做"风筝实验"。

Test 3

真题测试

31. Which of the following statements is INCORRECT?

A. The British constitution includes the Magna Carta of 1215.

B. The British constitution includes Parliamentary acts.

C. The British constitution includes decisions made by courts of law.

D. The British constitution includes one single written constitution.

32. The first city ever founded in Canada is

    A. Quebec.   B. Vancouver.

    C. Toronto.   D. Montreal.

33. When did the Australian Federation officially come into being?

    A. 1770.   B. 1788.

    C. 1900.   D. 1901.

34. *The Emancipation Proclamation* to end the slavery plantation system in the South of the U.S. was issued by

    A. Abraham Lincoln.   B. Thomas Paine.

    C. George Washington.   D. Thomas Jefferson.

真题点评

31. [答案] D [考点] 英国政治。

[精析] 注意题目要求选出不正确的。选项中都是关于英国宪法的描述。选项D提到英国有一个独立的成文宪法，不正确，故选D。据了解，英国宪法与绝大多数国家宪法不同，不是一个独立的文件，它由成文法(statute law)、习惯法(common law)、惯例(conventions)组成。主要有《大宪章》(*Magna Carta*)、人身保护法(1679年)、《权利法案》(1689年)、议会法(parliamentary act)以及历次修改的选举法、市自治法、郡议会法等。

32. [答案] A [考点] 加拿大历史。

[精析] 魁北克城(Quebec City)原为印第安人居留地，法国探险家萨米埃尔·德·尚普兰于1608年建魁北克城，它是加拿大建立的第一个城市、魁北克省省会、加拿大东部重要城市和港口。

要点归纳

> 加拿大主要城市：
> - 首都：Ottawa（渥太华）   - 第一大城市：Toronto（多伦多）
> - 第二大城市：Montreal（蒙特利尔）   - 第三大城市：Vancouver（温哥华）

33. [答案] D [考点] 澳大利亚历史。

[精析] 1900年，澳大利亚六个殖民地的居民举行了一人一票的全民公决，投票决定是否把六个殖民地统一成一个联邦国家。投票结果是六个地方要统一，建立起一个单一的澳大利亚联邦。1901年1月1日，六个殖民区统一成为联邦，澳大利亚联邦成立，同时通过第一部宪法。因此，澳大利亚联邦正式成立是在1901年，故选D。1770年，英国航海家库克船长(Captain James Cook)发现澳大利亚东海岸，将其命

名为"新南威尔士"，并宣布这片土地是英国的属土。1788年1月26日，由菲利普船长率领的一支有6艘船的船队正式在澳大利亚杰克逊港(Port Jackson)建立起第一个英国殖民区，该地区后来人口不断增长而发展成为澳大利亚现今的第一大城市悉尼。

34. [答案] A [考点] 美国历史。

[精析]《解放黑人奴隶宣言》(*Emancipation Proclamation*)是总统林肯在1863年1月1日颁布的一项旨在使美国南部叛乱州的黑人奴隶成为自由民众的法令。1863年元旦，林肯颁布了《解放黑人奴隶宣言》，宣布叛乱诸州的奴隶获得自由并得到保障。但《解放黑人奴隶宣言》不适用于没有参加叛乱的边界蓄奴州。1865年和1868年，国会分别通过了宪法第13、14条修正案，才正式废除奴隶制。托马斯·潘恩(Thomas Paine)是英裔美国思想家、作家、政治活动家。乔治·华盛顿(George Washington)是美国的第一位总统。托马斯·杰斐逊(Thomas Jefferson)是《独立宣言》的起草者之一，同时还是美国的第三任总统。

Test 4

31. The Head of State of New Zealand is

    A. the governor-general.

    B. the Prime Minister.

    C. the high commissioner.

    D. the monarch of the United Kingdom.

32. The capital of Scotland is

    A. Glasgow.   B. Edinburgh.

    C. Manchester.   D. London.

33. Who wrote the *Declaration of Independence* and later became the U.S. President?

    A. Thomas Jefferson.   B. George Washington.

    C. Thomas Paine.   D. John Adams.

34. Which of the following cities is located on the eastern coast of Australia?

    A. Perth.   B. Adelaide.

    C. Sydney.   D. Melbourne.

31. [答案] D [考点] 新西兰政治常识。

[精析] 题目问的是新西兰的国家元首。新西兰以前是英国的殖民地，它的国家元首是英国的君主 (the monarch of the United Kingdom)，而总督 (the governor-general）代表英国君主行使管理权。众议院普选产生的多数党的领导人就是总理（the Prime Minister）。故选D。

32. **[答案]** B **[考点]** 英国地理概况。

[精析] 苏格兰的首府是爱丁堡（Edinburgh）。格拉斯哥（Glasgow）是苏格兰最大的工商业城市和港口，英国第三大城市，位于苏格兰中部低地，跨克莱德河。曼彻斯特（Manchester）位于英格兰西北部平原，伦敦（London）是英格兰首府。

要点归纳

大不列颠及北爱尔兰联合王国（英国）四个行政分区首府：
- 英格兰（England）：伦敦（London）   • 苏格兰（Scotland）：爱丁堡（Edinburgh）
- 威尔士（Wales）：加的夫（Cardiff）
- 北爱尔兰（Northern Ireland）：贝尔法斯特（Belfast）

---

33. **[答案]** A **[考点]** 美国历史人物。

[精析] 《独立宣言》是由托马斯·杰斐逊等人起草的，托马斯·杰斐逊后来成为美国的第三届总统。故选A。乔治·华盛顿（George Washington）是美国的第一任总统。托马斯·潘恩（Thomas Paine）是美国殖民地时期的英裔美国思想家、作家。约翰·亚当斯（John Adams）是美国第二任总统。

34. **[答案]** C **[考点]** 澳大利亚地理概况。

[精析] 悉尼（Sydney）位于澳大利亚东部太平洋沿岸，是澳大利亚最大的城市和港口。珀斯（Perth）位于澳大利亚西南角的斯旺河（Swan River）畔，是西澳大利亚州（Western Australia）的首府，也是澳大利亚第四大城市。阿德莱德（Adelaide）位于澳大利亚南部，南澳大利亚州首府和港口。墨尔本（Melbourne）位于澳大利亚东南角，是澳大利亚的第二大城市。故选C。

Test 5

真题测试

31. The largest city in Canada is
    A. Vancouver.   B. Montreal.
    C. Toronto.   D. Ottawa.

32. According to the United States Constitution, the legislative power is invested in
    A. the Federal Government.   B. the Supreme Court.
    C. the Cabinet.   D. the Congress.

34

33. Which of the following is the oldest sport in the United States?

    A. Baseball.   B. Tennis.

    C. Basketball.   D. American football.

34. The head of the executive branch in New Zealand is

    A. the President.   B. the Governor-General.

    C. the British monarch.   D. the Prime Minister.

真题点评

31. [答案] C [考点] 加拿大地理概况。

[精析] 加拿大最大的城市是多伦多，它是安大略省的省会，全国的工业和商业中心，是加拿大湖区的一个重要港口城市。

32. [答案] D [考点] 美国政治制度。

[精析] 美国宪法规定美国的立法权属于国会。联邦政府 (the Federal Government) 包括美国的立法、行政和司法机关，美国的司法权属于最高法院 (the Supreme Court)。内阁 (the Cabinet) 是英国的官方体制。

要点归纳

美国实行联邦制 (the Federal System)，实行三权分立：

- 立法权 (legislative) 属于国会 (the Congress)
- 行政权 (executive) 属于美国总统 (the President)
- 司法权 (judicial) 属于美国联邦最高法院 (the Supreme Court)

33. [答案] A [考点] 美国体育。

[精析] 现代棒球运动 (baseball) 源于英国而发展于美国，1839年，美国纽约州古帕斯镇举行了有史以来的首次棒球比赛。网球 (tennis) 在美国源于1874年，当时在百慕大度假的美国人玛丽·奥特布里奇女士在观看了英国军官的网球比赛后，对这项体育活动颇感兴趣，于是将网球规则、网拍和网球带到纽约。篮球 (basketball) 是1891年12月初由美国马萨诸塞州普林菲尔德 (Springfield) 市基督教青年会国际训练学校的体育教师詹姆斯·奈史密斯 (James Naismith) 博士发明的。美国足球，美式橄榄球 (American Football) 是由英国的橄榄球直接演变过来的，19世纪中叶在美国盛行，现代美式足球在1874年哈佛大学对蒙特利尔麦基尔大学的三场系列赛中发展起来。综上所述，故选A。

34. [答案] D [考点] 新西兰政治制度。

[精析] 英国女王是新西兰的国家元首，女王任命的总督 (the Governor-General) 作为其代表行使管理权。总督与内阁组成的行政会议是法定的最高行政机构 (executive branch)，内阁掌握实权，由议会多数党组成，而多数党的最高领导人当选总理 (the Prime Minister)，故选D。

Test 6

31. The majority of the current population in the UK are descendants of all the following tribes respectively EXCEPT

    A. the Anglos.   B. the Celts.

    C. the Jutes.   D. the Saxons.

32. The Head of State of Canada is represented by

    A. the Monarch.   B. the President.

    C. the Prime Minister.   D. the Governor-general.

33. The *Declaration of Independence* was written by

    A. Thomas Jefferson.   B. George Washington.

    C. Alexander Hamilton.   D. James Madison.

34. The original inhabitants of Australia were

    A. the Red Indians.   B. the Eskimos.

    C. the Aborigines.   D. the Maoris.

31. [答案] C [考点] 英国历史知识。

[精析] 题目问的是现在大多数的英国人都是哪些民族的后裔,凯尔特人(Celts)主要是苏格兰高地民族、爱尔兰人和威尔士人的祖先。5世纪中期,由朱特人(Jutes)、撒克逊人(Saxons)和安格鲁人(Anglos)构成的日耳曼部落入侵大不列颠,其中安格鲁人和撒克逊人占多数,成为英国人的祖先,而朱特人占少数,在发展中被同化而逐渐消亡,所以朱特人不是英国人的祖先,故选C。

32. [答案] D [考点] 加拿大政治。

[精析] 加拿大、澳大利亚和新西兰都是英联邦的成员,它们的国家元首都是英国国王或女王,但代表者为总督(governor-general)。故本题选D。

33. [答案] A [考点] 美国历史。

[精析] 《独立宣言》是由托马斯·杰斐逊(Thomas Jefferson)、约翰·亚当斯(John Adams)和本杰明·富兰克林(Benjamin Franklin)等人组成的委员会起草的。乔治·华盛顿(George Washington)是美国的第一任总统。亚历山大·汉密尔顿(Alexander Hamilton)是美国的开国元勋之一,也是宪法的起草人之一,是美国的第一任财政部长。詹姆斯·麦迪逊(James Madison)是美国的第四任总统。故本题选A。

34. [答案] C　[考点] 澳大利亚历史。

[精析] 土著居民(the Aborigines)是澳大利亚的原住民，故选C。

> **要点归纳**
>
> 英语国家的原住民：
> - 美国：印第安人(the Indians)
> - 澳大利亚：土著居民(the Aborigines)
> - 新西兰：毛利人(the Maori)
> - 加拿大：爱斯基摩人或因纽特人、印第安人（the Eskimos or Inuit and Indians）

Test 7

(真题测试)

31. The President during the American Civil War was

A. Andrew Jackson.

B. Abraham Lincoln.

C. Thomas Jefferson.

D. George Washington.

32. The capital of New Zealand is

A. Christchurch.

B. Auckland.

C. Wellington.

D. Hamilton.

33. Who were the natives of Australia before the arrival of the British settlers?

A. The Aborigines.

B. The Maori.

C. The Indians.

D. The Eskimos.

34. The Prime Minister in Britain is head of

A. the Shadow Cabinet.

B. the Parliament.

C. the Opposition.

D. the Cabinet.

(真题点评)

31. [答案] B　[考点] 美国历史人物。

[精析] 美国内战时期任职的总统为亚伯拉罕·林肯。选项A中的安德鲁·杰克逊是美国的第七届总统，他在内战前任职；他是美国历史上第一位民主党总统。托马斯·杰斐逊是美国历史上第三位总统，也是《独立宣言》的起草者。乔治·华盛顿则是美国历史上的第一位总统。

32. [答案] C　[考点] 新西兰地理概况。

[精析] 新西兰的首都是惠灵顿。基督城和奥克兰都是新西兰的港口城市，汉密尔顿则位于新西兰怀卡托河畔。

33. ［答案］A ［考点］澳大利亚历史。

［精析］澳大利亚原为土著人（the Aborigines）居住，直到1770年美国航海家詹姆斯·库克在澳大利亚东海岸登陆，并宣布澳大利亚为英国殖民地。毛利人(the Maori)是新西兰原住居民，印第安人（the Indians)是美洲的原住居民。爱斯基摩人(the Eskimos)是北极居民。

34. ［答案］D ［考点］英国政治常识。

［精析］英国首相主持内阁事务，负责分配大臣们的职能，定期会见女王，向女王报告政府事务。

Test 8

真题测试

31. _____ is the capital city of Canada.

    A. Vancouver   B. Ottawa

    C. Montreal   D. York

32. U.S. presidents normally serve a (n) _____ term.

    A. two-year   B. four-year

    C. six-year   D. eight-year

33. Which of the following cities is NOT located in the Northeast, U.S.?

    A. Huston.   B. Boston.

    C. Baltimore.   D. Philadelphia.

34. _____ is the state church in England.

    A. The Roman Catholic Church   B. The Baptist Church

    C. The Protestant Church   D. The Church of England

真题点评

31. ［答案］B ［考点］加拿大地理。

［精析］加拿大的首都是渥太华(Ottawa)，蒙特利尔(Montreal)是加拿大第二大城市，温哥华(Vancouver)是加拿大西部的工业中心。

32. ［答案］B ［考点］美国政治常识。

［精析］美国总统的任期一般为4年，并且只可连任一次。

33. ［答案］A ［考点］美国地理常识。

［精析］休斯敦是位于美国南部的墨西哥湾沿岸城市，不是东北部城市，故选A。

34. ［答案］D ［考点］英国宗教。

［精析］英格兰国教是英格兰教会(the Church of England)。

第三章
英语文学知识

第一节 美国文学

从殖民地时期起，欧洲殖民者和清教徒翻开了美国文学史的第一页。这之后很长一段时间内，美国文学一直受到欧洲文化的影响，这是美国文学发展的第一阶段，即"殖民地时期"。

美国独立后，民族文学开始发展，这是美国文学发展的第二个阶段。在此期间，出现了一批早期的美国作家，代表人物是本杰明·富兰克林(Benjamin Franklin)。

18世纪末、19世纪初，美国文学开始进入繁荣发展的阶段，即"浪漫主义时期"(Romanticism)。南北战争时期，美国文学进入了全盛阶段，产生了强调个性主义和直觉的早期浪漫主义(Pre-Romanticism)，以及超验主义文学(Transcendentalism)。该时期是美国前所未有的文学变动时代，涌现了一大批优秀的作家和作品。他们赋予当时美国文学以深度和力量，也促进了浪漫主义高潮的来临，即后浪漫主义时期(Post-Romanticism)。

南北战争后，美国社会动荡不安，这时的作品更注重于揭露社会的阴暗面，美国的民族文学进一步发展，出现了许多带有本土色彩和批判现实主义的作品。美国文学由此进入了第四个发展阶段"现实主义时期"(Realism)。这个时期有以亨利·詹姆斯(Henry James)为代表的"现实主义文学"(Realism)，以马克·吐温(Mark Twain)为代表的"本土色彩文学"(Local Colorism)，以及以斯蒂芬·克莱恩(Stephen Crane)、西奥多·德莱塞(Theodore Dreiser)和杰克·伦敦(Jack London)为代表的"美国自然主义文学"(American Naturalism)。

一战后，美国人陷入战后的茫然，美国文学也开始进入了"现代主义时期"(Modernism)。

下面我们就对各个时期的重点知识进行具体介绍。

1 殖民地时期（16世纪末—17世纪中期）

Some of the American literature in this period were pamphlets and writings extolling the benefits of the colonies to both a European and colonist audience. Captain John Smith(约翰·史密斯)could be considered the first American author with his works: *A True Relation of Virginia* (《关于弗吉尼亚的真实叙述》, 1608).

2 独立革命时期（17世纪中期—18世纪末）

Most of the revolutionary writing is political, and poetry came into being.

Writer	Time	Works and Contribution
Benjamin Franklin 本杰明·富兰克林	1706~1790	• A member of the committee to draft *The Declaration of Independence*（《独立宣言》起草委员会成员） • *Poor Richard's Almanac*（《穷理查德年鉴》） *The Autobiography*（《自传》）
Thomas Paine 托马斯·潘恩	1737~1809	• Pamphlets: *Common Sense*（《常识》） *The American Crisis*（《美国危机》）
Thomas Jefferson 托马斯·杰斐逊	1743~1826	• The drafter of *The Declaration of Independence* • The third president of America.
Philip Freneau 菲利普·弗瑞诺	1752~1832	• Considered as "Poet of the American Revolution"（美国独立革命的诗人）and "Father of America Poetry"（美国诗歌之父） • Poem: *The Wild Honey Suckle*（《野忍冬花》）

③ **浪漫主义时期**（18世纪末—19世纪中后期）

American romanticism was also called American Renaissance （美国文艺复兴）. American Romantics attached more importance to the feelings, intuitions and emotions than reason and common sense. Transcendentalism（超验主义）marked the maturity of American Romanticism.

Writer	Time	Works and Contribution
Washington Irving 华盛顿·欧文	1783~1859	• Was called "Father of American Literature"（美国文学之父）, best known for his short stories and the first American writer to achieve international fame • Short stories: *Rip Van Winkle*（《瑞普·凡·温克尔》） *The Legend of Sleepy Hollow*（《睡谷的传说》） • Other writings: *The Sketch Book*（《见闻札记》）, which marked the beginning of the American Romanticism.
William Cullen Bryant 威廉·柯伦·布赖恩特	1794~1878	• The first American lyric poet of distinction • Poems: *To a Waterfowl*（《致水鸟》） *Thanatopsis*（《死亡随想》）

Writer	Time	Works and Contribution
James Fenimore Cooper 詹姆斯·费尼莫尔·库珀	1789~1851	• Novelist • In *Leatherstocking Tales*（《皮袜子五部曲》）, the most famous one is *The Last of Mohicans*（《最后的莫西干人》）.
Ralph Waldo Emerson 拉尔夫·沃尔多·爱默生	1803~1882	• Head of the Transcendental Movement(超验主义中心人物) • Essayist and poet • Essay: *Nature*（《论自然》）, regarded as "the manifesto of American Transcendentalism"（美国超验主义的宣言）.
Henry David Thoreau 亨利·大卫·梭罗	1817~1862	• Writer and great thinker • *Walden*（《瓦尔登湖》） *Civil Disobedience*（《论公民的不服从》）
Henry Wadsworth Longfellow 亨利·沃兹沃思·朗费罗	1807~1882	• The first American poet to write the narrative poems • *The Song of Hiawatha*（《海华沙之歌》） *Evangeline*（《伊万杰琳》） *A Psalm of Life*（《人生礼赞》） Translation of Dante's *Divine Comedy*（《神曲》）
Nathaniel Hawthorne 纳撒尼尔·霍桑	1804~1864	• He was considered to be the first writer of fiction. • Symbolic novel: *The Scarlet Letter*（《红字》） • Novel: *The House of the Seven Gables*《有七个尖角阁楼的房子》 Short story: *Mosses from an Old Manse*（《古屋青苔》）
Edgar Allan Poe 埃德加·爱伦·坡	1809~1849	• Novelist, poet and critic • He was considered "the Father of American detective stories". • Poems: *The Raven*（《乌鸦》） *Annabel Lee*（《安娜贝尔·李》） *To Helen*（《致海伦》） • Novel: *The Fall of the House of Usher*（《厄舍古屋的倒塌》）
Herman Melville 赫尔曼·梅尔维尔	1819~1891	• Novelist • Novel: *Moby Dick*（《白鲸》）

Writer	Time	Works and Contribution
Emily Dickinson 埃米莉·迪金森	1830~1886	• Poet • The theme of her works is usually religion, life and death, love and marriage. • Poems: *Because I Could Not Stop for Death*（《因为我不能等待死亡》） *I'm Nobody. Who Are You?*（《我是无名小卒！你是谁？》）
Walt Whitman 沃尔特·惠特曼	1819~1892	• Great democratic poet • He is the first great American poet to use free verse（自由诗体）in poetry. • Poetry collection: *Leaves of Grass*（《草叶集》），which marked the end of the American Romanticism.

4 现实主义时期（19世纪中期—20世纪初）

American industrialization and the development of the Far West promote American literature to step into realism. Most literary works of this period are novels, and have some major features, such as straightforward or matter-of-fact manner, focus on commonness of the lives of the common people, writers holding objective rather than idealistic view of human nature.

Writer	Time	Works and Contribution
Harriet Beecher Stowe 哈丽雅特·比彻·斯托	1811~1896	• Novel: *Uncle Tom's Cabin*（《汤姆叔叔的小屋》）
Henry James 亨利·詹姆斯	1843~1916	• Henry James, along with Mark Twain and William Dean Howells are 3 representatives of American realism. • He was considered the founder of psychological realism（心理分析小说）. • Novels: *The Portrait of a Lady*（《贵妇人画像》） *The Wings of the Dove*（《鸽翼》） *The Ambassadors*（《大使》） *The Golden Bowl*（《金碗》） *Daisy Miller*（《黛西·米勒》）

Writer	Time	Works and Contribution
Mark Twain 马克·吐温	1835~1910	• One of America's first and foremost realists and humorists • William Faulkner called Twain "the father of American literature." • Novels: *The Celebrated Jumping Frog of Calaveras County*（《卡拉维拉斯郡著名的跳蛙》） *The Gilded Age*（《镀金时代》） *The Adventures of Tom Sawyer*（《汤姆·索亚历险记》） *The Prince and the Pauper*（《王子与贫儿》） *The Adventures of Huckleberry Finn*（《哈克贝利·费恩历险记》）
Stephen Crane 斯蒂芬·克莱恩	1871~1900	• Novelist • Novel: *The Red Badge of Courage*（《红色英勇勋章》）
Theodore Dreiser 西奥多·德莱塞	1871~1945	• One of America's greatest Naturalist writers • Novels: *Sister Carrie*（《嘉莉妹妹》） *An American Tragedy*（《美国悲剧》） *Trilogy of Desire*（《欲望三部曲》）, which includes *The Financier*（《金融家》）, *The Titan*（《巨人》）*and The Stoic*（《斯多葛》）
Jack London 杰克·伦敦	1876~1916	• Naturalist writer • Novels: *The Call of the Wild*（《野性的呼唤》） *Love of Life*（《热爱生命》） *Martin Eden*（《马丁·伊登》）
O. Henry 欧·亨利	1862~1910	• Naturalist writer and was famous for his short stories • Most famous short stories: *The Gift of the Magi*（《麦琪的礼物》） *The Cop and the Anthem*（《警察与赞美诗》）

⑤ 现代主义时期（20世纪初）

American modernism started at the turn of the 20th century with its core period between World War I and World War II and continued into the 21st century. And modernism displayed its momentum first in the movement of Imagism(意象派).

Writer	Time	Works and Contribution
Ernest Hemingway 欧内斯特·海明威	1899~1961	• Novelist • Spokesman of the Lost Generation（迷惘的一代） • He won the Nobel Prize in Literature in 1954. • The first novel: *The Sun Also Rises*（《太阳照样升起》） • Famous novels: *A Farewell to Arms*（《永别了，武器！》） *For Whom the Bell Tolls*（《丧钟为谁而鸣》） *The Old Man and the Sea*（《老人与海》）
Ezra Pound 埃兹拉·庞德	1885~1972	• The father of modern American poetry（美国现代诗歌之父）and one of the most important imagist poets（意象派诗人） • Epic poem: *The Cantos*（《诗章》），the most frequently read poem in it is *In a Station of the Metro*（《在地铁站》）.
Robert Frost 罗伯特·弗罗斯特	1874~1963	• His poetry focused on the landscape and people in New England, so he is considered "the New England poet."（新英格兰诗人） • Poetry collections: *Mending Wall*（《修墙》） *The Road Not Taken*（《未选择的路》） • Poems: *Stopping by the Woods on a Snowy Evening*（《雪夜林边小驻》） *Desert Places*（《荒芜地带》）
T. S. Eliot 托马斯·斯特思斯·艾略特	1888~1965	• American-born English poet • He was awarded the Nobel Prize in Literature in 1948. • Poems: *The Waste Land*（《荒原》） *Four Quarters*（《四个四重奏》）
William Faulkner 威廉·福克纳	1897~1962	• Novelist • He was the most important southern writer of the 20th century, and won 1949 Nobel Prize in Literature. • Novels: *The Sound and the Fury*（《喧哗与骚动》） *Light in August*（《八月之光》） *Absalom, Absalom*（《押沙龙，押沙龙！》）

Writer	Time	Works and Contribution
Francis Scott Fitzgerald 弗朗西斯·司各特·菲茨杰拉德	1896~1940	• Novelist • Spokesman of the Jazz Age(爵士乐时代) • Novels: *The Great Gatsby*(《了不起的盖茨比》) *Tender Is the Night*(《夜色温柔》)
John Steinbeck 约翰·斯坦贝克	1902~1968	• Novelist • Received the Nobel Prize for Literature in 1962 • Novel: *The Grapes of Wrath*(《愤怒的葡萄》)
Eugene Gladstone O'Neill 尤金·格拉德斯通·奥尼尔	1888~1953	• American playwright, received Nobel Prize for Literature in 1936 and won Pulitzer Prize 4 times • Play: *The Hairy Ape*(《毛猿》)

第二节 英国文学

在英国文学史上，盎格鲁-撒克逊人统治英国前，英国没有留下书面的文学作品。盎格鲁-撒克逊人入侵英国以后，他们的史诗《贝奥武夫》流传了下来，成为古英语时期最古老的英语文学作品。1066年诺曼入侵后，受欧洲大陆语言的影响，英国文学逐渐发展起来，其中以用韵文写的骑士传奇故事（Romance）最为盛行，这是英国文学发展的第一个时期——中古英语文学（Medieval English），14世纪是中古英语文学发展的繁荣时期。

从16世纪开始，英国文学受到了开始于14世纪的欧洲文艺复兴的影响，进入了它发展的第二个阶段"文艺复兴时期"（English Renaissance）。这一时期的诗歌创作异常活跃，有大批的诗集出版，但文学上最为繁荣的是伊丽莎白女王时期的戏剧，其中最著名的剧作家是莎士比亚（William Shakespeare），同时，散文在这一时期也有一定的发展。

17世纪中期，英国文学受到欧洲启蒙运动(The Enlightenment)的影响，进入它发展的第三个阶段"新古典主义时期"（Neoclassicism）。这一时期散文得到了快速发展，以亚历山大·蒲柏（Alexander Pope）和丹尼尔·笛福（Daniel Defoe）等为代表人物。

从18世纪中期到19世纪中期，诗歌在英国文学史上得到了快速的发展，涌现出了一批优秀的代表诗人，如威廉·华兹华斯（William Wordsworth）、乔治·戈登·拜伦（George Gordon Byron）和珀西·比希·雪莱（Percy Bysshe Shelley）等，这是英国文学的浪漫主义时期(Romanticism)。

维多利亚时期的英国文学(Victorian Literature)以小说为主要文学形式，文学作品也更加关注社会的现实问题。著名的批判现实主义小说家有查尔斯·狄更斯(Charles Dickens)、威廉·梅克皮斯·萨克雷(William Makepeace Thackeray)、勃朗特姐妹(Bronte sisters)。这一时期的诗歌具有标新立异的特点，罗伯特·布朗宁(Robert Browning)将诗歌和小说结合起来，创造了新的诗歌形式——"戏剧独白诗"(dramatic monologue)。

进入20世纪以后，小说也是英国文学的主要文学形式，但涌现了许多不同的流派，其中奥斯卡·王尔德(Oscar Wilde)是颓废派(Decadence)和唯美主义文学(Aestheticism)的代表人物，乔伊斯(Joyce)是意识流(Stream of Consciousness)的代表人物，弗吉尼亚·伍尔夫(Virginia Woolf)是现代主义(Modernism)的代表人物。

下面我们就对各个时期的重点知识进行具体介绍。

1 中古英语文学（8世纪~15世纪）

The Old English literature is exclusively a verse literature in oral form. Pagan（异教的）poetry *Beowulf* was regarded as the beginning of the Old English literature. And after

Norman Conquest, Romance（传奇）became the prevailing form of literature and was regarded as the epitome of the Middle Ages.

Writer	Time	Works and Contribution
口头传诵	公元 5 世纪	• *Beowulf*(《贝奥武夫》): The national epic（史诗） of the English people, and the oldest poem in English language
Geoffrey Chaucer 杰弗里·乔叟	1343~1400	• "The father of English poetry"; "the father of English fiction"; the 14th century is called "Age of Chaucer" • A collection of stories: *The Canterbury Tales*（《坎特伯雷故事集》）

2 文艺复兴时期（16世纪~17世纪中期）

The English Renaissance in English cultural history is sometimes referred to as "the age of Shakespeare" or "the Elizabethan era", the first period in English and British history to be named after a reigning monarch（执政君主）. And the most distinctive achievement of Elizabethan literature is the drama, followed by lyrical poetry. In the same period, one of the best essayists in English literature, Francis Bacon（弗朗西斯·培根）, wrote more than 50 excellent essays.

Writer	Time	Works and Contribution
Edmund Spencer 埃德蒙·斯宾塞	1552~1599	• "The poets' poet"（诗人中的诗人） • *The Faerie Queene*（《仙后》）, an epic poem and fantastical allegory
Thomas More 托马斯·莫尔	1478~1535	• A leading Renaissance humanist（人文主义者）and an opponent of the Protestant Reformation（宗教改革） • Prose writer • *Masterpiece: Utopia*（《乌托邦》）
Francis Bacon 弗朗西斯·培根	1561~1626	• The founder of English materialist philosophy（唯物主义哲学） • The first essayist in England • Essays: *Of Studies*（《论学习》） *Of Travel*（《论旅行》） *Of Wisdom*（《论智慧》）

Writer	Time	Works and Contribution
Christopher Marlowe 克里斯托弗·马洛	1564~1593	• Playwright, belongs to "University Wit"(大学才子) • He first made blank verse(无韵诗). • Play: *The Tragic History of Doctor Faustus*(《浮士德博士的悲剧》)
William Shakespeare 威廉·莎士比亚	1564~1616	• The greatest English playwright, and one of the founders of realism in English literature • He wrote 37 plays(16 comedies, 11 tragedies and 10 historical plays), 154 sonnets(十四行诗) and some long poems. • Four Comedies: *A Midsummer Night's Dream*(《仲夏夜之梦》) *The Merchant of Venice*(《威尼斯商人》) *As You Like It*(《皆大欢喜》) *Twelfth Night*(《第十二夜》) • Four Tragedies: *Hamlet*(《哈姆雷特》) *Othello*(《奥赛罗》) *King Lear*(《李尔王》) *Macbeth*(《麦克白》) • Major historical plays: *Henry IV*(《亨利四世》) *Henry V*(《亨利五世》)
John Donne 约翰·多恩	1572~1631	• A poet, and a major representative of the metaphysical poets(玄学派诗人) • Poems: *The Songs and Sonnets*(《歌谣与十四行诗》) *A Valediction: Forbidding Mourning*(《别离辞·节哀》)
John Milton 约翰·弥尔顿	1608~1674	• The greatest poet in the Revolution period • Epic poems: *Paradise Lost*(《失乐园》) *Paradise Regained*(《复乐园》) • Tragedy: *Samson Agonistes*(《力士参孙》)

3 新古典主义时期（17世纪中期~18世纪）

The Neoclassical Period is from the Restoration Period to the appearance of *Lyrical Ballads*（《抒情歌谣集》）, which is the beginning of the English Romanticism. In this period, British literature was under the influence of Enlightenment Movement（启蒙运动）. The main literary stream of this period was realism. Prose had a rapid development. The novel was born and folks wrote fictional novels as a way of telling stories to each other about what was going on in their lives and world. When mass literacy was becoming a reality, newspapers and magazines came into being.

Writer	Time	Works and Contribution
John Bunyan 约翰·班扬	1628~1688	• Prose writer • Allegorical novel: *The Pilgrim's Progress*(《天路历程》)
John Dryden 约翰·德莱顿	1631~1700	• Poet, playwright and literary critic(文学评论家), the most notable representative of English Classicism in the Restoration period • He was called "the Father of English Criticism". • He established the heroic couplet(英雄双韵体) as a standard form of English poetry. • Play: *All for Love* (《一切为了爱》)
Alexander Pope 亚历山大·蒲柏	1688~1744	• Poet • The 18th century was called "the Age of Pope". • The representative writer of the neo-classical school（新古典主义学派） • Poems: *The Rape of the Lock* (《夺发记》) *An Essay on Man* (《论人类》)
Samuel Johnson 塞缪尔·约翰逊	1709~1784	• Neo-classical writer and lexicographer（字典编纂者） • Dictionary: *A Dictionary of the English Language* (《英语词典》)
Daniel Defoe 丹尼尔·笛福	1660~1731	• Realist novelist • "Father of English and European Novels" • Novel: *Robinson Crusoe* (《鲁滨逊漂流记》)
Jonathan Swift 乔纳森·斯威夫特	1667~1745	• Realist novelist • Novel: *Gulliver's Travels* (《格列佛游记》) • Satirical essay: *A Modest Proposal* (《一个小小的建议》)
Henry Fielding 亨利·菲尔丁	1707~1754	• Realist novelist, the founder of English realistic novels • Novel: *The History of Tom Jones, a Foundling* (《弃儿汤姆·琼斯的历史》)

Writer	Time	Works and Contribution
William Blake 威廉·布莱克	1757~1827	• Pre-romantic poet • Poetry collection: *Songs of Innocence*（《天真之歌》）, including the famous poem *The Lamb*（《羔羊》）; *Songs of Experience*（《经验之歌》）, including the famous poems *The Tiger*（《老虎》）, *London*（《伦敦》）, *The Chimney Sweeper*（《扫烟囱的小孩》）
Robert Burns 罗伯特·彭斯	1759~1796	• Pre-romantic poet • The national poet of Scotland • Poems: *A Red, Red Rose*（《一朵红红的玫瑰》） *Auld Lang Syne*（《友谊天长地久》）

4 浪漫主义时期（18世纪中期~19世纪中期）

The Romantic period is an age of poetry beginning with the appearance of *Lyrical Ballads* and ending with the death of Walter Scott. William Wordsworth, Samuel Taylor Coleridge, Robert Southey（罗伯特·骚塞）, are Romantic poets of the First Generation, and they are also called the Lake Poets（湖畔派诗人）. George Gordon Byron, Percy Bysshe Shelley, John Keats are "second generation" Romantic poets.

Writer	Time	Works and Contribution
William Wordsworth 威廉·华兹华斯	1770~1850	• "Poet Laureate"（桂冠诗人） • *Lyrical Ballads*（《抒情歌谣集》）: joint work by Wordsworth and Coleridge, in which the best known poems by Wordsworth are *Tintern Abbey*（《丁登寺旁》）and *Lines Written in Early Spring*（《写于早春》） • Poems: *I Wandered Lonely as a Cloud*（《我好似一朵流云独自漫游》） *The Solitary Reaper*（《孤独的割麦女》）
Samuel Taylor Coleridge 塞缪尔·泰勒·柯勒律治	1772~1834	• A great poet and a literary critic • Lyrical Ballads: joint work by Wordsworth and Coleridge, in which the best known poem by Coleridge is *The Rime of the Ancient Mariner*（《古舟子咏》）

Writer	Time	Works and Contribution
George Gordon Byron 乔治·戈登·拜伦	1788~1824	• Poet • Narrative poems: *Childe Harold's Pilgrimage* （《恰尔德·哈罗德游记》） *Don Juan*（《唐璜》） • Lyrical poems: *She Walks in Beauty*（《她走在美的光影里》） *When We Two Parted*（《昔日依依别》）
Percy Bysshe Shelley 珀西·比希·雪莱	1792~1822	• Poet • Drama: *Prometheus Unbound*（《解放了的普罗米修斯》） • Poems: *Ode to the West Wind*（《西风颂》） *To a Skylark*（《云雀颂》）
John Keats 约翰·济慈	1795~1821	• Poet • Poems: *Ode on a Grecian Urn*（《希腊古瓮颂》）, *Ode to a Nightingale*（《夜莺颂》）, *To Autumn*（《秋颂》）
Charles Lamb 查尔斯·兰姆	1775~1834	• The best essayist in the age • Children's book: *Tales from Shakespeare*（《莎士比亚戏剧故事集》）
Walter Scott 沃尔特·司各特	1771~1832	• Scottish historical novelist • Novel: *Ivanhoe*（《艾凡赫》）
Jane Austen 简·奥斯汀	1775~1817	• First English woman novelist • Novels: *Pride and Prejudice*（《傲慢与偏见》） *Sense and Sensibility*（《理智与情感》） *Emma*（《爱玛》）

⑤ 维多利亚时期（19世纪早期~20世纪初期）

A new literary trend, Critical Realism （批判现实主义）, appeared in Victoria period. Novel is the main literary form of this time, and there are also poems and proses.

Writer	Time	Works and Contribution

Charles Dickens
查尔斯·狄更斯
	1812~1870	• Most popular English novelist of the Victorian era
		• Representative works:
		  Pickwick Papers（《匹克威克外传》）
		  Oliver Twist（《雾都孤儿》）
		  The Old Curiosity Shop（《老古玩店》）
		  Dombey and Son（《董贝父子》）
		  David Copperfield（《大卫·科波菲尔》）
		  Great Expectations（《远大前程》）
		  A Tale of Two Cities（《双城记》）

William Makepeace Thackeray 威廉·梅克皮斯·萨克雷	1811~1863	• Novelist • Representative work: *Vanity Fair*（《名利场》）
Charlotte Bronte 夏洛蒂·勃朗特	1816~1855	• English novelist, the eldest of the Bronte sisters（勃朗特三姐妹） • Representative work: *Jane Eyre*（《简·爱》）
Emily Bronte 埃米莉·勃朗特	1818~1848	• The second eldest of the Bronte sisters • Representative work: *Wuthering Heights*（《呼啸山庄》）
Anne Bronte 安妮·勃朗特	1820~1849	• The youngest one of the Bronte sisters • Representative work: *Agnes Grey*（《艾格尼斯·格雷》）
George Eliot 乔治·艾略特	1819~1880	• Novelist • Representative works: *The Mill on the Floss*（《弗洛斯河上的磨坊》） *Silas Marner*（《织工马南传》）
Alfred Tennyson 阿尔弗雷德·丁尼生	1809~1892	• English poet, and Poet Laureate during much of Queen Victoria's reign • Short lyric: *Break, Break, Break*（《拍岸曲》）
Robert Browning 罗伯特·布朗宁	1812~1889	• English poet and playwright, famous for mastery of dramatic monologues（戏剧独白诗） • Poems: *My Last Duchess*（《我的前公爵夫人》） *Meeting at Night*（《深夜幽会》）

6 现代主义时期（19世纪末）

The modern English novel gives a realistic presentation of life of the common English people. In this period, literary trends such as symbolism（象征主义）, the stream of consciousness（意识流）and naturalism（自然主义）gradually take the place of realism.

Writer	Time	Works and Contribution
Oscar Wilde 奥斯卡·王尔德	1854~1900	• Irish writer, poet, and prominent aesthete（唯美主义者） • The representative among the writers of aestheticism（唯美主义）and decadence（颓废派文艺） • Novel: *The Picture of Dorian Gray*（《道林·格雷的画像》） • Collection of stories: *The Happy Prince*（《快乐王子》）
Thomas Hardy 托马斯·哈代	1840~1928	• Novelist • Representative works: *The Mayor of Casterbridge*（《卡斯特桥市长》） *Tess of the D'urbervilles*（《德伯家的苔丝》） *Jude the Obscure*（《无名的裘德》）
George Bernard Shaw 萧伯纳	1856~1950	• Irish Dramatist • Dramas: *Man and Superman*（《人与超人》） *Major Barbara*（《巴巴拉少校》） *Pygmalion*（《皮格马利翁》）
William Butler Yeats 威廉·巴特勒·叶芝	1865~1939	• Irish poet and playwright • Poems: *Sailing to Byzantium*（《航向拜占庭》） *The Second Coming*（《第二次降临》） *Leda and the Swan*（《丽达与天鹅》）
D. H. Lawrence 大卫·赫伯特·劳伦斯	1885~1930	• Novelist • Novel: *Sons and Lovers*（《儿子与情人》） *The Rainbow*（《虹》） *Women in Love*（《恋爱中的女人》） *Lady Chatterley's Lover*（《查泰莱夫人的情人》）

Writer	Time	Works and Contribution
James Joyce 詹姆斯·乔伊斯	1882~1941	<ul><li>Irish novelist</li><li>The founder of the Stream of Consciousness（意识流）</li><li>Novels: *Dubliners*（《都柏林人》） *A Portrait of the Artist as a Young Man*（《一个青年艺术家的画像》） *Ulysses*（《尤利西斯》） *Finnegans Wake*（《芬尼根守灵夜》）</li></ul>
Virginia Woolf 弗吉尼亚·伍尔夫	1882~1941	<ul><li>A representative of Modernism（现代主义）and one of the great innovative novelists of the 20th century</li><li>Novels: *Mrs. Dalloway*（《戴洛维夫人》） *To the Lighthouse*（《到灯塔去》） *The Waves*（《海浪》）</li><li>Essays: *A Room of One's Own*（《自己的房间》） *Three Guineas*（《三枚金币》）</li></ul>

Test 1

真题测试

35. Who is the author of *The Waste Land*?
    A. George Bernard Shaw.　　　　B. W. B. Yeats.
    C. Dylan Thomas.　　　　　　　D. T. S. Eliot.

36. Which of the following novelists wrote *The Sound and the Fury*?
    A. William Faulkner.　　　　　B. Ernest Hemingway.
    C. Scott Fitzgerald.　　　　　　D. John Steinbeck.

37. "The lettuce was lonely without tomatoes and cucumbers for company" is an example of
    A. exaggeration.　　　　　　　B. understatement.
    C. personification.　　　　　　　D. synecdoche.

真题点评

35. [答案] **D** [考点] 文学作家及作品。

[精析]《荒原》(*The Waste Land*)是美国诗人艾略特最著名的一首长诗,这首诗是献给庞德的。在诗歌中,他用典的范围极广,从莎士比亚到但丁,从佛经到民歌等。正是这部寻求精神家园的诗歌,使得艾略特扬名于世。萧伯纳是爱尔兰剧作家,1925年获诺贝尔文学奖,是英国现代杰出的现实主义戏剧作家。他的著名作品有《圣女贞德》(*Saint Joan*)和历史剧《卖花女》(*Pygmalion*)。叶芝是爱尔兰著名诗人,被称为"二十世纪最伟大的英语诗人",代表作是《茵纳斯弗利岛》(*The Lake Isle of Innisfree*)。托马斯,威尔士诗人、作家,他的诗歌围绕生、欲、死三大主题,著名的作品是《牛奶树下》(*Under Milk Wood*)和《不要温和地走进那个良夜》(*Do Not Go Gentle into That Good Night*)。

36. [答案] **A** [考点]美国作家及作品。

[精析]《喧哗与骚动》(*The Sound and the Fury*)是美国著名小说家威廉·福克纳(William Faulkner, 1897–1962)的代表作。福克纳另两部著名作品是《八月之光》(*Light in August*)和《献给艾米莉的玫瑰花》(*A Rose for Emily*)。欧内斯特·海明威(Ernest Hemingway),美国小说家,代表作有《老人与海》(*The Old Man and the*

55

Sea)、《太阳照样升起》(*The Sun Also Rises*)、《永别了，武器》(*A Farewell to Arms*)、《丧钟为谁而鸣》(*For Whom the Bell Tolls*)等。司各特·菲茨杰拉德(Scott Fitzgerald)，美国作家，他的著名小说《了不起的盖茨比》(*The Great Gatsby*)是"迷惘的一代"的代表作。约翰·斯坦贝克(John Steinbeck)，美国作家，代表作是《愤怒的葡萄》(*The Grapes of Wrath*)。

37. [答案] C　[考点] 文学修辞。

[精析] "莴苣没有西红柿和黄瓜的陪伴显得很孤独。"是拟人的修辞方法。拟人 (personification)就是把事物人格化，把本来不具备人的一些动作和感情的事物变成和人一样，这一手法是中外作家都常用的修辞手法之一。夸张(exaggeration)指为了启发听者或读者的想象力和加强所说的话的力量，用夸大的词语来形容事物。含蓄陈述(understatement)即把表示现象的状态、程度、形象、数量、作用等特征性的东西故意说得特别低、小，此种修辞格正好跟夸张相反。提喻(synecdoche)通常是用局部来代替整体，或整体来代替局部的修辞手法。

Test 2

真题测试

35. Virginia Woolf was an important female _____ in the 20th-century England.
   A. poet　　　　　　　　　　　　　B. biographer
   C. playwright　　　　　　　　　　D. novelist

36. _____ refers to a long narrative poem that records the adventures of a hero in a nation's history.
   A. Ballad　　　　　　　　　　　　B. Romance
   C. Epic　　　　　　　　　　　　　D. Elegy

37. Which of the following best explores American myth in the 20th century?
   A. *The Great Gatsby*.　　　　　　B. *The Sun Also Rises*.
   C. *The Sound and the Fury*.　　　D. *Beyond the Horizon*.

真题点评

35. [答案] D　[考点] 英国文学之作家贡献。

[精析] 弗吉尼亚·伍尔夫(Virginia Woolf)是20世纪意识流(stream of consciousness)小说的代表人物之一，被誉为"20世纪现代主义与女性主义的先锋之一"，《墙上的斑点》(*The Mark on the Wall*)是她第一篇典型的意识流作品，其最著名的代表作品还有《达洛维夫人》(*Mrs. Dalloway*)、《灯塔行》(*To the Lighthouse*)、《雅各的房间》(*Jacob's Room*)。

36. [答案] C [考点] 文学基本概念。

[精析] 史诗或叙事诗 (epic) 指的就是叙述英雄传说或民族重大历史事件的古代叙事长诗；民谣（ballad）则指的是民间流行的歌谣，它盛行于15世纪；传奇故事（romance）是中世纪盛行的一种文学形式，主要以散文或叙事诗的形式描述骑士等贵族英雄人物的生活和事迹；挽歌 (elegy) 是写给死者表达悲伤情感的诗歌。

37. [答案] A [考点] 美国文学之作家作品。

[精析]《了不起的盖茨比》(The Great Gatsby) 是20世纪美国小说家弗朗西斯·司各特·菲茨杰拉德 (Francis Scott Fitzgerald) 的代表作品。这部作品发表于1925年，以20世纪20年代的纽约市及长岛为背景，设定在现代化的美国社会中上阶层的白人圈内，真实地反映了美国当时的社会现状。《了不起的盖茨比》奠定了弗朗西斯·司各特·菲茨杰拉德在现代美国文学史上的地位，他因此成为20世纪20年代"爵士时代"的发言人和"迷惘的一代"的代表作家之一。

Test 3

(真题测试)

35. _____ is best known for the technique of dramatic monologue in his poems.

　　A. William Blake

　　B. W. B. Yeats

　　C. Robert Browning

　　D. William Wordsworth

36. *The Financier* is written by

　　A. Mark Twain.

　　B. Henry James.

　　C. William Faulkner.

　　D. Theodore Dreiser.

37. In literature a story in verse or prose with a double meaning is defined as

　　A. allegory.

　　B. sonnet.

　　C. blank verse.

　　D. rhyme.

(真题点评)

35. [答案] C [考点] 英国文学作家及其贡献。

[精析] 英国维多利亚时期著名诗人罗伯特·布朗宁（Robert Browning, 1812~1889）对英国诗歌的最大贡献是他发展并完善了戏剧独白诗（Dramatic monologue），故选C。威廉·布莱克 (William Blake) 是19世纪英国浪漫派诗人，主要诗作有诗集《天真之歌》(Song of Innocence)、《经验之歌》(Song of Experience) 等。威廉·巴特勒·叶芝（William Butler Yeats），爱尔兰诗人、剧作家，是"爱尔兰文艺复兴运动"的领袖，也是艾比剧院 (Abbey Theatre) 的创建者之一，被诗人艾略特誉为"当代最伟大的诗人"。威廉·华兹华斯 (William Wordsworth) 是英国的浪漫主义诗人，属"湖畔派"诗人，1843年被授予"桂冠诗人"的称号。

36. ［答案］D ［考点］美国文学之作家作品。

［精析］《金融家》(*The Financier*, 1912)是美国现实主义时期小说家西奥多·德莱塞 (Theodore Dreiser)创作的《欲望三部曲》(*Trilogy of Desire*)中的第一部。其他两部 是《巨人》(*The Titan*, 1914)和《斯多葛》(*The Stoic*, 1947)。

37. ［答案］A ［考点］文学基本概念。

［精析］通过讲故事来说明道理的文学体裁是寓言(allegory)。故事既包含故事本身 的字面意思，又包括其隐含的比喻意义，故选A。十四行诗(sonnet)是一种格律严 谨的抒情诗体。英国十四行诗以莎士比亚最为出名，诗由三节四行诗和两行对句 组成，每行10个音节，韵式为ABAB, CDCD, EFEF, GG。克里斯托弗·马洛是第一 个将无韵体(blank verse)运用到戏剧中的英国戏剧家。韵律(rhyme)是诗歌声韵和 节奏，以及诗歌的押韵规则。

Test 4

真题测试

35. *Ode to the West Wind* was written by

    A. William Blake.   B. William Wordsworth.

    C. Samuel Taylor Coleridge.   D. Percy B. Shelley.

36. Who among the following is a poet of free verse?

    A. Ralph Waldo Emerson.   B. Walt Whitman.

    C. Herman Melville.   D. Theodore Dreiser.

37. The novel *Sons and Lovers* was written by

    A. Thomas Hardy.   B. John Galsworthy.

    C. D. H. Lawrence.   D. James Joyce.

真题点评

35. ［答案］D ［考点］英国文学作家及其作品。

［精析］《西风颂》(*Ode to the West Wind*) 是英国第二代浪漫主义诗人雪莱(Percy Bysshe Shelley)的作品，《西风颂》中最著名的佳句是"冬天到了，春天还会远吗？" (If Winter comes, can Spring be far behind?) 雪莱还著有《解放了的普罗米修斯》 (*Prometheus Unbounded*)、《致云雀》(*To a Skylark*)等作品。

36. ［答案］B ［考点］美国文学作家及其贡献。

［精析］自由诗体(free verse)是由惠特曼(Walt Whitman)创造的，这种新诗体的创 作不受传统格律和韵脚的限制和束缚。惠特曼的代表作是《草叶集》(*Leaves of Grass*)，它标志着美国浪漫主义时期的结束。爱默生(Ralph Waldo Emerson)是美 国超验主义(Transcendentalism)的倡导者，代表作《论自助》(*Self-Reliance*)。梅尔维

尔(Herman Melville)是美国浪漫主义后期的小说家，代表作是《白鲸》(*Moby Dich*)。德莱塞(*Theodore Dreiser*)是美国自然主义的代表人物，代表作有"欲望三部曲"(*Trilogy of Desire*)和《嘉莉妹妹》(*Sister Carrie*)。

37. [答案] C [考点] 英美文学之作家作品。
    [精析]《儿子与情人》(*Sons and Lovers*)是20世纪英国最独特和最有争议作家之一的戴维·赫伯特·劳伦斯(D. H. Lawrence)的长篇小说，通常人们把《儿子与情人》看做是一部带有自传性质的长篇小说，因为故事内容取材于劳伦斯的早年生活。

Test 5

真题测试

35. *The Canterbury Tales*, a collection of stories told by a group of pilgrims on their way to Canterbury, is an important poetic work by
    A. William Langland.   B. Geoffrey Chaucer.
    C. William Shakespeare.   D. Alfred Tennyson.
36. Who wrote *The American*?
    A. Herman Melville.   B. Nathaniel Hawthorne.
    C. Henry James.   D. Theodore Dreiser.
37. All of the following are well-known female writers in 20th-century Britain EXCEPT
    A. George Eliot.   B. Iris Jean Murdoch.
    C. Doris Lessing.   D. Muriel Spark.

真题点评

35. [答案] B [考点] 英美文学之文学作品。
    [精析]《坎特伯雷故事集》(*The Canterbury Tales*) 是英国作家乔叟(Geoffrey Chaucer)的小说。作品描写一群香客聚集在伦敦一家小旅店里，准备去坎特伯雷城朝圣。店主人建议香客们在往返途中各讲两个故事，看谁讲得最好。《坎特伯雷故事集》包括了23个故事。作品广泛地反映了资本主义萌芽时期的英国社会生活，揭露了教会的腐败、教士的贪婪和伪善，谴责了扼杀人性的禁欲主义，肯定了世俗的爱情生活。它是英国文学史上现实主义的第一部典范。乔叟首创的英雄双韵体(Heroic Couplet) 为以后的英国诗人所广泛采用，因而乔叟被誉为"英国诗歌之父"。故选B。
36. [答案] C [考点] 英美文学之文学作品。
    [精析]《美国人》(*The American*) 是美国现实主义时期作家亨利·詹姆斯(Henry James) 的长篇小说，他是美国现实主义时期的三大代表作家之一，其他两位为豪威尔斯(William Dean Howells)和马克·吐温(Mark Twain)。

詹姆斯的主要作品：

- 长篇小说：《鸽翼》(*The Wings of the Dove*)、《大使》(*The Ambassadors*)、《金碗》(*The Golden Bowl*)、《贵妇人的画像》(*The Portrait of a Lady*)
- 中短篇小说：《黛西·米勒》(*Daisy Miller*)

37. [答案] A [考点] 英美文学作家生平年代。

[精析] 乔治·艾略特（George Eliot, 1819~1880）是英国维多利亚时代著名作家之一；艾丽丝·简·默多克(Iris Jean Murdoch, 1919~1999)是战后英国文坛最具影响力的小说家之一；多丽丝·莱辛（Doris Lessing, 1919年10月22日~）是当代英国最重要的作家之一，被誉为继伍尔夫之后最伟大的女性作家，第11位女性诺贝尔文学奖获得者；穆丽尔·斯帕克(Muriel Spark, 1918年~)是苏格兰女作家，于20世纪50年代开始文学创作。

Test 6

35. Which of the following novels was written by Emily Bronte?

A. *Oliver Twist.*　　　　　　　　B. *Middlemarch.*

C. *Jane Eyre.*　　　　　　　　　D. *Wuthering Heights.*

36. William Butler Yeats was a (n) _____ poet and playwright.

A. American　　　　　　　　　B. Canadian

C. Irish　　　　　　　　　　　D. Australian

37. *Death of a Salesman* was written by

A. Arthur Miller.　　　　　　　B. Ernest Hemingway.

C. Ralph Ellison.　　　　　　　D. James Baldwin.

35. [答案] D [考点] 英国文学作家及作品。

[精析] 埃米莉·勃朗特（Emily Bronte）是勃朗特三姐妹中的老二，她的代表作是《呼啸山庄》(*Wuthering Heights*)；《雾都孤儿》(*Oliver Twist*)是英国作家查尔斯·狄更斯(Charles Dickens)的作品；《米德尔马契》(*Middlemarch*)是英国作家乔治·艾略特(George Eliot)的作品。

勃朗特三姐妹及其代表作：

- 夏洛蒂·勃朗特(Charlotte Bronte)　　《简·爱》(*Jane Eyre*)

- 埃米莉·勃朗特(Emily Bronte) 《呼啸山庄》(*Wuthering Heights*)
- 安妮·勃朗特(Anne Bronte) 《艾格尼斯·格雷》(*Agnes Grey*)

36. [答案]C [考点]爱尔兰文学作家及流派。

[精析]威廉·巴特勒·叶芝(William Butler Yeats)是爱尔兰的诗人和剧作家。

37. [答案]A [考点]美国文学作家及作品。

[精析]《推销员之死》(*Death of a Salesman*)是当代美国剧作家亚瑟·米勒(Arthur Miller)的代表作。

要点归纳

欧内斯特·海明威(Ernest Hemingway),美国小说家,代表作品有:
- 《太阳照样升起》(*The Sun Also Rises*) 《永别了,武器》(*A Farewell to Arms*) 《丧钟为谁而鸣》(*For Whom the Bell Tolls*)《老人与海》(*The Old Man and the Sea*)
- 拉尔夫·埃里森(Ralph Ellison),美国当代黑人作家,代表作品有: 《看不见的人》或《隐形人》(*Invisible Man*)
- 詹姆斯·鲍德温(James Baldwin),美国黑人作家,代表作品有: 《向苍天呼吁》(*Go Tell It on the Mountain*)

Test 7

真题测试

35. Which of the following writers is a poet of the 20th century?

　　A. T. S. Eliot.　　　　　　　　　　B. D. H. Lawrence.

　　C. Theodore Dreiser.　　　　　　　D. James Joyce.

36. The novel *For Whom the Bell Tolls* is written by

　　A. Scott Fitzgerald.　　　　　　　B. William Faulkner.

　　C. Eugene O'Neil.　　　　　　　　D. Ernest Hemingway.

37. _____ is defined as an expression of human emotion which is condensed into fourteen lines.

　　A. Free verse　　B. Sonnet　　　　C. Ode　　　　D. Epigram

真题点评

35. [答案]A [考点]英美文学作家及其时代。

[精析]托马斯·斯特恩斯·艾略特(Thomas Stearns Eliot)是美国现代主义时期的代表诗人。劳伦斯(D. H. Lawrence)是英国20世纪著名的小说家,西奥多·德莱赛(Theodore Dreiser)的美国自然主义时期的著名小说家,詹姆斯·乔伊斯(James Joyce)是爱尔兰的意识流作家。

36. [答案] D [考点] 英美文学之文学作品。

[精析]《丧钟为谁而鸣》(For Whom the Bell Tolls) 是美国现代小说家欧内斯特·海明威(Ernest Hemingway)的代表作之一。

37. [答案] B [考点] 文学基本概念。

[精析] 十四行诗(sonnet)是一种抒情短诗，一般来说有14行，每一行有特定的韵律，行与行之间有固定的押韵格式。

Test 8

(真题测试)

35. The novel *Emma* is written by

    A. Mary Shelley.   B. Charlotte Bronte.

    C. Elizabeth C. Gaskell.   D. Jane Austen.

36. Which of following is NOT a romantic poet?

    A. William Wordsworth.   B. George Elliot.

    C. George G. Byron.   D. Percy B. Shelley.

37. William Sidney Porter, known as O. Henry, is most famous for

    A. his poems.   B. his plays.

    C. his short stories.   D. his novels.

(真题点评)

35. [答案] D [考点] 英美文学之作家作品。

[精析]《爱玛》是英国作家简·奥斯汀(Jane Austen)的作品，她的代表作还有《傲慢与偏见》(*Pride and Prejudice*)，《理智与情感》(*Sense and Sensibility*)。

36. [答案] B [考点] 英美文学之作家流派。

[精析] William Wordsworth, George G. Byron, Percy B. Shelley都是英国浪漫主义诗人的代表人物，而George Elliot是维多利亚时期的小说家，不是诗人。

37. [答案] C [考点] 美国文学作家作品风格。

[精析] O. Henry(欧·亨利)是美国批判现实主义作家William Sidney Porter的笔名，他是世界著名的短篇小说家，曾被誉为"美国现代短篇小说之父"。

第四章
英语语言学

　　语言学部分涉及的知识点比较多,但是主要考点集中在基本概念及运用方面,具体说来,包括:语言学基本概念、语言学基本知识、语言学基本概念的实例分析、语言学家及其代表理论观点。

　　人文知识部分重在考查知识面,涉及范围广,但是并不需要深入挖掘,因此编者只针对重要的概念和知识点进行讲解。同时,为了便于考生理解和使用本书,编者用英文给出基本概念和解释,在必要的时候加注中文。

第一节 语言学概念

1 语言的特点和功能

(1) Features of Language 语言的特点

1) **Creativity**:可创造性,即语言的使用者可以理解并创造无限数量的句子。

2) **Duality**:二重性,指语言是声音和意义双重结构组成的系统。

3) **Arbitrariness**:任意性,即语言所表达的概念与其相对应的声音符号间的关系是任意的。

4) **Displacement**:移位性,指我们用语言可以表达许多不在场的东西。

5) **Cultural Transmission**:文化传递性,指语言是一种传递文化的方式。

6) **Interchangeability**:可交换性,即同一个语言共同体内的成员可以传递、接受信息。

7) **Reflexivity**:自反性,指人类的语言可以被用来描述语言本身,即"元语言"。

(2) Functions of Language 语言的功能

1) **Informative**:信息功能,即语言可以用来传递信息,在功能语言学中称之为概念功能(ideational function)。

2) **Interpersonal**:人际功能,指人们通过语言来建立、维持其社会地位。

3) **Performative**:施为功能,指人们通过语言来实现让他人完成某个任务的功能。此概念来自Austin和Searle,属于语用学(Pragmatics)的范畴。

4) **Emotive**:感情功能,指语言可以改变听众的感情。

5）**Phatic Communion**：交感功能，指人们使用特定的表达方式，如"你好"等，来维持相互间的关系。

6）**Recreational**：娱乐功能，指人们可以使用语言进行娱乐活动，如唱歌等。

7）**Metalingual**：元语言功能，指人类可以使用语言来谈论、改变语言本身。

② 语言学的主要分支

语言学就是对语言的科学研究。

（1）Internal Branches: Intra-Disciplinary Divisions 内部分支

1）**Phonetics**（语音学）: the study of speech sounds（研究语音）.

2）**Phonology**（音系学）: the study of the rules governing the structure, distribution and sequencing of speech sounds and the shape of syllables（研究语音和音节的结构、分布和序列）.

3）**Morphology**（形态学）: the study of the minimal units of meaning—morphemes and word-formation processes, that is, the internal organization of words（研究意义的最小单位——语素和成词过程，即单词的内部构造）.

4）**Syntax**（句法学）: the study of principles of forming and understanding correct English sentences（研究造句的规则）.

5）**Semantics**（语义学）: the study of how meaning is encoded in a language（研究意义如何在语言中编码）.

6）**Pragmatics**（语用学）: the study of meaning in context（研究语境中的意义）.

（2）External Branches: Inter-Disciplinary Divisions 外部分支：跨学科分支，即宏观语言学分支

1）**Psycholinguistics**（心理语言学）: to study the interrelation of language and mind.

2）**Sociolinguistics**（社会语言学）: to study the characteristics of language varieties, language functions and speakers as the three interact and change within a speech community.

3）**Anthropological Linguistics**（人类语言学）: to study the emergence of language and the divergence of language over thousands of years.

4）**Computational Linguistics**（计算机语言学）: to study the use of computers to process or produce human language.

③ 语音学 Phonetics

（1）Sub-Branches of Phonetics 语音学分支

1）**Articulatory phonetics**（发音语音学）: the production of speech sounds.

2）**Acoustic phonetics**（声学语音学）: the physical properties of speech sounds.

3）**Auditory phonetics**（听觉语音学）: the perceptive mechanism of speech sounds.

（2）Groups of Speech Sounds 语音分类

Consonants（辅音）and Vowels（元音）

④ 音系学 Phonology

（1）Phonemes and Allophones 音位和音位变体

1）**Phoneme**（音位）: a distinctive, abstract sound unit with a distinctive feature（在某一语言中具有区别意义的最小语音单位）.

2）**Allophones**（音位变体）: the variants of a phoneme.

3）**Contrastive Distribution**（对立分布）: the typical to be found in Minimal Pairs（最小语音对）. A Minimal Pair refers to two words which differ from each other by only one distinctive sound （one phoneme）and which also differ in meaning, for example, *bear* and *pear*.

4）**Complementary Distribution**（互补分布）: allophones that are not found in the same position（从不出现在相同环境中的音位变体）.

5）**Free Variation** （自由变体）: If segments appear in the same position but the mutual substitution does not result in change of meaning, they are said to be in free variation （同一个词由于某种原因发成了两个音，这种差异可能来自方言或者习惯等）.

（2）Suprasegmental Features 超音段特征

The principle suprasegmental features are syllable, stress, tone and intonation.

⑤ 形态学 Morphology

（1）Morpheme 词素

1）**Morpheme**: the smallest meaningful unit of language （最小的有意义的语言单位）.

2）**Free Morphemes**（自由语素）**and Bound Morphemes**（黏着语素）
- Morphemes constituting words by themselves are called free morphemes. They are roots（词根）of words.

- Morphemes always attached to free morphemes to form new words are called bound morphemes. They are affixes（词缀）of words, which can be further divided into Inflectional Affixes（屈折词缀）and Derivational Affixes(派生词缀).

  Inflexional morphemes in modern English indicate case and number of nouns, tense and aspect of verbs, and degree of adjectives and adverbs.

  Derivational morphemes are bound morphemes added to existing forms to construct new words.

（2）**Word Formation** 词的形成

　　1）**Derivation**(派生): length + en→lengthen

　　2）**Compounding**(复合): book + shelf→bookshelf

　　3）**Lexical Change Proper**(特有的词汇变化)

- Invention(新创词语): nylon
- Blending(混成词): transfer + resister→transistor
- Abbreviation(缩写词): advertisement→ad
- Acronym(首字母缩写词): World Trade Organization→WTO
- Back-formation(逆构词法): editor→edit
- Borrowing(外来词): Kung-fu

　　4）**Semantic Change**(语义变化)

- Broadening(词义扩大): task tax imposed→a piece of work
- Narrowing(词义缩小): deer beast→a particular kind of animal
- Meaning shift(词义转移): bead prayer→the prayer bead→small, ball-shaped piece of glass, metal or wood

⑥ 句法学 Syntax

（1）**Traditional Grammar** 传统语法

　　1）In traditional grammar, a sentence is considered a sequence of words which are classified into parts of speech.

　　2）Sentences are analysed in terms of grammatical functions of words: subjects, objects, verbs（predicates）, predicatives...

　　3）Nouns: number, case, gender...

　　4）Verbs: tense, aspect, voice...

　　5）Agreement in number/person/gender

（2）**Structural Grammar** 结构主义语法

　　1）It was founded by Saussure, who distinguishes the linguistic competence of the speaker and the actual phenomena or data of linguistics as Langue（语言）and Parole（言语）.

2）Structural grammar arose out of **an attempt to deviate from traditional grammar**. It deals with the inter-relationships of different grammatical units. In the concern of structural grammar, words are not just independent grammatical units, but are inter-related to one another.

3）**Key concepts**: Syntagmatic and Paradigmatic relations（组合关系和聚合关系）, Structure and System（结构与系统）, Immediate constituents（直接成分）, Endocentric and Exocentric constructions（向心结构与离心结构）.

（3）**Transformational-Generative（TG）Grammar 转换生成语法**

1）It was founded by **Noam Chomsky,** who believes that language is somewhat innate—The Innateness Hypothesis（天赋假说）and that children are born with a Language Acquisition Device（语言习得机制）, which consists of three elements: a hypothesis-maker（假设标记）, linguistic universal（语言普遍现象）and an evaluation procedure（评估程序）.

2）Chomsky distinguishes a language user's underlying knowledge about the system of rules and the actual use of language in concrete situation as Competence（语言能力）and Performance（语言运用）. TG Grammar takes the ideal speaker's linguistic competence as the object of study.

3）The Grammar has **five stages of development**: the Classical Theory, the Standard Theory, the Extended Standard Theory, the Revised Extended Standard Theory and the Minimalist program.

（4）**Systematic Functional Grammar 系统功能语法**

1）It was founded by **M. A. K. Halliday** and takes actual uses of language as the object of study.

2）The Grammar has **two components**: Systematic Grammar and Functional Grammar.

3）**Key concepts**: Theme and Rheme（主位和述位）, Communicative Dynamism（交际动力）, the three meta-functions of language—Ideational function（概念功能）, Interpersonal function（交际功能）and Textual function（文本功能）.

7 语义学 Semantics

Definition of Meaning 意义的定义

1）**G. Leech and his 7 types of meaning**: Conceptual meaning（概念意义）, Connotative meaning（内涵意义）, Social meaning（社会意义）, Affective meaning(情感意义), Reflected meaning(反映意义), Collocative meaning(搭配意义), Thematic meaning(主题意义).

2) **The conceptual view**（概念主义观点）: semantic triangle（语义三角）by Ogden and Richards—Symbol or Form, Referent, and Thought or Reference.

3) **Contextualism**（语境主义）: to base meaning on context; a representative of the approach was J. R. Firth.

4) **Behaviorism**（行为主义）: the meaning of a language form is the situation in which the speaker utters it and the response it calls forth in the hearer; a supporter of the approach was Bloomfield, who was a principle representative of American Structuralism（美国结构主义）.

5) **Key Concepts:**
- Lexical sense relations(词汇涵义关系): Synonymy(同义关系), Polysemy(一词多义).
- Homonymy（同音或同形异义关系）: Hyponymy（上下义关系）, Antonymy(反义关系).
- Sentential sense relations（语句涵义关系）: Tautology（同义反复句）, Contradiction(自相矛盾句), Inconsistency(矛盾关系), Synonymousness（同义关系）, Entailment（衍推关系）, Presupposition（预设关系）, Semantically Anomalousness(语义反常句).

8 语用学 Pragmatics

（1）Speech Act Theory 言语行为理论

1) **The first major theory** in the study of language in use.

2) **Founded by John Langshaw Austin.**

3) **The major idea**: things can be done with word.

4) **Two types of sentences**: Performative and Constative(行事话语与叙事话语).

5) **Theory of the Illocutionary**（行事行为理论）: Locutionary Act（言内行为）, Illocutionary Act(言外行为), Perlocutionary Act(言后行为).

（2）Conversational Implicature 会话含义理论

1) Proposed by **Herbert Paul Grice**.

2) **The Cooperative Principles**（合作原则）: Quantity Maxim（数量准则）, Quality Maxim(质量准则), Relation Maxim(关系准则), Manner Maxim(方式准则).

Test 1

真题测试

38. In English if a word begins with a [1] or a [r], then the next sound must be a vowel. This is a(n)

    A. assimilation rule.　　　　　　　B. sequential rule.

    C. deletion rule.　　　　　　　　　D. grammar rule.

39. Which of the following is an example of clipping?

    A. APEC.　　　　　　　　　　　　B. Motel.

    C. Xerox.　　　　　　　　　　　　D. Disco.

40. The type of language which is selected as appropriate to a particular type of situation is called

    A. register.　　　　　　　　　　　B. dialect.

    C. slang.　　　　　　　　　　　　D. variety.

真题点评

38. [答案] B　[考点] 语言学概念的实例分析。

　　[精析] 序列规则(sequential rule)是语言学中的专业术语,是指在某个特殊语言里规范音素组合的规则,题中所给例子是典型的序列规则。同化规则(assimilation rule)指的是一个语音片段通过复写其他的一个音位特征从而使两个音素显得相近。这种现象常出现在鼻音[n]里。省略原则(deletion rule)即有的音素省而不发,但相应的字母能被拼写出来,如:g在sign这个单词里是不发声的。语法规则(grammar rule)包括组合规则和聚合规则,像构词法和句法都属于组合规则范畴。

39. [答案] D　[考点] 语言学概念的实例分析。

　　[精析] clipping是指只截取较长单词前面几个字母来代替整个单词的缩写情况,Disco 是 discotheque 的缩写,故属于此类。APEC 是 Asia-Pacific Economic Cooperation的缩写,属于只取首字母的缩写词(acronym);motel是motor、hotel两词组合而来,属于合成词(blending)。Xerox是"富士施乐"的意思,属于商标名称(trade name)。

构词法：

- 派生词(Derivation)：从已存在的单词上形成的词，如：sing→singer。
- 复合词(Compounding)：把两个词放在一起，如：without。
- 新造词(Coinage)：为了某种目的而创造的词，如：walkman。
- 缩写(Clipping)：以开头几个字母代替整个单词的缩写，如：expo=exposition。
- 合成词(Blending)：从两个词里各取一部分，如：smog=smoke+fog。
- 首字母缩写词(Acronym)：取每个词的首字母，如：IT=information technology。
- 外借词(Borrowing)：从其他语言里借来的词，如：monsieur。

40. ［答案］A　［考点］语言学基本概念——语域。

［精析］根据某种语境的独特语言特征所构成的表达类型就是一个语域(register)，所以register在这里不是"注册"的意思，而是指"语域"，是社会语言学和语用学的常用概念。dialect意为"方言"，它是语言的变体，根据性质，方言可分地域方言和社会方言。slang意为"俚语"或"行话"，用于非正式场合，跟词汇一样，也经过换义、语义扩大、语义缩小、截短法、缩略词、褒义化、贬义化、夸张、委婉说法等流行于民间。variety是指"语言变体"，由具备相同社会特征的人在相同的社会环境中所普遍使用的某种语言表现形式，如果一些词语只有女性使用，这些词语就称为女性变体，如果只有男性使用，就称为男性变体。

Test 2

真题测试

38. _____ is defined as the study of the relationship between language and mind.

　A. Semantics　　　　　　　　　　　B. Pragmatics

　C. Cognitive linguistics　　　　　　　D. Sociolinguistics

39. A vowel is different from a consonant in English because of

　A. absence of obstruction.　　　　　　B. presence of obstruction.

　C. manner of articulation.　　　　　　D. place of articulation.

40. The definition "the act of using, or promoting the use of, several languages, either by an individual speaker or by a community of speakers" refers to

　A. Pidgin.　　　　　　　　　　　　B. Creole.

　C. Multilingualism.　　　　　　　　D. Bilingualism.

真题点评

38. ［答案］C　［考点］语言学基本概念——认知语言学。

[精析] 认知语言学(Cognitive linguistics)的主要观点是语言的创建、学习及运用，基本上都必须能够通过人类的认知加以解释，因为认知能力是人类学习知识的根本，由此可知，认知语言学主要研究的是语言与人的理解力的关系，故选C；社会语言学(Sociolinguistics)主要研究的是社会各层面对语言运用的影响，包含文化准则、社会规范或情境，同时也研究社会本质和差别对语言的影响，如族群、宗教、地位、性别、教育程度、年纪等；语义学(Semantics)研究的是词语在词汇、句子、篇章等自然语言中的意义；语用学(Pragmatics)是专门研究语言的理解和使用的学问，它研究在特定情境中的特定话语，研究如何通过语境来理解和使用语言。

39. [答案] A [考点] 语言学基本知识。
[精析] 在发辅音时，气流在声带的某些位置可能受到阻挡，而在发元音时，气流不会受到阻挡，由此可知，元音与辅音的区别就是元音中没有气流的阻挡。

40. [答案] C [考点] 语言学基本概念——多语制。
[精析] 提倡个人或群体同时使用多种语言被称为复语制或多语制(Multilingualism)；Bilingualism指的是能使用两种语言；皮钦语(Pidgin)是不同语种的人们在商业交往中发展起来的混杂语言；克里奥尔语(Creole)是指一种混合多种语言词汇、有时也掺杂其他一些语言语法的语言，这个词用以泛指所有的"混合语"。

Test 3

真题测试

38. _____ refers to the learning and development of a language.
　　A. Language acquisition　　　　B. Language comprehension
　　C. Language production　　　　D. Language instruction

39. The word "Motel" comes from "motor + hotel". This is an example of _____ in morphology.
　　A. backformation　　　　　　B. conversion
　　C. blending　　　　　　　　D. acronym

40. Language is the tool of communication. The symbol "Highway Closed" on a highway serves
　　A. an expressive function.　　　B. an informative function.
　　C. a performative function.　　　D. a persuasive function.

真题点评

38. [答案] A [考点] 语言学概念——语言习得。
[精析] 语言习得(language acquisition)、语言产生(language production)和语言理解(language comprehension)是心理语言学(psycholinguistics)主要研究的三个方面。

语言习得指的是儿童天生就拥有学习语言的能力，语言是人类的特性。语言理解指的是人类能够根据不同的语言结构理解不同的句子含义。语言产生指的是人类在对话中为表达自己的观点所采取的方式。

39. [答案]C [考点]语言学概念的实例分析。

[精析]通过"motor hotel"组合成一个词motel，属于形态学(morphology)中词的变化(lexical change proper)中的混成词(blending)。

> **要点归纳**
>
> 特有的词汇变化：
> - 新创词汇(invention)例如：Coke。
> - 混成词(blending)例如：smoke fog→smog。
> - 首字母缩写词(acronym)例如：WTO→World Trade Organization。
> - 缩写词(abbreviation)例如：advertisement→ad。
> - 逆构词(back-formation)例如：hawker→hawk。
> - 类推构词(analogical creation)例如：work的过去式wrought→worked。
> - 外来词(borrowing)例如：kung-fu 来自中国。

40. [答案]B [考点]语言学概念的实例分析。

[精析]高速公路上"高速公路封闭"告示牌是为了给人们基本的信息，获得一个事实情况。应该是语言的信息功能(informative function)。

> **要点归纳**
>
> 语言的基本功能：
> - 信息功能(informative function)，传达事实信息。
> - 人际功能(interpersonal function)，建立和维护人在社会中的地位。
> - 施为功能(performative function)，在各种仪式中的用语，例如：婚礼用语。
> - 情感功能(emotive function)，用于抒发人情感，如：damn it...。
> - 交感性谈话（phatic function），用于人们相互寒暄时的语言。例如：good morning。
> - 娱乐功能(recreational function)，仅为娱乐的语言，例如：唱歌。
> - 元语言功能(metalingual function)，用语言来解释语言本身。

Test 4

> **真题测试**

38. The study of the mental processes of language comprehension and production is
    A. corpus linguistics.
    B. sociolinguistics.
    C. theoretical linguistics.
    D. psycholinguistics.

39. A special language variety that mixes languages and is used by speakers of different languages for purposes of trading is called
    A. dialect.   B. idiolect.

    C. pidgin.   D. register.

40. When a speaker expresses his intention of speaking, such as asking someone to open the window, he is performing
    A. an illocutionary act.   B. a perlocutionary act.

    C. a locutionary act.   D. none of the above.

真题点评

38. ［答案］D ［考点］语言学概念——心理语言学。

［精析］心理语言学(psycholinguistics)是研究语言活动中的心理过程的学科。题干中的"语言表达和语言理解"就是语言活动，由此可知，题干描述的应属于心理语言学范畴，故选D。选项A中的语料库语言学(corpus linguistics)是一门与语料库直接有关的语言学科。语料库是载有语言信息的大量语言资料的集合，这些语言资料可以是书面材料，也可以是自然会话的转写材料。选项B中的社会语言学(sociolinguistics)主要研究语言和社会的各种关系，使用语言学的材料来描写和解释社会行为。选项C中的理论语言学(theoretical linguistics)所研究的是从具体的语言现象中总结、归纳出普遍的系统的理论和规律，并用这个理论指导各个具体语言的学习研究。

39. ［答案］C ［考点］语言学概念——洋泾浜语。

［精析］由不同语言混合，并用于母语不同的语言群体进行贸易交流的语言变体是洋泾浜语(pidgin)。故选C。选项A中的方言(dialect)是语言的变体，根据性质，方言可分地域方言和社会方言，地域方言是语言因地域方面的差别而形成的变体，是全民语言的不同地域上的分支。社会方言是同一地域的社会成员因为在职业、阶层、年龄、性别、文化教养等方面的社会差异而形成不同的社会变体。选项B中的习语(idiolect)指那些常用在一起，具有特定形式的词组，其蕴含的意义往往不能从词组中单个词的意思推测而得。习语通常包括成语、俗语、格言、歇后语、谚语、俚语、行话等。选项D中的语域(register)是语言使用的场合或领域的总称。

40. ［答案］A ［考点］语言学概念的实例分析。

［精析］由语言行为本身而随之产生了一些行为属于言外行为（an illocutionary act），故选A。言外行为是由约翰·奥斯汀（John Austin）提出的言语行为理论(speech act theory)中的三种行为中的一种。

言语行为理论的三种行为：
- 言内行为（a locutionary act），即说出词、短语和分句的行为，它是通过句法、词汇和音位来表达字面意义的行为。
- 言外行为（an illocutionary act），即表达说话者的意图的行为，它是在说某些话时所实施的行为。
- 言后行为（a perlocutionary act），是通过某些话所实施的行为，或讲某些话所导致的行为，它是话语所产生的后果或所引起的变化，它是通过讲某些话所完成的行为。

Test 5

38. Which of the following is NOT a design feature of human language?

    A. Arbitrariness.　　　　　　　　　　B. Displacement.

    C. Duality.　　　　　　　　　　　　 D. Diachronicity.

39. What type of sentence is "Mark likes fiction, but Tim is interested in poetry."?

    A. A simple sentence.　　　　　　　 B. A coordinate sentence.

    C. A complex sentence.　　　　　　　D. None of the above.

40. The phenomenon that words having different meanings have the same form is called

    A. hyponymy.　　　　　　　　　　　B. synonymy.

    C. polysemy.　　　　　　　　　　　 D. homonymy.

38. [答案] D　[考点] 语言学基本知识。

    [精析] 历时性（diachronicity）不是语言的区别性特征。历时语言学（diachronic linguistics）从纵向历史进程角度来研究语言。

    要点归纳

    人类语言的区别性特征：
    - 任意性（arbitrariness）　　　　　 ● 双重性（duality）
    - 可创造性（creativity）　　　　　　● 移位性（displacement）

39. [答案] B　[考点] 语言学概念的实例分析。

    [精析] 英语的句子根据语法形式（句子结构）可分为简单句、并列句和复合句。简单句（simple sentence）的基本形式是由一个主语加一个谓语构成。并列句（coordinate sentence）是两个或两个以上的简单句用并列连词连在一起构成的句子，

并列连词有：and, but, or, so等。并列句中的各简单句意义同等重要, 相互之间没有从属关系, 是平行并列的关系。复合句（complex sentence）由一个主句(principal clause)和一个或一个以上的从句(subordinate clause)构成, 主要分为定语从句、状语从句和名词性从句。题干中的例句由but这个表转折的并列连词连接, 属于并列句, 故选B。

40. [答案]D [考点]语言学概念的实例分析。

[精析]题干中提到的是同形异义词（homographs）, 属于同音同形异义关系（homonymy)的一种。

> **要点归纳**
>
> 主要的词义关系(major sense relations)有：
> - 同义关系(synonymy)
> - 一词多义(polysemy)
> - 反义关系(antonymy)
> - 同音同形异义(homonymy)
> - 上下义关系(hyponymy)

Test 6

真题测试

38. _____ refers to the study of the internal structure of words and the rules of word formation.

A. Phonology   B. Morphology

C. Semantics   D. Sociolinguistics

39. The distinctive features of a speech variety may be all the following EXCEPT

A. lexical.   B. syntactic.

C. phonological.   D. psycholinguistic.

40. The word tail once referred to "the tail of a horse", but now it is used to mean "the tail of any animal." This is an example of

A. widening of meaning.   B. narrowing of meaning.

C. meaning shift.   D. loss of meaning.

真题点评

38. [答案]B [考点]语言学概念——形态学。

[精析]形态学(morphology)是对单词的结构和形式的研究, 包括词尾变化、派生和合成词的构成等。音位学(phonology)主要研究的是语言的发音模式和各音之间发生变化的规则。语义学(semantics)主要研究语言单位的意思, 主要是单词和句子的意思。社会语言学(sociolinguistics)主要研究受社会和文化因素影响的语言和语言行为。

39. [答案]D [考点]语言学基本概念。

[精析]言语变体(speech variety)是语言使用者所使用的具有一定区别性特征的变体。语体的差异主要是通过不同的发音(phonological)、不同的语法结构(syntactic)或不同的词汇(lexical)选择来实现的,并不包括心理语言学(psycholinguistics),故选D。

40. [答案]A [考点]语言学概念的实例分析。

[精析]题干中提到"尾巴"在以前是指马的尾巴,但现在用来指任何一种动物的尾巴,题目问这是什么的例子。明显,以前用于特指,现在用于泛指,这属于词语意义扩大的情况。

要点归纳

语义变化(semantic change)主要有五种:
- 词义扩大(broadening)
- 词义缩小(narrowing)
- 俗词源(folk etymology)
- 词义转移(meaning shift)
- 词类转移(class shift)

Test 7

真题测试

38. What essentially distinguishes semantics and pragmatics is the notion of
    A. reference.   B. meaning.
    C. antonymy.   D. context.

39. The words "kid, child, offspring" are examples of
    A. dialectal synonyms.   B. stylistic synonyms.
    C. emotive synonyms.   D. collocational synonyms.

40. The distinction between parole and langue was made by
    A. Halliday.   B. Chomsky.
    C. Bloomfield.   D. Saussure.

真题点评

38. [答案]D [考点]语言学概念区分——语义学和语用学。

[精析]区分语义学和语用学最本质的因素是是否考虑了语言使用过程中的语境(context)因素。

39. [答案]B [考点]语言学概念的实例分析。

[精析]kid、child、offspring这三个单词都意为"孩子",但kid一般用于口语之中,

child一般用于书面语或较为正式的口语之中，offspring则常用于较为正式的文体之中，因此三者应为文体同义词。

英语词汇的同义关系(synonymy)包括：

- 方言同义词 (dialectal synonyms)：指不同方言中表示同一概念的词汇，例如：英式英语的autumn和美式英语的fall。
- 文体同义词 (stylistic synonyms)：指风格或者正式程度不同的词汇，例如：kid、child、offspring。
- 感情同义词 (synonyms that differ in their emotive or evaluative meaning)：指含义相同，但是表示说话人的不同情感或者观点态度的词汇，例如：collaborator和accomplice。
- 固定搭配同义词(collocational synonyms)：指用在不同固定搭配中的同义词，例如：accuse...of...和charge...with...。
- 语义区别同义词(semantically different synonyms)：指语义略有不同的单词。

40. ［答案］D ［考点］语言学家及其代表理论。

［精析］言语(parole)和语言(langue)的区别是由瑞士语言学家F. de Saussure于20世纪早期提出的。语言(langue)指的是语言系统的整体，而言语(parole)则指某个个体在实际语言使用环境中说出的具体话语。

Test 8

38. Syntax is the study of

    A. language functions.   B. sentence structures.

    C. textual organization.   D. word formation.

39. Which of the following is NOT a distinctive feature of human language?

    A. Arbitrariness.   B. Productivity.

    C. Cultural transmission.   D. Finiteness.

40. The speech act theory was first put forward by

    A. John Searle.   B. John Austin.

    C. Noam Chomsky.   D. M. A. K. Halliday.

38. ［答案］B ［考点］语言学概念——句法。

［精析］Syntax句法：It is the study of the rules governing the ways different constituents are combined to form a sentence in a language. 句法学主要研究句子的结构，故选B。

39. [答案]D [考点]语言学的基本理论。

[精析]人类语言的区别性特征主要有任意性(arbitrariness)、双重性(duality)、可创造性(creativity)、移位性(displacement)。根据creativity这个特征看出语言是可以无限创造的，因此不具有finiteness这种性质，故选D。

40. [答案]B [考点]语言学家及其代表理论。

[精析]"言语行为"理论最早是由John Austin在1969年提出来的。

Model Test 1

1. Which of the following does NOT belong to a political division on the island of Great Britain?

    A. England.

    B. Wales.

    C. Ireland.

    D. Scotland.

2. _____ is the world's largest exporter of mutton.

    A. New Zealand

    B. Australia

    C. Canada

    D. America

3. Which of the following does NOT belong to the first English-American colonies?

    A. New Mexico.

    B. Connecticut.

    C. Delaware.

    D. Virginia.

4. The Statue of Liberty is located

    A. in Arizona.

    B. at Boston Harbor.

    C. in Washington.

    D. at New York Harbor.

5. Which of the following novels were NOT developed by James Fenimore Cooper?

    A. Local novels.

    B. Sea novels.

    C. The American frontier novels.

    D. Novels about the revolutionary past.

6. Who is the author of *The Grapes of Wrath*?

    A. John Steinbeck.

    B. Eugene O'Neill.

    C. F. Scott Fitzgerald.

    D. Theodore Dreiser.

7. _____ marked the end of the American romanticism.

    A. *Song of Myself*

    B. *Leaves of Grass*

    C. *Walden*

    D. *The Raven*

8. The function of the sentence "A nice day, isn't it?" is

    A. informative.

    B. phatic.

    C. directive.

    D. performative.

9. Which of the following words is entirely arbitrary?

    A. Book.

    B. Crash.

    C. Beautiful.

    D. Newspaper.

10. Which of the following is NOT a branch of phonetics?
    A. Articulatory Phonetics.   B. Arbitrary Phonetics.
    C. Auditory Phonetics.   D. Acoustic Phonetics.

Model Test 2

1. The ancestors of the English are
   A. Celts.   B. Anglo-Saxons.
   C. Scots.   D. Irish.
2. Canada was originally one colony of
   A. England.   B. America.
   C. Australia.   D. Spain.
3. The traditional dividing line in America between "east" and "west" is
   A. the Appalachians.   B. the Rockies.
   C. the Mississippi River.   D. the Rio Grande River.
4. New Englanders were originally known as _____, which come to stand for all Americans.
   A. Yankees   B. Uncle Sam
   C. Hippies   D. Puritans
5. _____ was usually regarded as the first American writer.
   A. Captain John Smith.   B. William Bradford.
   C. Anne Bradstreet.   D. Thomas Paine.
6. Who is considered the father of modern English poetry?
   A. William Langland.   B. Philip Sidney.
   C. Edmund Spenser.   D. Geoffrey Chaucer.
7. The Spenserian Stanza refers to
   A. a free style.   B. a nine-line verse stanza.
   C. a free verse stanza.   D. nine-line poems.
8. The word "_____" is NOT a free morpheme.
   A. children   B. book
   C. sing   D. use
9. Syntactic categories contain all the following types EXCEPT
   A. meanings that words express.   B. linguistic items the words use.
   C. affixes that words take.   D. structures in which the words can occur.
10. Analysis of meaning includes
    A. predication analysis and semantics analysis.
    B. componential analysis and semantics analysis.
    C. semantics analysis and structural analysis.
    D. componential analysis and predication analysis.

Model Test 3

1. The largest city in New Zealand is
    A. Auckland.
    B. Christchurch.
    C. Dunedin.
    D. Wellington.

2. The three largest cities in Canada do NOT include
    A. Toronto.
    B. Quebec.
    C. Ottawa.
    D. Vancouver.

3. The First Continental Congress was held in 1774 in
    A. New York.
    B. Washington.
    C. Philadelphia.
    D. Louisiana.

4. The first known settlers of Britain were
    A. the Celts.
    B. the Anglo-Saxons.
    C. the Brythons.
    D. the Iberians.

5. _____ first introduced rationalism to England.
    A. Alexander Pope
    B. Samuel Pepys
    C. Daniel Defoe
    D. Samuel Richardson

6. Who wrote one of the most enduring classic poems *Ode to the West Wind*?
    A. William Wordsworth.
    B. Alfred Tennyson.
    C. Percy Shelley.
    D. Robert Burns.

7. American _____ was also called American Renaissance.
    A. Transcendentalism
    B. Realism
    C. Modernism
    D. Romanticism

8. Pragmatics is different from other linguistic branches because _____ get involved in it.
    A. listeners
    B. speakers
    C. followers
    D. grammars

9. The publication of Saussure's work *Course in General Linguistics* marked the beginning of
    A. the modern grammar.
    B. the pragmatics.
    C. the modern linguistics.
    D. the semantics.

10. _____ are NOT a minimal pair in English.
    A. "sink" and "zinc"
    B. "ben" and "pen"
    C. "teach" and "tough"
    D. "bat" and "pat"

Model Test 4

1. The official name of Great Britain is
   A. the United Kingdom.
   B. the United Kingdom of Great Britain.
   C. the United Kingdom of Great Britain and Ireland.
   D. the United Kingdom of Great Britain and Northern Ireland.

2. For nearly _____ years Britain was under the Roman occupation.
   A. 300   B. 400
   C. 500   D. 600

3. _____ is the capital of New South Wales, and the oldest and largest city in Australia.
   A. Melbourne   B. Sydney
   C. Darwin   D. Canberra

4. Which of the following is NOT the major newspaper or magazine in the USA?
   A. *New York Times.*   B. *Washington Post.*
   C. *National Geography.*   D. *Financial Times.*

5. The American literature around the Revolution of Independence experienced an age of
   A. sin and predestination.   B. enlightenment.
   C. reason and order.   D. philosophical movement.

6. _____ was considered as the "poet of the American revolution".
   A. Thomas Jefferson   B. Benjamin Franklin
   C. Thomas Paine   D. Philip Freneau

7. Shakespeare wrote all the following works EXCEPT
   A. *Hamlet.*   B. *King Lear.*
   C. *Wuthering Heights.*   D. *Othello.*

8. Which of the following do NOT belong to "open class words"?
   A. Articles.   B. Nouns.
   C. Adjectives.   D. Adverbs.

9. The words "baggage" and "luggage" are
   A. dialectal synonyms.
   B. synonyms differing in emotive meaning.
   C. collocationally-restricted synonyms.
   D. synonyms differing in styles.

10. The meaning of an utterance is based on
    A. the hearer.   B. the speaker.
    C. sentence meaning.   D. the context.

Model Test 5

1. Australia and New Zealand were first discovered by the _____ explorer.
   A. Dutch
   B. English
   C. Spanish
   D. French

2. _____ is generally regarded as the beginning of modern world history.
   A. The English Civil War
   B. The American Civil War
   C. The World War I
   D. The World War II

3. Under _____, Wales was conquered.
   A. Edward I
   B. Edward II
   C. Henry II
   D. Henry III

4. The natives of America are the _____.
   A. British
   B. Hispanics
   C. Mexicans
   D. Indians

5. _____ is often regarded as the founder of the English domestic novel.
   A. Henry Fielding
   B. Samuel Pepys
   C. Samuel Richardson
   D. Daniel Defoe

6. The modern English novel gives a(n) _____ presentation of life of the common people.
   A. realistic
   B. idealistic
   C. prophetic
   D. romantic

7. What is the name of the woman poet who had her *The Tenth Muse Lately Sprung up in America*?
   A. Anne Bradstreet.
   B. Maria Edgeworth.
   C. Jane Austen.
   D. Emily Dickinson.

8. There are _____ morphemes in the word "uncomfortably".
   A. three
   B. four
   C. five
   D. six

9. _____ is a linguistic variety used by people living in the same geographical region.
   A. Sociolect
   B. Idiolect
   C. Regional dialect
   D. Ethnic dialect

10. Traditional behaviourists think that _____ are keys to language development.
    A. imitation and habit formation
    B. imitation and practice
    C. generalization and learning
    D. discrimination and generalization

Model Test 6

1. The _____ were the forerunners of the Conservative Party.
   A. Whigs   B. Liberal Party
   C. Tories   D. reformists

2. _____ is the largest province in Canada geographically.
   A. Ontario   B. Quebec
   C. Saskatchewan   D. Manitoba

3. The United Kingdom is a _____, with a king or a queen as its head.
   A. federal state   B. constitutional monarchy
   C. feudal country   D. constitutional state

4. At first, the capital of the US was in
   A. Washington.   B. Boston.
   C. Philadelphia.   D. Los Angeles.

5. Which of the following female writers did NOT belong to the Bronte Sisters?
   A. Anne Bronte.   B. Charlotte Bronte.
   C. Emily Bronte.   D. Mary Bronte.

6. _____ was the first American playwright to win the Nobel Prize.
   A. Arthur Miller   B. Eugene Gladstone O'Neil
   C. Tennessee Williams   D. Bernard Malamud

7. In 1900, Jack London published his first collection of short stories, named
   A. *The Son of the Wolf.*   B. *The Sea Wolf.*
   C. *The Law of Life.*   D. *White Fang.*

8. The relationship between the words "color" and "black" is
   A. synonymy.   B. antonymy.
   C. polysemy.   D. hyponymy.

9. In linguistics, the fact that a lexical item may undergo a shift in meaning is called
   A. losing of meaning.   B. widening of meaning.
   C. meaning-shift.   D. narrowing of meaning.

10. _____ provides great philosophical insight into the nature of the linguistic communication.
    A. The CP Theory   B. The Speech Act Theory
    C. The Universal Grammar   D. The Principle of Conversation

Model Test 7

1. The first American president to be elected from the Republican Party was
   A. Abraham Lincoln.   B. James Monroe.
   C. James Madison.   D. Thomas Jefferson.

2. _____ is the leading state in oil and natural gas deposits in the US.
   A. Iowa   B. New York
   C. California   D. Texas

3. _____ is the longest river in Canada.
   A. The Murray River   B. The Mackenzie River
   C. The St. Lawrence   D. The Clutha River

4. The Privy Council was called _____ in the British history.
   A. the Great Council   B. the Democratic Party
   C. the Liberal Party   D. the King's Council

5. The dividing line between the nineteenth century and the contemporary American literature is
   A. World War I.   B. the Great Depression.
   C. World War II.   D. the Civil War.

6. All the following writers belong to "the Beat Generation" EXCEPT
   A. Lawrence Ferlinghetti.   B. Allen Ginsberg.
   C. William Burroughs.   D. John Updike.

7. "Poetry is Spontaneous" was put forward by
   A. Charles Lamb.   B. William Wordsworth.
   C. Robert Burns.   D. William Blake.

8. Which of the following is NOT the specific instance of directives?
   A. Advising.   B. Inviting.
   C. Warning.   D. Swearing.

9. Idiolect may combine all the following elements EXCEPT
   A. age variations.   B. gender variations.
   C. time variations.   D. regional variations.

10. Homophones are often employed to create puns for all the following effects EXCEPT
    A. ridicule.   B. humor.
    C. sarcasm.   D. redundancy.

Model Test 8

1. British Prime Minister is appointed by
   A. the monarch.
   B. the House of Lords.
   C. the House of Common.
   D. the public.

2. The US Congress has the power to make these laws EXCEPT of
   A. the regulation of foreign trade.
   B. marriage.
   C. defense.
   D. naturalization.

3. Canada is a country with as many as _____ nationalities.
   A. 40
   B. 60
   C. 80
   D. 100

4. The following animals are unique to Australia EXCEPT
   A. emus.
   B. kangaroos.
   C. koalas.
   D. tigers.

5. Which of the following is NOT a black author?
   A. James Baldwin.
   B. Alan Ginsberg.
   C. Richard Wright.
   D. Ralph Ellison.

6. _____ can be regarded as typically belonging to the school of Romantic literary.
   A. *Jane Eyre*
   B. *Sons and Lovers*
   C. *Don Juan*
   D. *Ulysses*

7. _____ is Hemingway's first true novel which portrays "the lost generation".
   A. *A Farewell to Arms*
   B. *The Old Man and the Sea*
   C. *For Whom the Bell Tolls*
   D. *The Sun Also Rises*

8. The theory of universal grammar was proposed by
   A. Chomsky.
   B. Saussure.
   C. Sapir.
   D. Firth.

9. The word "girl" originally meant "young person of either sex", but now it means "young people of female sex". This is an example of
   A. meaning-shift.
   B. loss of meaning.
   C. widening of meaning.
   D. narrow of meaning.

10. According to the speech act theory, a speaker might be performing all the following acts when speaking EXCEPT
    A. illocutionary act.
    B. perlocutionary act.
    C. performative act.
    D. locutionary act.

Model Test 9

1. _____ is the largest and busiest port on the Great Lakes.
   A. New York   B. Huston
   C. Chicago   D. Salt Lake City

2. _____ claimed that Australia and New Zealand belonged to Britain in 1770.
   A. Abel Tasman   B. Christopher Columbus
   C. James Cook   D. Amerigo Vespucci

3. _____ is the largest city and the chief port of the United States.
   A. New York City   B. Washington D.C.
   C. San Francisco   D. Los Angeles

4. _____ is the key to Industrial Revolution.
   A. Steam engine   B. Railway engine
   C. Cotton textile   D. Coal mining

5. _____ was NOT written by Charles Dickens.
   A. *David Copperfield*   B. *Oliver Twist*
   C. *Sons and Lovers*   D. *A Tale of Two Cities*

6. The term "metaphysical poetry" is commonly used to name the works of the 17th
   century writers who wrote under the influence of
   A. John Milton.   B. John Donne.
   C. John Keats.   D. John Bunyan.

7. The leader of the imagist movement in American literature is
   A. Thomas Stearns Eliot.   B. Robert Frost.
   C. Wallace Stevens.   D. Ezra Pound.

8. All the following words contain the inflectional affixes EXCEPT
   A. watches.   B. longer.
   C. notes.   D. useful.

9. Phrases that are formed of more than one word usually contain all the following
   elements EXCEPT
   A. complement.   B. head.
   C. specifier.   D. affix.

10. Contextual features exclude the _____ when an utterance is made.
    A. place   B. participants
    C. purpose   D. time

Model Test 10

1. Which of the following is NOT a part of New England?
   A. Maine.   B. California.
   C. Vermont.   D. Rhode Island.

2. The two party names of Whigs and Tories originated with
   A. the English Civil War.   B. the Glorious Revolution.
   C. the Industrial Revolution.   D. the Restoration.

3. Ottawa is located in the Ottawa Valley in the eastern part of the province of
   A. Manitoba.   B. Ontario.
   C. Saskatchewan.   D. Quebec.

4. Which of the following is NOT a state of Australia?
   A. Canberra.   B. Tasmania.
   C. Queensland.   D. South Australia.

5. In the mid-18th century, a new literary movement called _____ came to Europe and then to England.
   A. classicism   B. restoration
   C. romanticism   D. realism

6. William Faulkner was the foremost American _____ writer of the 20th century.
   A. black   B. southern
   C. western   D. New England

7. *The Great Gatsby* is written by
   A. Francis Scott Fitzgerald.   B. Ernest Hemingway.
   C. Sinclair Lewis.   D. John Steinbeck.

8. Which of the following does NOT belong to the methods of the addition of new words?
   A. Acronyms.   B. Borrowing.
   C. Form-shift.   D. Coinage.

9. Mode of discourse is concerned with
   A. how communication is carried out.
   B. where communication is carried out.
   C. when communication is carried out.
   D. who carries out the communication.

10. "Promising" belongs to
    A. representatives.
    B. commissives.
    C. expressives.
    D. directives.

Model Test 11

1. The term "Father of Waters" is used to refer to _____ in the US.
   A. the Nile River   B. the Amazon River
   C. the Hudson River   D. the Mississippi River

2. _____ is the heart of century-old French presence in North America.
   A. Quebec   B. Alberta
   C. Ontario   D. Nova Scotia

3. The _____ are the fastest growing racial and ethnic group in the United States.
   A. Asian-Americans   B. Mexico-Americans
   C. blacks   D. Indians

4. The general election in Britain is held every _____ years.
   A. three   B. four
   C. five   D. six

5. Ezra Pound's major work of poetry is the long poem called
   A. *Polite Essays.*   B. *Make It New.*
   C. *High Selwyn Mauberley.*   D. *The Cantos.*

6. *Pride and Prejudice* is one of the best known novels written by
   A. Anne Bronte.   B. Jane Austen.
   C. Mary Shelly.   D. Robert Southey.

7. Which of the following is NOT one of the "Lake Poets"?
   A. Samuel Taylor Coleridge.   B. John Keats.
   C. William Wordsworth.   D. Robert Southey.

8. The relationship between "begin" and "commence" is
   A. semantically diffcrent synonyms.   B. collocational synonyms.
   C. dialectal synonyms.   D. stylistic synonyms.

9. The criteria to determine a word's category include all the following EXCEPT
   A. inflection.   B. distribution.
   C. meaning.   D. style.

10. The same word has the same _____ meaning to all the speakers of the same language.
    A. conceptual   B. lexical
    C. affective   D. associative

Model Test 12

1. _____ is known as the automobile capital of the world.
   A. London   B. Los Angeles
   C. Toronto   D. Detroit

2. The oldest British daily newspaper is
    A. *Daily Express.*   B. *The Times.*
    C. *Financial Times.*   D. *The Observer.*

3. _____ is the capital of Wales.
    A. Dublin   B. Edinburgh
    C. Cardiff   D. New Castle

4. The city of _____, which was formerly known as Port Jackson, is the place of the earliest colonial settlement in Australia.
    A. Melbourne   B. Sydney
    C. Perth   D. Darwin

5. George Bernard Shaw was a(n)
    A. playwright.   B. poet.
    C. novelist.   D. essayist.

6. The famous short story *The Fall of the House of Usher* was written by
    A. Charles Dickens.   B. Edgar Allen Poe.
    C. John Richardson.   D. Henry Savery.

7. Most of Thomas Hardy's novels are set in Wessex,
    A. a crude region in England.   B. a fictional primitive region.
    C. a remote rural area.   D. Hardy's hometown.

8. The study of how sounds are put together and used to convey meaning in communication is
    A. morphology.   B. general linguistics.
    C. phonology.   D. semantics.

9. The word "tofu" is a _____ one.
    A. clipped   B. blended
    C. derived   D. borrowed

10. The transformational-generative grammar was proposed by
    A. John Austin.   B. Noam Chomsky.
    C. John Searle.   D. M.A.K. Halliday.

Model Test 13

1. The Statue of Liberty was given to American people by _____ as a gift.
    A. Britain   B. France
    C. Canada   D. Italy

2. Which of the following languages is NOT spoken in Scotland?
    A. English.   B. Scottish.
    C. Gaelic.   D. Denish.

3. Around _____ of New Zealanders are found in North Island.
   A. 3/4   B. 1/2
   C. 3/5   D. 2/5

4. The _____ victory was a great turning point of the War of Independence.
   A. New York City   B. Trenton
   C. Saratoga   D. New Jersey

5. "The Vanity Fair" is a well-known part in
   A. *The Pilgrim's Progress.*
   B. *Grace Abounding to the Chief of Sinners.*
   C. *The Life and Death of Mr. Badman.*
   D. *The Holy War.*

6. In 1954, _____ was awarded the Nobel Prize for literature for his "mastery of the art of modern narration".
   A. T. S. Eliot   B. Ernest Hemingway
   C. John Steinbeck   D. William Faulkner

7. The Rabbit series were written by
   A. Ezra Pound.   B. Mark Twain.
   C. Sinclair Lewis.   D. John Updike.

8. According to the componential analysis, the words "boy" and "man" differ in the feature of
   A. adult.   B. male.
   C. human.   D. gender.

9. Which of the following is NOT the change in the meaning of words?
   A. Specification of meaning.   B. Narrowing of meaning.
   C. Meaning-shift.   D. Widening of meaning.

10. The dialect which is influenced by social status is
    A. regional dialect.   B. idiolect.
    C. sociolect.   D. ethnic dialect.

Model Test 14

1. The District of Manhattan is in the city of
   A. New York.   B. Chicago.
   C. San Francisco.   D. Washington D.C..

2. Apart from Paris, France, Montreal is regarded as the largest _____ city in the world, known as "Paris the Second".
   A. Spanish-speaking   B. Portuguese-speaking
   C. German-speaking   D. French-speaking

3. Which of the following is NOT a natural zone of Scotland?

    A. The highlands in the north.   B. The central lowlands.

    C. The east uplands.   D. The south uplands.

4. The victory at _____ was the turning point of the American Civil War.

    A. Gettysburg   B. Philadelphia

    C. Louisiana   D. Gadsden

5. John Steinbeck, author of _____, was awarded the Nobel Prize for Literature in 1962.

    A. *The Grapes of Wrath*   B. *Invisible Man*

    C. *The Winds of War*   D. *To Kill a Mockingbird*

6. What is regarded as the first American prose epic?

    A. *Nature.*   B. *The Scarlet Letter.*

    C. *Walden.*   D. *Moby Dick.*

7. John Dryden was all of the following EXCEPT

    A. a literary critic.   B. a short story writer.

    C. a poet.   D. a dramatist.

8. A(n) _____ is a phonetic unit or segment.

    A. phone   B. phoneme

    C. allophone   D. sound

9. The subject area of _____ is on the borders of linguistics and literature.

    A. mathematical linguistics   B. anthropological linguistics

    C. neurolinguistics   D. linguistic stylistics

10. The word "smog" comes from "smoke + fog". This is an example of _____ in morphology.

    A. backformation   B. conversion

    C. blending   D. acronym

Model Test 15

1. It was _____ who brought Christianity to Britain.

    A. the Dutch   B. the French

    C. the Roman   D. the Spanish

2. Yellow Stone National Park is located in

    A. the northern part of Wyoming.   B. the western part of Wyoming.

    C. the southern part of Wyoming.   D. the eastern part of Wyoming.

3. The Parliament of Canada consists of the Senate and

    A. the House of Lords.   B. the House of Commons.

    C. the Upper House.   D. the House of Representatives.

4. _____ forms a natural boundary between Mexico and the United States.

    A. The Ohio River　　　　　　　　　B. The Mississippi River

    C. The Rio Grande River　　　　　　　D. The Ruhr River

5. Which of the following figures does NOT belong to "The Lost Generation"?

    A. Ezra Pound.　　　　　　　　　　　B. William Carlos Williams.

    C. Robert Frost.　　　　　　　　　　　D. Theodore Dreiser.

6. Who is described by Mark Twain as a boy with "a sound heart and a deformed conscience"?

    A. Tom Sawyer.　　　　　　　　　　　B. Huckleberry Finn.

    C. Jim.　　　　　　　　　　　　　　　D. Tony.

7. The novel *Gulliver's Travels* was written by

    A. John Bunyan.　　　　　　　　　　　B. Jonathan Swift.

    C. Tobias Smollett.　　　　　　　　　　D. Laurence Sterne.

8. Speech _____ refers to any distinguishable form of speech used by a speaker.

    A. change　　　　　　　　　　　　　　B. act

    C. variety　　　　　　　　　　　　　　D. usage

9. The word "motherland" is a(n)

    A. clipped word.　　　　　　　　　　　B. compound.

    C. blended word.　　　　　　　　　　　D. acronym.

10. Classification of vowels are made according to all the following EXCEPT

    A. the openness of the mouth.　　　　　B. the position of the tongue.

    C. the shape of the lip.　　　　　　　　D. the sound of the vowels.

Model Test 16

1. The capital of New Zealand is

    A. Dunedin.　　　　　　　　　　　　　B. Christchurch.

    C. Wellington.　　　　　　　　　　　　D. Auckland.

2. Britain is separated from the rest of Europe by _____ in the south.

    A. the English Channel　　　　　　　　B. the North Sea

    C. the Pacific Ocean　　　　　　　　　D. the Atlantic Ocean

3. It was _____ who made Washington the capital of the United States.

    A. George Washington　　　　　　　　B. Thomas Jefferson

    C. John Adams　　　　　　　　　　　　D. Abraham Lincoln

4. The Witan (council or meeting of the wisemen) created by the Anglo-Saxons is the basis of the present British

    A. Parliament.　　　　　　　　　　　　B. Government.

    C. Monarchy.　　　　　　　　　　　　D. Privy Council.

5. During the first decade of the 20th century, _____ became an international tendency.

    A. modernism   B. romanticism

    C. realism   D. pre-modernism

6. _____ is the most successful religious allegory in the English language.

    A. *The Holy War*   B. *The Pilgrim's Progress*

    C. *Exodus*   D. *Genesis*

7. *The Flea* was written by

    A. William Shakespeare.   B. Philip Sidney.

    C. Thomas More.   D. John Donne.

8. The study of _____ does not form the core of linguistics.

    A. pragmatics   B. morphology

    C. syntax   D. neurolinguistics

9. If the study of meaning is conducted in the context of language use, _____ comes into being.

    A. pragmatics   B. syntax

    C. morphology   D. semantics

10. Language is the tool of communication. The symbol "Road Work Ahead" on a highway serves

    A. an expressive function.   B. an informative function.

    C. a performative function.   D. a persuasive function.

Model Test 17

1. Australia was originally one colony of

    A. America.   B. Britain.

    C. Canada.   D. France.

2. _____ is the most important river in Scotland.

    A. Severn River   B. River Clyde

    C. Thames River   D. River Nevis

3. All the Representatives in the US are elected every _____ years.

    A. two   B. three

    C. four   D. five

4. The longest and the most important river in the USA is

    A. the Columbia River.   B. the Mississippi River.

    C. the Ohio River.   D. the Colorado River.

5. The Romantic Period of American literature started with the publication of Washington Irving's
   A. *The Sketch Book.*   B. *Tales of a Traveler.*
   C. *The Alhambra.*   D. *A history of New York.*
6. Who is regarded as a "worshipper of nature"?
   A. John Keats.   B. William Blake.
   C. William Wordsworth.   D. Jane Austen.
7. _____ is not one of Shakespeare's romantic love comedies.
   A. *Twelfth Night*   B. *As You Like It*
   C. *The Merchant of Venice*   D. *Romeo and Juliet*
8. Which of the following words is NOT a compound word?
   A. Unusual.   B. Football.
   C. Icy-cold.   D. Rainbow.
9. The syntactic component provides the _____ for a sentence.
   A. structure   B. meaning
   C. lexicon   D. rule
10. Predication analysis is proposed by British linguist
   A. N. Chomsky.   B. G. Leech.
   C. M.A.K. Halliday.   D. Saussure.

Model Test 18

1. _____ is Australia's largest and most diverse industry.
   A. Mining   B. Manufacturing
   C. Fishing   D. Agriculture
2. _____ is known as "the father of the British navy".
   A. St. Augustine   B. King Alfred
   C. Julius Caesar   D. Emperor Claudius
3. The first English colony in America was founded at
   A. Virginia.   B. Plymouth.
   C. Georgia.   D. Carolina.
4. The largest groups of Native Americans are found on
   A. the Great Plains.   B. the Colorado Plateau.
   C. Hawaii.   D. the Great Lakes.
5. The first official version of the Bible known as the Great Bible was revised in the
   A. 15th century.   B. 16th century.
   C. 17th century.   D. 18th century.

6. How many lines does a sonnet have?

   A. 9.　　　　　　　　　　　　　　B. 10.

   C. 14.　　　　　　　　　　　　　D. 18.

7. Mark Twain is well-known for his

   A. frontier theme.　　　　　　　　B. international theme.

   C. symbolism.　　　　　　　　　　D. local color.

8. _____ act refers to the act of expressing the speaker's intention.

   A. Locutionary　　　　　　　　　B. Illocutionary

   C. Perlocutionary　　　　　　　　D. Spontaneous

9. The distinction between langue and parole is similar to that between

   A. speech and writing.　　　　　　B. prescriptive and descriptive.

   C. competence and performance.　　D. synchronic and diachronic.

10. Which of the following words is different from others in word formation?

    A. UN.　　　　　　　　　　　　　B. AIDS.

    C. WTO.　　　　　　　　　　　　D. DOZER.

Model Test 19

1. The highest federal judicial authority in the US is

   A. the Congress.　　　　　　　　　B. the president.

   C. the Supreme Court.　　　　　　D. the Senate.

2. One of the most far-reaching consequences of World War II was that it hastened the end of

   A. the Commonwealth.　　　　　　B. the British Empire.

   C. the Industrial Revolution.　　　D. America's empire.

3. The Grand Banks, the world's greatest fishing grounds, are located in _____ in Canada.

   A. the Atlantic Provinces　　　　　B. Lawrence—Great Lakes Provinces

   C. the Prairie Provinces　　　　　D. the Province of British Columbia

4. The capital of South Australia is

   A. Canberra.　　　　　　　　　　B. Brisbane.

   C. Adelaide.　　　　　　　　　　D. Darwin.

5. _____ is the first important English essayist and the founder of modern science in England.

   A. Philip Sidney　　　　　　　　　B. Francis Bacon

   C. Edmund Spenser　　　　　　　D. William Caxton

6. In American Literature history, the period before the American Civil War is generally referred to as

   A. the Realistic Period.　　　　　　B. the Romantic Period.

   C. the Modern Period.　　　　　　D. the Naturalist Period.

7. The best example of Hawthorne's symbolism is the recreation of Puritan Boston in
   A. *Mosses from an Old Manse.*   B. *The Scarlet Letter.*
   C. *The House of the Seven Gables.*   D. *The Marble Faun.*
8. Competence refers to
   A. the ideal language user's knowledge of the rules of his language.
   B. the ideal knowledge of meaning of sentences.
   C. what speakers can do with certain languages.
   D. the realization of the language user's knowledge in utterances.
9. _____ means the lack of a logical connection between the form of something and its expression in sounds.
   A. Abstractness   B. Arbitrariness
   C. Duality   D. Displacement
10. When a speaker expresses his intention of speaking, such as asking someone else to do him a favor, he is performing
    A. an illocutionary act.   B. a perlocutionary act.
    C. a locutionary act.   D. none of the above.

Model Test 20

1. The British monarchy can be traced back to _____ century.
   A. the 6th   B. the 7th
   C. the 8th   D. the 9th
2. Alaska lies in the _____ of North America, stretching southward from the Arctic Ocean to the Pacific.
   A. northwestern part   B. southwestern part
   C. northeastern part   D. southeastern part
3. _____ became the financial and commercial center of Australia because of the gold rushes.
   A. Canberra   B. Darwin
   C. Melbourne   D. Sydney
4. _____ is the chemical capital of the world.
   A. Huston   B. London
   C. Edinburgh   D. Paris
5. American author _____'s book *The Red Badge of Courage* published in 1895 brought him international fame.
   A. Alex Haley   B. Norman Mailer
   C. Stephen Crane   D. John Steinbeck

6. Daniel Defoe's novels mainly focus on
   A. the struggle of the unfortunate for mere existence.
   B. the struggle of the shipwrecked persons for security.
   C. the struggle of the pirates for wealth.
   D. the desire of the criminals for property.

7. The 18th century England is known as the _____ in history.
   A. Romanticism   B. Classicism
   C. Renaissance   D. Enlightenment

8. The different phones that can represent a phoneme in different phonetic environments are called the _____ of that phoneme.
   A. allophones   B. phones
   C. allomorph   D. phonetics

9. _____ answers such question as how infants acquire their first language.
   A. Anthropological linguistics   B. Applied linguistics
   C. Sociolinguistics   D. Psycholinguistics

10. What type of sentence is "Tom likes basketball, but his brother is interested in football."?
    A. A simple sentence.   B. A coordinate sentence.
    C. A complex sentence.   D. None of the above.

Model Test 21

1. The *British North America Act* of 1867 established Canada as a
   A. colony.   B. protectorate.
   C. dominion.   D. sphere of influence.

2. The US ranks first in the production and export of
   A. rice.   B. wheat.
   C. corn.   D. gold.

3. _____ was the first nationwide working class movement in Britain.
   A. The Agricultural Enclosure   B. The People's Charter
   C. The Industrial Revolution   D. The Chartist Movement

4. _____ music is perhaps America's greatest contribution to the world of popular music.
   A. Blues   B. Waltz
   C. Rock   D. Jazz

5. The novel *Sister Carrie* was written by
   A. Sherwood Anderson.   B. Stephen Crane.
   C. Theodore Dreiser.   D. William Dean Howells.

6. _____ flourished in the Elizabethan Age more than any other form of literature.

    A. Novel   B. Poetry

    C. Essay   D. Drama

7. Who is the most outstanding of all the transcendental writers in American literature?

    A. Washington Irving.   B. James Fenimore Cooper.

    C. Ralph Waldo Emerson.   D. Henry David Thoreau.

8. The meaning that can be found in the dictionary is the _____ meaning of a word.

    A. iconic   B. cultural

    C. connotative   D. denotative

9. The form of a given language used in a certain geographical region is called

    A. dialect.   B. pidgin.

    C. register.   D. style.

10. The phrases "accuse of" and "charge with" are

    A. dialectal synonyms.   B. semantically different synonyms.

    C. stylistic synonyms.   D. collocational synonyms.

Model Test 22

1. Whose presidential term is the longest in the US?

    A. Franklin Roosevelt.   B. George Washington.

    C. Thomas Jefferson.   D. Abraham Lincoln.

2. _____ is the second largest city of Canada.

    A. Corner Brook   B. Toronto

    C. Montreal   D. Vancouver

3. Christopher Columbus was a(n) _____ navigator.

    A. British   B. Spanish

    C. Portuguese   D. Italian

4. _____ is the oldest of the Australian states.

    A. New South Wales   B. South Australia

    C. Queensland   D. Victoria

5. _____ is a folk legend brought to England by Anglo-Saxons from their continental homes; it is a long poem of over 3,000 lines and the national epic of the English people.

    A. *Beowulf*

    B. *Sir Gawain and the Green Knight*

    C. *The Canterbury Tales*

    D. *King Arthur and His Knights of the Roundtable*

6. The father of English poetry, the author of *Troilus and Criseyde* is also the one of
   A. *Romeo and Juliet.*
   B. *The Faerie Queen.*
   C. *Tamburlaine.*
   D. *The Canterbury Tales.*

7. The group of Shakespeare plays known as "romance" or "reconciliation plays" is
   A. *Merchant of Venice; As You Like It.*
   B. *The Tempest; Pericles, Prince of Tyre; The Winter's Tale.*
   C. *Romeo and Juliet; Antonym and Cleopatra.*
   D. *The Tempest; Pericles, Prince of Tyre; The Winter's Tale; Cymbeline.*

8. The study of language acquisition is generally known as
   A. theoretical linguistics.
   B. psycholinguistics.
   C. applied linguistics.
   D. historical linguistics.

9. The history of English is usually divided into _____ major periods.
   A. three
   B. four
   C. five
   D. two

10. The morpheme "scope" in the common word "telescope" is a(n)
   A. bound morpheme.
   B. bound form.
   C. inflectional morpheme.
   D. free morpheme.

Model Test 23

1. The world's largest volcano Mauna Loa is located on
   A. Alaska.
   B. the Colorado Plateau.
   C. Hawaii.
   D. the Great Lakes.

2. Enclosure in Britain introduced _____ into rural relationships.
   A. a new partnership
   B. a new class hostility
   C. a new class
   D. a new world

3. _____ is the capital city of Australia.
   A. Darwin
   B. Melbourne
   C. Canberra
   D. Sydney

4. As a consequence of the Industrial Revolution, _____ became the source of the nation's wealth.
   A. towns
   B. machines
   C. farms
   D. factories

5. "He has a servant called Friday." "He" in the quoted sentence is a character in
   A. Henry fielding's *Tom Jones.*
   B. John Bunyan's *The Pilgrim's Progress.*
   C. Richard Brinsley Sheridan's *The School for Scandal.*
   D. Daniel Defoe's *Robinson Crusoe.*

6. *Gulliver's Travels* was written by
    A. Daniel Defoe.   B. Charles Dickens.
    C. Jonathan Swift.   D. Joseph Addison.

7. William Wordsworth is generally known as a _____ poet.
    A. romantic   B. realistic
    C. naturalistic   D. neo-classic

8. The study of the production of speech sounds is of great interest to those working in
    A. articulatory phonetics.   B. acoustic phonetics.
    C. auditory phonetics.   D. phonology.

9. Which of the following is NOT a branch of Macrolinguistics?
    A. Sociolinguistics.   B. Psycholinguistics.
    C. Historical linguistics.   D. Computational linguistics.

10. The words "rain" and "reign" are examples of
    A. synonyms.   B. polysemies.
    C. hyponymies.   D. homonymies.

Model Test 24

1. *The Declaration of Independence* was drafted by
    A. George Washington.   B. Thomas Jefferson.
    C. John Locke.   D. Abraham Lincoln.

2. The first king of England is
    A. James I.   B. Henry I.
    C. Egbert.   D. John.

3. Canada is made up of _____ provinces and three territories.
    A. five   B. eight
    C. six   D. ten

4. _____ is "the Space City of the USA".
    A. Detroit   B. Boston
    C. Houston   D. Chicago

5. The first American writer who gained international fame was
    A. Mark Twain.   B. R. W. Emerson.
    C. Washington Irving.   D. Walt Whitman.

6. _____ published in 1789 marked the beginning of Romanticism in English poetry.
    A. *Lucy Poems*   B. *Lyrical Ballads*
    C. *My Heart Leaps Up*   D. *To the Cuckoo*

7. *Paradise Lost* is the masterpiece of
   A. Robert Burns.
   B. William Shakespeare.
   C. John Milton.
   D. William Blake.

8. Children can speak before they can read or write shows that language is
   A. arbitrary.
   B. used for communication.
   C. productive.
   D. basically vocal.

9. The meaning of "yellow" to Chinese is different from that to western people, and the different meanings of "yellow" are its _____ meanings.
   A. associative
   B. conceptual
   C. cognitive
   D. stylistic

10. All the following topics are studied in pragmatics EXCEPT
    A. conversation.
    B. politeness.
    C. deixis.
    D. context.

Model Test 25

1. _____ is the only organ which has the power to interpret the Constitution in the US.
   A. The Federal Government
   B. The House of Representatives
   C. The Senate
   D. The Supreme Court

2. The highest mountain in Britain is
   A. Boleyn.
   B. Scafell.
   C. Ben Nevis.
   D. Snowdonia.

3. The first immigrants in the American history came from
   A. France.
   B. England and Netherlands.
   C. Russia.
   D. Spain and Portugal.

4. Nearly _____ of Canada's trade is with America including exports and imports.
   A. 1/3
   B. 1/2
   C. 2/3
   D. 3/4

5. Which of the following is NOT written by Eugene Gladstone O'Neill?
   A. *Anna Christie.*
   B. *The Iceman Cometh.*
   C. *Long Day's Journey into Night.*
   D. *Invisible Man.*

6. William Langland wrote for
   A. the common people.
   B. the court.
   C. the royal family.
   D. the monks.

7. Which of the following is NOT a dominant figure of the American Realistic Period?
   A. William Dean Howells.
   B. Theodore Dreiser.
   C. Henry James.
   D. Mark Twain.

8. N. Chomsky is a great _____ linguist.
   A. American   B. Canadian
   C. French   D. Swiss

9. _____ are bound morphemes because they cannot be used as separate words.
   A. Affixes   B. Stems
   C. Roots   D. Derivations

10. According to the predication analysis, the predication of the sentence "It is snowing."
    is a
    A. one-place predication.   B. two-place predication.
    C. three-place predication.   D. no-place predication.

Model Test 26

1. _____ was the first president to resign in American history.
   A. Lincoln   B. Nixon
   C. Clinton   D. Bush

2. Which sport is regarded as a major British industry?
   A. Tennis.   B. Golf.
   C. Horse racing.   D. Boxing.

3. Melbourne is the capital of
   A. Tasmania.   B. Queensland.
   C. Victoria.   D. New South Wales.

4. Most immigrants to the United States are now from
   A. Asia.   B. Europe.
   C. Africa.   D. Asian and Hispanic countries.

5. _____ is often acclaimed as the literary spokesman of the Jazz Age.
   A. F. Scott Fitzgerald   B. Ernest Hemingway
   C. Sinclair Lewis   D. John Steinbeck

6. The real main stream of the English Renaissance is
   A. the Elizabethan poetry.   B. the Elizabethan drama.
   C. the Elizabethan novel.   D. the Elizabethan essay.

7. _____ is not only a prose writer but also a king of Wessex.
   A. Adam Bede   B. King Arthur
   C. Alfred the Great   D. Venerable Bede

8. There are _____ morphemes in the word "desirability".
   A. two   B. three
   C. four   D. five

9. Application of the transformational rules yields _____ structure.
   A. deep
   B. new
   C. surface
   D. complex

10. _____ is the study of language processing.
    A. Psycholinguistics
    B. Semantics
    C. Sociolinguistics
    D. Pragmatics

Model Test 27

1. Which part of Britain is always fighting?
   A. England.
   B. Scotland.
   C. Wales.
   D. Northern Ireland.

2. With regard to its size, the USA is the _____ country in the world.
   A. largest
   B. second largest
   C. third largest
   D. fourth largest

3. Big Ben is in
   A. London.
   B. New York.
   C. Washington.
   D. Liverpool.

4. The largest city in Australia is
   A. Canberra.
   B. Sydney.
   C. Melbourne.
   D. Queensland.

5. *Don Juan* was written by
   A. Percy Bysshe Shelley.
   B. John Keats.
   C. George Gordon Byron.
   D. William Wordsworth.

6. Henry James was most famous for
   A. his poems.
   B. his plays.
   C. his novels.
   D. his short stories.

7. Which of the following is NOT a representative of Modernism?
   A. Mark Twain.
   B. Earnest Hemingway.
   C. Ezra Pound.
   D. Robert Frost.

8. The study of internal organization of words is
   A. semantics.
   B. morphology.
   C. syntax.
   D. phonology.

9. The distinction between competence and performance was made by
   A. Halliday.
   B. Saussure.
   C. Bloomfield.
   D. Chomsky.

10. The words "toys, walks, John's" can be examples of

    A. free morphemes.   B. compounds.

    C. inflectional affixes.   D. derivations.

Model Test 28

1. What is the highest mountain in Britain?

    A. Scafell.   B. Ben Nevis.

    C. The Cotswold.   D. The Forth.

2. The nation's capital city Washington D.C. and New York are located in

    A. the American West.   B. the Great Plains.

    C. the Midwest.   D. the Middle Atlantic States.

3. The American president involved in Watergate Scandal was

    A. Richard Nixon.   B. George Bush.

    C. Andrew Jackson.   D. Bill Clinton.

4. Quebec province in Canada has a strong _____ culture.

    A. British   B. German

    C. French   D. Italian

5. Francis Scott Fitzgerald was famous for

    A. *The Great Gatsby*.   B. *The Sound and the Fury*.

    C. *A Farewell to Arms*.   D. *The Grapes of Wrath*.

6. Which of the following writers is a novelist of the 20th century?

    A. John Keats.   B. Charles Lamb.

    C. Walter Scott.   D. James Joyce.

7. _____ is the effect of language in which the intended meaning is the opposite of what is stated.

    A. Metaphor   B. Simile

    C. Personification   D. Irony

8. Among the following, _____ is NOT one of the functions of adult's language according to Halliday.

    A. the Ideational Function   B. the Syntactic Function

    C. the Interpersonal Function   D. the Textual Function

9. Theme and rheme are terms in _____ of syntax.

    A. the Traditional Approach   B. the Structural Approach

    C. the Functional Approach   D. the Generative Approach

10. Which of the following is a blending word?
    A. Lengthen.   B. Nylon.
    C. Edit.   D. Smog.

Model Test 29

1. The largest city of British Columbia in Canada is
   A. Ottawa.   B. Winnipeg.
   C. Vancouver.   D. Montreal.

2. Which of the following is not a British newspaper?
   A. *Daily Express.*   B. *Daily Mirror.*
   C. *The Wall Street Journal.*   D. *The Observer.*

3. The Midwest is America's most important _____ area.
   A. agricultural   B. industrial
   C. manufacturing   D. mining industry

4. The aim of President Roosevelt's New Deal was to save American
   A. economy.   B. democracy.
   C. society.   D. politics.

5. *Pygmalion* was written by
   A. William Butler Yeats.   B. Bernard Shaw.
   C. T. S. Eliot.   D. Virginia Woolf.

6. Emily Dickinson was regarded mainly as a(n)
   A. novelist.   B. poet.
   C. playwright.   D. essayist.

7. Which of the following is the representative of Realism?
   A. Washington Irving.   B. James Fenimore Cooper.
   C. Nathaniel Hawthorne.   D. Herman Melville.

8. Phatic communication refers to
   A. language's function of the expression of identity.
   B. social interaction of language.
   C. language's function of expressing itself.
   D. sociological use of language.

9. The Cooperative Principles were put forward by
   A. John Langshaw Austin.   B. J. Firbas.
   C. Herbert Paul Grice.   D. H. L. Smith.

10. According to _____, we could only say "The boy kicked the ball" instead of "Boy the ball kicked the".

A. syntagmatic relation
B. paradigmatic relation
C. endocentric construction
D. exocentric construction

Model Test 30

1. In 1066, _____ landed in England and built the Norman Empire.

A. Julius Caesar
B. Henry VIII
C. Oliver Cromwell
D. William the Conqueror

2. The Parliament of Australia consists of the House of Representatives and

A. the House of Commons.
B. the House of Lords.
C. the Senate.
D. the General.

3. The longest river in Britain is

A. the Mersey.
B. the Severn.
C. the Thames.
D. the Clyde.

4. Ten amendments introduced by James Madison in 1789 were added to the Constitution, which are known as

A. the Bill of Rights.
B. the Civil Rights.
C. Federalist Papers.
D. the Articles of Confederation.

5. *Uncle Tom's Cabin* was written by

A. Nathaniel Hawthorne.
B. Harriet Beecher Stowe.
C. Stephen Crane.
D. Eugene O'Neil.

6. Who is called "father of English and European novels"?

A. Mark Twain.
B. Daniel Defoe.
C. William Makepeace Thackeray.
D. David Herbert Lawrence.

7. A reference in a literary work to a person, a place or a thing in history or another work of literary is an

A. allegory.
B. archetype.
C. analogy.
D. allusion.

8. Which of the following is NOT a case in English?

A. Nominative.
B. Accusative.
C. Genitive.
D. Vocative.

9. _____ is often described as "father of modern linguistics"?

A. Saussure
B. Chomsky
C. Bloomfield
D. Halliday

10. Which of the following phrases is an example of an endocentric construction?
    A. On the shelf.   B. Beyond the words.
    C. An old man.   D. Without thinking.

Model Test 31

1. In Ireland, the head of the state is the president with a term of _____ years.
   A. 4   B. 5
   C. 6   D. 7

2. Which of the following is NOT in London?
   A. Brooklyn Bridge.   B. St. Paul's Cathedral.
   C. Westminster Abbey.   D. Buckingham Palace.

3. The capital of Australia is
   A. Melbourne.   B. Sydney.
   C. Darwin.   D. Canberra.

4. Which American university is with the longest history?
   A. Yale.   B. Oxford.
   C. Harvard.   D. Stanford.

5. Percy Bysshe Shelley was famous for
   A. *Ode to a Nightingale.*   B. *Ode to Autumn.*
   C. *The Rime of the Ancient Mariner.* D. *Prometheus Unbound.*

6. Who was the first great American poet to use free verse?
   A. Edgar Allen Poe.   B. Walt Whitman.
   C. Henry Wadsworth Longfellow.   D. Henry David Thoreau.

7. The Renaissance was a European phenomenon originated in
   A. France.   B. Britain.
   C. Italy.   D. Spain.

8. Semantics is the study of
   A. words.   B. sentences.
   C. context.   D. meaning.

9. Semantic triangle is made up of reference, symbol and
   A. referent.   B. meaning.
   C. thought.   D. words or phrases.

10. How many syllables does the word "syllable" have?
    A. 1.   B. 2.
    C. 3.   D. 4.

Model Test 32

1. _____ were the first inhabitants in Britain.
   A. The Normans
   B. The Celts
   C. The Iberians
   D. The Anglo-Saxons

2. *The Declaration of Independence* came from the theory of British philosopher
   A. Paul Revere.
   B. John Locke.
   C. Charles Cornwallis.
   D. Frederick Douglass.

3. Sydney is the capital city of
   A. New South Wales.
   B. Queensland.
   C. South Australia.
   D. Tasmania.

4. Which American president was at the same time period with Martin Luther King Jr.?
   A. John Kennedy.
   B. Abraham Lincoln.
   C. George Washington.
   D. Ronald Reagan.

5. *The Canterbury Tales* was written by
   A. Alfred the Great.
   B. Thomas Malory.
   C. Geoffrey Chaucer.
   D. Edmund Spencer.

6. Walt Whitman was a(n)
   A. playwright.
   B. essayist.
   C. poet.
   D. novelist.

7. Alexander Pope was the representative writer of
   A. Transcendentalism.
   B. Romanticism.
   C. Modernism.
   D. Neo-Classicism.

8. Psycholinguistics investigates the interrelation of language and
   A. a speech community.
   B. its diversity.
   C. human mind.
   D. human behavior.

9. The words "amaze" and "astound" are
   A. dialectal synonyms.
   B. semantically different synonyms.
   C. stylistic synonyms.
   D. collocational synonyms.

10. Functional Sentence Perspective was put forward by
    A. the London School.
    B. the Prague School.
    C. Boas and Sapir.
    D. Post-Bloomfieldian linguists.

Model Test 33

1. In history, Britain has been under the occupation of Romans for about _____ years.
   A. 800
   B. 600
   C. 200
   D. 400

2. The victory of _____ was the turning point of the War of Independence.

    A. Saratoga   B. Gettysburg

    C. Trenton   D. Yorktown

3. Which of the following is one of the world's greatest continental rivers?

    A. The Ohio River.   B. The Missouri River.

    C. The Hudson River.   D. The Mississippi River.

4. _____ was famous for his abdication because of his marriage with a divorced American.

    A. Edward VIII   B. Edward VII

    C. George VI   D. George VII

5. Which of the following was NOT a novel written by Mark Twain?

    A. *The Adventures of Tom Sawyer.*   B. *Great Expectations.*

    C. *Life on the Mississippi.*   D. *The Prince and the Pauper.*

6. John Keats was a poet of

    A. the 17th century.   B. the 18th century.

    C. the 19th century.   D. the 20th century.

7. _____ has no regular rhythm or line length.

    A. Ode   B. Epigram

    C. Sonnet   D. Free Verse

8. The study of _____ does NOT constitute the core of linguistics.

    A. Semantics   B. Syntax

    C. Pragmatics   D. Sociolinguistics

9. _____ are not minimal pair in English.

    A. "Bat" and "pat"   B. "Teach" and "cheat"

    C. "Sink" and "zinc"   D. "Fine" and "vine"

10. Syntax mainly deals with

    A. the rules governing the structure, distribution and sequencing of speech sounds.

    B. the minimal units of meaning—morphemes.

    C. principles of forming and understanding correct English sentences.

    D. how meaning is encoded in a language.

Model Test 34

1. Which of the following universities has the longest history?

    A. Yale.   B. Oxford.

    C. Harvard.   D. Stanford.

2. Between 1337 and 1453 the _____ took place in Britain.

    A. Wars of Roses   B. Black Death

    C. Hundred Years' War   D. Peasants Uprising

3. The capital city of Canada is
   A. Montreal.   B. Ottawa.
   C. Vancouver.   D. Quebec.
4. In Jan. 1918, American President _____ prepared his "Fourteen Point" as a basis of peace negotiation.
   A. Woodrow Wilson   B. William Howard Taft
   C. Warren Harding   D. John Calvin Coolidge, Jr.
5. The representatives of the Enlightenment in English literature were the following writers EXCEPT
   A. Joseph Addison.   B. Richard Steele.
   C. William Blake.   D. Alexander Pope.
6. The novel *Emma* is written by
   A. Jane Austen.   B. Elizabeth C. Gaskell.
   C. Charlotte Bronte.   D. Mary Shelley.
7. "The father of the English and European novel" is
   A. Geoffrey Chaucer.   B. Edmund Spenser.
   C. Francis Bacon.   D. Daniel Defoe.
8. Which is the branch of linguistics which studies the characteristics of speech sounds and provides methods for their description, classification and transcription?
   A. Phonetics.   B. Phonology.
   C. Semantics.   D. Pragmatics.
9. Who made the distinction between Langue and Parole?
   A. Leech.   B. Chomsky.
   C. Halliday.   D. Saussure.
10. "Fall" and "autumn" are _____ synonyms.
   A. stylistic   B. collocational
   C. dialectal   D. semantically different

Model Test 35

1. The real centre of power in the British Parliament is
   A. the King or the Queen.   B. the House of Commons.
   C. the House of Lords.   D. the Cabinet.
2. The natives of the Continent of North America are the
   A. Aborigines.   B. Maoris.
   C. Indians.   D. Inuits.

3. Among the most typical English sports, _____ has been existing since the 16th century.

A. rugby

B. cricket

C. boxing

D. football

4. What is the title of Canada's national anthem?

A. *O Canada*

B. *God Save The Queen*

C. *Canada My Country*

D. *True Patriot Love*

5. Keats' most important and mature poem form is _____.

A. ode

B. elegy

C. epic

D. sonnet

6. G. B. Shaw's play *Mrs. Warren's Profession* is a realistic exposure of the _____ in the English society.

A. slum landlordism

B. inequality between men and women

C. political corruption

D. economic exploitation of women

7. *The Preface to Shakespeare* and *Lives of the Poets* are the works of critic

A. G. B. Shaw.

B. Samuel Johnson.

C. Ben Johnson.

D. E. M. Foster.

8. What is the meaning relationship between the two words "tree & willow"?

A. Polysemy.

B. Homonymy.

C. Hyponymy.

D. Antonymy.

9. The words "color" and "idea" are called _____ because they can occur unattached.

A. derivational morphemes

B. bound morphemes

C. inflectional morphemes

D. free morphemes

10. _____ is the study of speech sounds.

A. Phonetics

B. Phonology

C. Syntax

D. Semantics

Model Test 36

1. The oldest part of British Parliament is

A. the House of Lords.

B. the House of Commons.

C. the Shadow of Cabinet.

D. the Chamber.

2. The national newspapers can be divided into _____ and national Sundays.

A. national dailies

B. national weeklies

C. national monthlies

D. national Saturdays

3. _____, the third largest city in Canada, is well known as Ice-Free Harbor.

A. Montreal

B. Quebec

C. Toronto

D. Vancouver

4. The President during the American Civil War was
   A. Andrew Jackson.   B. Abraham Lincoln.
   C. Thomas Jefferson.   D. George Washington.

5. *The Ring and the Book* is a masterpiece of
   A. Alfred Tennyson.   B. Robert Browning.
   C. Thomas Hardy.   D. Ralph Waldo Emerson.

6. Matthew Arnold is the writer of
   A. *Dover Beach.*   B. *My last Duchess.*
   C. *Break, Break, Break.*   D. *The Eagle.*

7. The writer of *Heart of Darkness* is also the one of
   A. *Time of Machine.*   B. *Jim.*
   C. *Lord Jim.*   D. *A Passage to India.*

8. The study of language development over a period of time is generally termed as _____
   linguistic.
   A. applied   B. diachronic
   C. comparative   D. synchronic

9. The letter combination "-ness" in the words "weakness", "darkness" is called a
   A. prefix.   B. suffix.
   C. free morpheme.   D. root.

10. "Words are names or labels for things." This view is called _____ in semantic theory.
    A. mentalism   B. conceptualism
    C. naming theory   D. contextualism

Model Test 37

1. All the following universities are located in New England EXCEPT
   A. Yale.   B. Harvard.
   C. MIT.   D. Berkeley.

2. *Wuthering Heights* is the masterpiece of
   A. Jane Austen.   B. Charlotte Bronte.
   C. Emily Bronte.   D. William Thackeray.

3. Which of the following is the oldest national Sunday newspaper in Britain?
   A. *The Times.*   B. *The Guardian.*
   C. *The Observer.*   D. *The Financial Times.*

4. In American history, Gilded Age is the years
    A. between the start of the 19th century and the end of the 19th century.
    B. between the Civil War and the start of the 20th century.
    C. from 1929 to 1933.
    D. from 1950 to 1975.

5. Wordsworth's poetry, divided by the subjects, falls into two major groups: one about nature and the other about
    A. human life.   B. human nature.
    C. social system.   D. human spirit.

6. Which of the following is NOT one of the *Leather Stocking Tales* by James F. Cooper?
    A. *The Pioneers.*   B. *The Last of the Mohicans.*
    C. *The Pathfinder.*   D. *The Crater.*

7. The Romantic Period in American Literary history started with the publication of
    A. Washington Irving's *The Sketch Book.*
    B. Washington Irving's *Tales of a Traveler.*
    C. Whitman's *Leaves of Grass.*
    D. James Fenimore Cooper's *Leather Stocking Tales.*

8. Which is the smallest unit of language in terms of relationship between expression and content?
    A. Word.   B. Morpheme.
    C. Allomorph.   D. Root.

9. "Long" and "short" are a pair of _____ antonyms.
    A. gradable   B. complementary
    C. reverse   D. converse

10. The word "language" is sometimes used to refer to the whole of a person's language called
    A. scientific language.   B. idiolect.
    C. colloquial language.   D. formal language.

Model Test 38

1. The Great Charter (Magna Carta) was signed by _____ in 1215.
    A. King Henry I   B. King John
    C. King William I   D. King Richard

2. The Capital of Northern Ireland is
    A. Swansea.   B. Cardiff.
    C. Rhonda.   D. Belfast.

3. The three largest cities in **Canada** do NOT include

A. Toronto.　　　　　　　　　B. Montreal.

C. Ottawa.　　　　　　　　　D. Vancouver.

4. The first American President who inaugurated in Washington City was

A. George Washington.　　　　B. Thomas Jefferson.

C. John Adams.　　　　　　　D. Abraham Lincoln.

5. The following plays are comedies by Shakespeare EXCEPT

A. *A Midsummer Night's Dream.*　B. *Twelfth Night.*

C. *The Merchant of Venice.*　　D. *The Tempest.*

6. *The Legend of Sleepy Hollow* is a short story written by

A. James Fenimore Cooper.　　B. Washington Irving.

C. Edgar Allan Poe.　　　　　D. Mark Twain.

7. _____ was considered to be the greatest dramatist in the 18th century.

A. Henry Fielding　　　　　　B. Jonathan Swift

C. Daniel Defoe　　　　　　　D. Richard B. Sheridan

8. The function of the sentence "Water starts to freeze at zero degree centigrade." is

A. interrogative.　　　　　　　B. directive.

C. informative.　　　　　　　D. performative.

9. _____ act expresses the intention of the speaker.

A. Locutionary　　　　　　　B. Illocutionary

C. Perlocutionary　　　　　　D. Speech

10. TG grammar was put forward by

A. Saussure.　　　　　　　　B. Leech.

C. Halliday.　　　　　　　　D. Noam Chomsky.

Model Test 39

1. _____ is the largest state of all the states of America.

A. Texas　　　　　　　　　　B. Alaska

C. California　　　　　　　　D. Hawaii

2. The capital of the Republic of Ireland is

A. Dublin.　　　　　　　　　B. Cardiff.

C. Belfast.　　　　　　　　　D. Edinburgh.

3. _____ is the only judicial branch which has the authority to explain the American Constitution.

A. The Supreme Court　　　　B. The President

C. The Senate　　　　　　　　D. The House of Representatives

4. The flag of the United Kingdom, is made up of _____ crosses.
   A. two   B. three
   C. four   D. five

5. _____ is the founder of English materialist philosophy.
   A. Christopher Marlowe   B. Francis Bacon
   C. Thomas More   D. Edmund Spencer

6. Ezra Pound is best known for his active involvement in
   A. the Beat Generation movement.
   B. the radical political protests.
   C. the poetic revolution.
   D. the school of Naturalism.

7. Which of the following was written by Harriet Beecher Stowe?
   A. *Roughing It in the Bush.*   B. *Walden.*
   C. *Adam Bede.*   D. *Uncle Tom's Cabin.*

8. The study of a language as it changes through time is _____ linguistic.
   A. comparative   B. diachronic
   C. up-to-date   D. descriptive

9. Among the three branches of phonetics, the most highly developed one is _____ phonetics.
   A. auditory   B. acoustic
   C. articulatory   D. none of the above three

10. The element "-es" in "pushes" is a(n)
    A. free morpheme.   B. derivational morpheme.
    C. root morpheme.   D. inflectional morpheme.

Model Test 40

1. The symbol of England is
   A. Thistle.   B. Shamrock.
   C. Daffodil.   D. Rose.

2. _____, the capital of Victoria, is Australia's second largest city.
   A. Melbourne   B. Brisbane
   C. Canberra   D. Adelaide

3. The first known settlers of Britain were the
   A. Iberians.   B. Jutes.
   C. Celts.   D. Anglo-Saxons.

4. In 1620, in order to escape religious persecution, 102 Pilgrims sailed to the America in Mayflower and established
   A. New York.   B. Georgia.
   C. Virginia.   D. Plymouth.
5. F. Scott Fitzgerald mainly shows the spiritual predicament of _____ in his fiction.
   A. the working class   B. the upper class
   C. the exiles in Paris   D. intellectuals and artists
6. Which of the following is NOT written by Theodore Dreiser?
   A. *Sister Carrie.*   B. *The Titan.*
   C. *Light in August.*   D. *Jennie Gerhardt.*
7. Which of the following is NOT the works of William Blake?
   A. *Poetical Sketches.*   B. *Songs of Innocence.*
   C. *The Marriage of Heaven and Hell.*   D. *The Tree of Liberty.*
8. The SF Grammar is developed by _____ on the basis of Firth's theories.
   A. Saussure   B. Leonard Bloomfield
   C. Halliday   D. Noam Chomsky
9. One way to analyze lexical meaning is
   A. predication analysis.   B. stylistic analysis.
   C. componential analysis.   D. proposition analysis.
10. The relation between "poultry" and "duck" is
   A. polysemy.   B. antonymy.
   C. homophony.   D. hyponymy.

Model Test 1

1. ［答案］C ［考点］英国地理概况。
   ［精析］大不列颠岛(Great Britain)上共有三个政治分区：英格兰(England)、苏格兰(Scotland)和威尔士(Wales)，而爱尔兰(全称：爱尔兰共和国)则是大不列颠岛之外的另一岛屿——爱尔兰岛上的国家。

   > 要点归纳
   >
   > - 英格兰(England)位于大不列颠岛南部，是面积最大、人口最稠密的地区；
   > - 苏格兰(Scotland)位于大不列颠岛北部，拥有三大自然区：北部高地、中部低地和南部山陵；
   > - 威尔士(Wales)位于大不列颠岛西部。

2. ［答案］A ［考点］新西兰经济概况。
   ［精析］新西兰是经济发达国家，畜牧业是其经济的基础。新西兰羊肉、奶制品和粗羊毛的出口量均居世界第一位。新西兰还是世界上最大的鹿茸生产国和出口国。

3. ［答案］A ［考点］美国历史概况。
   ［精析］新墨西哥并不是首批英属美国殖民地。

   > 要点归纳
   >
   > 首批英属美国殖民地共有13个州，具体包括：Virginia, Massachusetts, New Hampshire, Rhode Island, Connecticut, New York, New Jersey, Pennsylvania, Delaware, Maryland, North Carolina, South Carolina, Georgia。

4. ［答案］D ［考点］美国地理概况。
   ［精析］自由女神像位于纽约港。

5. ［答案］A ［考点］美国文学之作家贡献。
   ［精析］美国浪漫主义时期的代表人物James Fenimore Cooper发展了三种小说：有关过去革命的小说、海洋小说和美国边境小说。

6. ［答案］A ［考点］美国文学之作家作品。
   ［精析］*The Grapes of Wrath*(《愤怒的葡萄》)的作者是John Steinbeck，他是美国大萧条时期的主要作家。

7. ［答案］B ［考点］美国文学之作家贡献。

［精析］Walt Whitman的*Leaves of Grass*(《草叶集》)标志着美国浪漫主义时期的终结。

8. ［答案］B ［考点］语言学实例分析。

［精析］"今天天气不错，不是吗？"这句话的真正目的并不是和对方讨论具体的天气，而是展开对话之前的铺垫，其功能是交际性的。

9. ［答案］A ［考点］语言学实例分析。

［精析］四个单词中只有book是随意创造出来的。crash是拟声词(onomatopoetic word)；newspaper由news和paper组合而成；beautiful是由beauty演变而来的。

10. ［答案］B ［考点］语言学基本概念。

［精析］语音学的三大分支是：发音语音学（Arituculatory Phonetics）、听觉语音学（Auditory Phonetics）和声学语音学（Acoustic Phonetics）。

Model Test 2

1. ［答案］B ［考点］英国历史概况。

［精析］英格兰人的祖先是Anglo-Saxons(盎格鲁-撒克逊人)，而苏格兰、威尔士和爱尔兰人都属于Celts(凯尔特人)的后裔。

2. ［答案］A ［考点］加拿大历史概况。

［精析］加拿大原本是英法殖民地，后来英法战争爆发，法国将该殖民地送给了英国。

3. ［答案］C ［考点］美国地理概况。

［精析］密西西比河是美国传统的东西方分界线。

4. ［答案］A ［考点］美国历史概况。

［精析］Yankee一词原本用于指代新英格兰人，现在则用于代表美国人，俗称美国佬。

5. ［答案］A ［考点］美国文学作家及其贡献。

［精析］John Smith一般被看成是第一位美国作家，其作品*A True Relation of Virginia*(《关于弗吉尼亚的真实叙述》)被认为是美国文学史上的第一部作品。

6. ［答案］D ［考点］英国文学作家及其贡献。

［精析］Geoffrey Chaucer被看成是现代英国诗歌之父，其代表作为*The Canterbury Tales*(《坎特伯雷故事集》)。

7. ［答案］B ［考点］文学概念。

［精析］斯宾塞诗节指的是斯宾塞在自己的诗中所用的九行诗节。

8. ［答案］A ［考点］语言学实例分析。

［精析］自由词素（free morpheme）指的是可独立出现、独立成词的词素，而children 是由自由词素child衍化而来的。

9. ［答案］B ［考点］语言学基本概念。

［精析］句法学的分类主要有单词所表达的含义、单词所用的词缀、单词出现的结构等。

10. ［答案］D ［考点］语言学基本概念。

［精析］意义分析包括成分分析（componential analysis）和述谓分析（predication analysis）。

Model Test 3

1. ［答案］A ［考点］新西兰城市概况。

［精析］海港城市奥克兰是新西兰最大的城市。新西兰首都是惠灵顿。

2. ［答案］C ［考点］加拿大城市概况。

［精析］加拿大的三大城市不包括渥太华。

3. ［答案］C ［考点］美国历史概况。

［精析］第一次大陆会议和第二次大陆会议的召开地点都是Philadelphia（费城）。

4. ［答案］D ［考点］英国历史概况。

［精析］人们所知的英国最早的居民是Iberians（伊比利亚人）。

5. ［答案］A ［考点］英国文学之作家及其贡献。

［精析］将理性主义介绍到英国的是新古典主义时期的代表人物Alexander Pope。

6. ［答案］C ［考点］英国文学之作家作品。

［精析］*Ode to the West Wind*（《西风颂》）的作者是Percy Shelley，他是英国浪漫主义时期的著名诗人。

要点归纳

Percy Shelley的代表作品有：

- *Queen Mab*（《麦布女王》）   • *Ode to a Skylark*（《云雀颂》）
- *A Defence of Poetry*（《诗辩》）• *PrometheusUnbound*（《解放了的普罗米修斯》）

7. ［答案］D ［考点］美国文学之基本文学概念。

［精析］美国的浪漫主义时期又被称为美国的文艺复兴时期。

120

8. [答案] B [考点] 语言学基本概念。

[精析] 语用学与其他语言学分支的差别在于它的研究与说话者，即语言使用者有关。

9. [答案] C [考点] 语言学基本知识。

[精析] Saussure所写的*Course in General Linguistics*(《普通语言学教程》)标志着现代语言学的开端。

10. [答案] C [考点] 语言学实例分析。

[精析] 最小对立体是指除了出现在同一位置上的一个音之外其余都相同的两个语音组合，题目中的A、B、D三组都是最小对立体。

Model Test 4

1. [答案] D [考点] 英国政治概况。

[精析] 英国的官方名称是大不列颠及北爱尔兰联合王国（the United Kingdom of Great Britain and Northern Ireland）。

2. [答案] B [考点] 英国历史概况。

[精析] 罗马人克劳迪厄斯(Claudius)于公元43年占领不列颠，在接下来的将近400年间，英国一直处于罗马人的占领之下。

3. [答案] B [考点] 澳大利亚地理概况。

[精析] 悉尼是澳大利亚新南威尔士州的首府，同时也是澳大利亚历史最悠久、面积最大的城市。

4. [答案] D [考点] 美国文化概况。

[精析] *Financial Times*(《金融时报》)是英国著名的报纸，并不是美国的报纸。

5. [答案] C [考点] 美国文学基本知识。

[精析] 独立革命时期的美国文学强调理性和秩序。

6. [答案] D [考点] 美国文学之作家贡献。

[精析] Philip Freneau被看成是"美国革命的诗人"，同时也是美国18世纪最杰出的诗人。

7. [答案] C [考点] 英国文学之作家作品。

[精析] *Wuthering Heights*(《呼啸山庄》)的作者是埃米莉·勃朗特(Emily Bronte)，而非莎士比亚。

8. [答案] A [考点] 语言学基本概念。

[精析] 开放性单词(open class words)包括名词、动词、形容词和副词，而冠词属

于封闭性单词。

9. ［答案］A ［考点］语言学实例分析。
［精析］baggage和luggage都意为"行李"，但前者用于美国，后者用于英国，两者只是应用的地域不同，属于dialectal synonyms。

10. ［答案］C ［考点］语言学基本概念。
［精析］话语的含义（utterance meaning）是以所说句子的含义为基础的。

Model Test 5

1. ［答案］A ［考点］澳大利亚和新西兰历史概况。
［精析］澳大利亚和新西兰最初是由荷兰探险家Abel Tasman于1642年发现的。

2. ［答案］A ［考点］英国历史概况。
［精析］英国内战通常被看做是现代世界史的开端。

3. ［答案］D ［考点］英国历史概况。
［精析］威尔士是在亨利三世的统治之下被占领的。

4. ［答案］D ［考点］美国历史概况。
［精析］美国的土著居民是当地的印第安人。

5. ［答案］C ［考点］英国文学之作家贡献。
［精析］Samuel Richardson通常被看成是英国本土小说的创始人。

6. ［答案］A ［考点］英国文学之文学流派。
［精析］英国现代小说主要是对普通大众生活进行现实的描述和展现。

7. ［答案］A ［考点］美国文学之作家作品。
［精析］*The Tenth Muse Lately Sprung up in America*（《美国新崛起的第十位缪斯女神》）是美国女诗人Anne Bradstreet的代表作。

8. ［答案］B ［考点］语言学实例分析。
［精析］uncomfortably是由un-, comfort, -able, -ly组成的。

9. ［答案］C ［考点］语言学基本概念。
［精析］地域方言（regional dialect）指的是生活在同一地理区域内的人所使用的语言变体。

10. ［答案］D ［考点］语言学家基本理论。
［精析］传统行为主义者认为识别和概括是语言学习进步的关键。

Model Test 6

1. [答案] C [考点] 英国政治概况。
   [精析] 英国保守党的前身是托利党。托利党人是指那些支持世袭王权、不愿废除国王的人。

2. [答案] B [考点] 加拿大地理概况。
   [精析] 魁北克省是加拿大面积最大的省。

3. [答案] B [考点] 英国政治概况。
   [精析] 英国是君主立宪制国家，国家首脑为国王或女王。

4. [答案] C [考点] 美国历史概况。
   [精析] 美国建国之初政府地处费城。

5. [答案] D [考点] 英国文学之作家生平。
   [精析] 勃朗特三姐妹指的是：Charlotte Bronte、Emily Bronte和Anne Bronte。

6. [答案] B [考点] 美国文学之作家生平。
   [精析] Eugene Gladstone O'Neill是美国现代戏剧的奠基人，也是美国首位获得诺贝尔文学奖的戏剧作家。

7. [答案] A [考点] 美国文学之作家作品。
   [精析] *The Son of the Wolf*(《狼之子》)出版于1900年，是Jack London的首部短篇小说合集。

8. [答案] D [考点] 语言学实例分析。
   [精析] "颜色"和"黑色"属于上下义关系。

9. [答案] C [考点] 语言学基本概念。
   [精析] 在语言学中，语句含义的改变被称为意义转移(meaning-shift)。

10. [答案] B [考点] 语言学基本理论。
    [精析] 言语行为理论(Speech Act Theory)将言语行为分为言内行为、言外行为和言后行为这三类，有助于人们更深入地分析语言交际的本质。

Model Test 7

1. [答案] A [考点] 美国政治概况。
   [精析] 美国历史上第一位共和党总统是Abraham Lincoln。

2. ［答案］D ［考点］美国地理概况。
［精析］得克萨斯州是美国石油和天然气储量最大的州。

3. ［答案］B ［考点］加拿大地理概况。
［精析］马更些河（the Mackenzie River）是加拿大最长的河流，流经加拿大地盾（Canadian Shield）与西部落基山脉（the Rocky Mountains）之间，全长1600公里。

4. ［答案］D ［考点］英国政治概况。
［精析］枢密院在英国历史上又称国王议会，原本是政府行政权力的源泉。

5. ［答案］A ［考点］美国文学。
［精析］美国现代文学与之前的分界线是第一次世界大战。

6. ［答案］D ［考点］美国文学之作家流派。
［精析］John Updike并不是美国文学"垮掉的一代"的代表作家。

7. ［答案］B ［考点］英国文学。
［精析］William Wordsworth认为"所有的好诗都是激情的自然流露"。

8. ［答案］D ［考点］语言学基本概念。
［精析］指令类（directives）言语行为包括：inviting, suggesting, requesting, advising, warning, threatening, ordering, 而swearing属于阐述类（representatives）。

9. ［答案］C ［考点］语言学基本概念。
［精析］个人方言结合了以下几个因素：地域变化、社会变化、性别变化和年龄变化。

10. ［答案］D ［考点］语言学基本概念。
［精析］在双关语中使用同义词主要是为了制造幽默、讽刺、嘲笑等效果。

Model Test 8

1. ［答案］A ［考点］英国政治概况。
［精析］在英国大选中获多数议席的政党组建政府，其领袖由君主任命为首相。

2. ［答案］B ［考点］美国政治概况。
［精析］美国的立法机关是美国国会，但婚姻不属于其立法范围。

3. ［答案］D ［考点］加拿大地理概况。
［精析］加拿大是个多民族国家，境内有多达100个民族。

4. ［答案］D ［考点］澳大利亚地理概况。
［精析］食火鸡、袋鼠和考拉都是澳大利亚特有的动物，老虎则并非如此。

5. [答案] B [考点] 美国文学之作家生平。
[精析] Alan Ginsberg并不是黑人作家。

6. [答案] C [考点] 英国文学之作家流派。
[精析] *Don Juan*(《唐璜》)是英国浪漫主义诗人Byron的经典之作。

7. [答案] D [考点] 美国文学。
[精析] *The Sun Also Rises*(《太阳照样升起》)是Hemingway第一部描写"失落的一代"的小说。

8. [答案] A [考点] 语言学家代表理论。
[精析] 普遍语法理论是由Chomsky提出的。

9. [答案] D [考点] 语言学实例分析。
[精析] girl一词最初指年轻男性或女性,现在则只用于表示年轻女性,这显然是词义的缩小。

10. [答案] C [考点] 语言学基本概念。
[精析] 依照言语行为理论,说话者在说话时可能实施言内行为(locutionary act)、言外行为(illocutionary act)和言后行为(perlocutionary act)。

Model Test 9

1. [答案] C [考点] 美国地理概况。
[精析] 芝加哥是五大湖地区最大、最繁忙的港口。

2. [答案] C [考点] 新西兰和澳大利亚历史概况。
[精析] 詹姆斯·库克船长1770年宣称占领澳大利亚和新西兰。Abel Tasman发现了澳大利亚和新西兰。Christopher Columbus发现了中美洲的圣萨尔瓦多岛。意大利航海家Amerigo Vespucci 1499年到达美洲,他认为哥伦布到达的这块大陆并不是亚洲,声称发现了一个新世界,之后美洲大陆就是用他的名字命名的。

3. [答案] A [考点] 美国地理概况。
[精析] 纽约是美国最大的城市,同时也是美国最主要的港口城市。

4. [答案] C [考点] 英国历史概况。
[精析] 英国工业革命最大的成就是纺织业的改革,因此纺织品是工业革命的关键所在。

5. [答案] C [考点] 英国文学之作家作品。
[精析] 《儿子与情人》(*Sons and Lovers*)是英国现代主义时期小说家大卫·赫伯特·劳伦斯(D. H. Lawrence)的代表作。

查尔斯·狄更斯(Charles Dickens)是英国维多利亚时期著名的小说家,其代表作有:

- *A Tale of Two Cities*(《双城记》)
- *David Copperfield*(《大卫·科波菲尔》)
- *Great Expectation*(《远大前程》)
- *Oliver Twist*(《雾都孤儿》)
- *Hard Times*(《艰难时世》)
- *The Old Curiosity Shop*(《老古玩店》)
- *Pickwick Papers*(《匹克威克外传》)

6. [答案]B [考点]英国文学之作家流派。
[精析] metaphysical poetry(玄学派诗歌)通常用于指17世纪受John Donne影响而写作的作家的作品。

7. [答案]D [考点]美国文学之作家贡献。
[精析] Ezra Pound是美国意象主义的先驱。

8. [答案]D [考点]语言学实例分析。
[精析]屈折词缀(inflectional affixes)不具有词汇意义,通常用于表示时态、单复数、比较级等语法变化。watches中的-es、longer中的-er和notes中的-s都属于屈折词缀。useful则属于派生词。

9. [答案]D [考点]语言学基本概念。
[精析]由一个以上的单词构成的短语通常包含中心语(head)、标志语(specifier)和补足语(complement)这几个要素。

10. [答案]C [考点]语言学基本概念。
[精析]语境因素包括时间、地点和会话参与者,并不包括目的。

Model Test 10

1. [答案]B [考点]美国地理概况。
[精析]新英格兰由六个州组成:Maine, New Hampshire, Vermont, Massachusetts, Rhode Island和Connecticut。该地区以多山、多山谷、多河流为特征。加利福尼亚州是美国西部太平洋沿岸的一个州。

2. [答案]B [考点]英国政治概况。
[精析]辉格党和托利党这两个政党名称起源于1688年的the Glorious Revolution(光荣革命)。

3. [答案]B [考点]加拿大地理概况。
[精析]渥太华地处加拿大安大略省东部的安大略谷。

4. ［答案］A　［考点］澳大利亚地理概况。

　　［精析］堪培拉(Canberra)是澳大利亚的首都，同时也是直辖区。

> **要点归纳**
>
> 澳大利亚共分为六个州和两个地区，其中六个州分别是：New South Wales、Victoria、Queensland、South Australia、West Australia和Tasmania；两个地区分别是Northern Territory和Canberra。

5. ［答案］C　［考点］英国文学之文学流派。

　　［精析］18世纪中期浪漫主义在欧洲兴起，随后传入英国。

6. ［答案］B　［考点］美国文学之作家生平。

　　［精析］William Faulkner是20世纪著名的美国南方作家。

7. ［答案］A　［考点］美国文学之作家作品。

　　［精析］*The Great Gatsby*(《了不起的盖茨比》)是Francis Scott Fitzgerald的作品。

8. ［答案］C　［考点］语言学基本概念。

　　［精析］新词的添加主要通过以下方式完成：coinage、clipped words、blending、acronyms、back-formation、functional-shift和borrowing。

9. ［答案］A　［考点］语言学基本概念。

　　［精析］话语方式主要研究进行交流的方式。

10. ［答案］B　［考点］语言学实例分析。

　　［精析］承诺类（commissive）言语行为是说话者对某些动作或行为进行的承诺，promising就是典型的例子。

Model Test 11

1. ［答案］D　［考点］美国地理概况。

　　［精析］美国的"众河之父"指的是密西西比河。

2. ［答案］A　［考点］加拿大历史概况。

　　［精析］加拿大魁北克(Quebec)至今仍然保留着法国的生活习惯和文化传统，是法国人在北美长期生活的见证。

3. ［答案］A　［考点］美国地理概况。

　　［精析］美国少数民族人口中增长最快的是亚裔美国人，亚裔美国人中又以华裔美国人居多。

4. 〔答案〕C 〔考点〕英国政治概况。

〔精析〕英国每五年举行一次大选。

5. 〔答案〕D 〔考点〕美国文学之作家作品。

〔精析〕长诗*The Cantos*(《诗章》)是Ezra Pound最伟大的作品。

6. 〔答案〕B 〔考点〕英国文学之作家作品。

〔精析〕*Pride and Prejudice*(《傲慢与偏见》)是英国著名女小说家Jane Austen的代表作之一。

7. 〔答案〕B 〔考点〕英国文学之作家流派。

〔精析〕英国早期浪漫主义"湖畔诗人"的代表人物是William Wordsworth, Samuel Taylor Coleridge和Robert Southey。

8. 〔答案〕D 〔考点〕语言学实例分析。

〔精析〕begin和commence是同义词，但两者风格不同，前者较为随意，后者较为正式。

9. 〔答案〕D 〔考点〕语言学基本概念。

〔精析〕决定词类的标准有屈折变化、分布和含义，并不包括风格。

10. 〔答案〕A 〔考点〕语言学基本概念。

〔精析〕同一个单词概念上的意义对于该语言的所有使用者而言都是一样的。

Model Test 12

1. 〔答案〕D 〔考点〕美国经济概况。

〔精析〕美国的底特律(Detroit)被称为"世界汽车之都"。

2. 〔答案〕B 〔考点〕英国文化概况。

〔精析〕英国历史最悠久的报纸是《泰晤士报》。

3. 〔答案〕C 〔考点〕英国地理概况。

〔精析〕威尔士首府是加的夫。

4. 〔答案〕B 〔考点〕澳大利亚历史概况。

〔精析〕曾冠名为杰克逊港的悉尼是澳大利亚最早的殖民据点。

5. 〔答案〕A 〔考点〕英国文学之作家流派。

〔精析〕萧伯纳(George Bernard Shaw)被认为是自莎士比亚以来英国最著名的剧作家。

6. ［答案］**B** ［考点］美国文学之作家作品。
   ［精析］*The Fall of the House of Usher*（《厄舍古屋的倒塌》）的作者是美国浪漫主义时期的代表人物Edgar Allen Poe。

7. ［答案］**B** ［考点］英国文学。
   ［精析］英国维多利亚时期的代表人物Thomas Hardy的大部分小说都以虚构的原始地区Wessex为背景。

8. ［答案］**C** ［考点］语言学基本概念。
   ［精析］对声音的组合方式以及交流过程中声音传递意义的方式所进行的研究属于音位学的研究范畴。

9. ［答案］**D** ［考点］语言学实例分析。
   ［精析］tofu(豆腐)在英语中属于外来词。

10. ［答案］**B** ［考点］语言学家代表理论。
    ［精析］转换生成语法（transformational-generative grammar）是Chomsky于1957年提出的语法研究模式，其主要内容是短语结构规则和转换规则。

Model Test 13

1. ［答案］**B** ［考点］美国历史概况。
   ［精析］美国的自由女神像是法国于1884年赠予美国人民的礼物。

2. ［答案］**D** ［考点］英国文化概况。
   ［精析］英语和苏格兰语是苏格兰的官方语言，现在盖尔语(Gaelic)也还在苏格兰高地地区使用，丹麦语是斯堪的纳维亚语言中的一种，主要在丹麦使用。

3. ［答案］**A** ［考点］新西兰地理概况。
   ［精析］新西兰的北岛居住着新西兰四分之三的人口。

4. [答案] C [考点] 美国历史概况。
[精析] "萨拉托加大捷"被认为是北美独立战争的转折点,并直接导致了美法联军的建立。

5. [答案] A [考点] 英国文学之作家作品。
[精析] *The Pilgrim's Progress*(《天路历程》)是17世纪英国文艺复兴后期作家John Bunyan的经典之作, *The Vanity Fair*(《名利场》)是其中最著名的一部分。

6. [答案] B [考点] 美国文学之作家贡献。
[精析] 1954年诺贝尔文学奖得主是美国的Ernest Hemingway。Hemingway是"迷惘的一代"的代表人物,以写小说见长。

7. [答案] D [考点] 美国文学之作家作品。
[精析] The Rabbit series(兔子系列)是John Updike(约翰·厄普代克)最为出色的作品。

8. [答案] A [考点] 语言学实例分析。
[精析] "男孩"和"男人"的主要区别在于前者是孩子,而后者是成年人。

9. [答案] A [考点] 语言学基本概念。
[精析] 单词意义的变化有三种:词义扩大(widening of meaning)、词义缩减(narrowing of meaning)和意义转移(meaning-shift)。

10. [答案] C [考点] 语言学基本概念。
[精析] 受社会阶层影响而产生的方言属于社会方言。

Model Test 14

1. [答案] A [考点] 美国地理概况。
[精析] 曼哈顿是美国纽约市著名的商业区,也是纽约的中心地带。

2. [答案] D [考点] 加拿大概况。
[精析] 蒙特利尔的法裔加拿大人占全市人口的三分之二,是除了法国巴黎以外世界上最大的法语城市,素有"小巴黎"之称。

3. [答案] C [考点] 英国地理概况。
[精析] 苏格兰有三大自然区:北部高地、中部低地及南部山陵。

4. [答案] A [考点] 美国历史概况。
[精析] 葛底斯堡大捷是美国内战的转折点。

5. [答案] A [考点] 美国文学之作家作品。

[精析] John Steinbeck凭借*The Grapes of Wrath*(《愤怒的葡萄》)于1962年获得了诺贝尔文学奖。

6. [答案] D [考点] 美国文学。

[精析] *Moby Dick*（《白鲸》）被看成是美国首部散文史诗，其作者是Herman Melville。而*Nature*(《论自然》)则被称为the manifesto of American transcendentalism。

7. [答案] B [考点] 英国文学之作家流派。

[精析] John Dryden是英国古典主义最杰出的代表，他是17世纪后期享有盛名的桂冠诗人，也是杰出的戏剧家和文艺评论家。

8. [答案] A [考点] 语言学基本概念。

[精析] 音素(phone)是语言单位或语音片段。

9. [答案] D [考点] 语言学基本概念。

[精析] 语言文体学(linguistic stylistics)是介于语言学和文学之间的研究领域。

10. [答案] C [考点] 语言学实例分析。

[精析] 通过"smoke +fog"组合成一个词smog属于形态学(morphology)中词的变化(lexical change proper)中的混成词(blending)。

Model Test 15

1. [答案] C [考点] 英国历史概况。

[精析] 罗马人在统治英国期间将基督教这种新的宗教带到了英国。

2. [答案] A [考点] 美国地理概况。

[精析] 美国黄石国家公园(Yellow Stone National Park)位于怀俄明州的北部地区，是世界上最古老的国家公园，也是美国最大的野生动物保护区。

3. [答案] B [考点] 加拿大政治概况。

[精析] 加拿大的议会包括参议院和众议院（the House of Commons），参众两院通过的法案由代表英国女王的总督签署后成为法律。

4. [答案] C [考点] 美国地理概况。

[精析] 格兰德河(Rio Grande River)是美国和墨西哥之间的天然界河。

5. [答案] D [考点] 美国文学之作家流派。

[精析] The Lost Generation(迷惘的一代)指的是第一次世界大战之后美国的文学流派，即现代主义文学，而Theodore Dreiser则是现实主义文学的代表人物，故选D。

6. ［答案］B ［考点］美国文学之作家作品。

［精析］在*The Adventures of Huckleberry Finn*（《哈克贝利·费恩历险记》）一书中，Mark Twain将主人公Finn描写成了带有a sound heart and a deformed conscience的男孩。

7. ［答案］B ［考点］英国文学之作家作品。

［精析］*Gulliver's Travels*（《格列佛游记》)的作者是Jonathan Swift。

8. ［答案］C ［考点］语言学基本概念。

［精析］言语变体(speech variety)指的是语言使用者所用的可分辨的言语形式。

9. ［答案］B ［考点］语言学实例分析。

［精析］motherland是mother和land组合而成的合成词。

10. ［答案］D ［考点］语言学基本概念。

［精析］元音的分类是依照舌头的位置、嘴张开的幅度、嘴唇的形状来决定的，与元音本身的发音无关。

Model Test 16

1. ［答案］C ［考点］新西兰地理概况。

［精析］新西兰的首都是惠灵顿(Wellington)，惠灵顿也是新西兰的第二大城市；达尼丁(Dunedin)是新西兰的第四大城市；基督城(Christchurch)是新西兰的第三大城市；奥克兰(Auckland)是新西兰的第一大城市。

2. ［答案］A ［考点］英国地理概况。

［精析］英国南面的英吉利海峡和东面的北海将其与欧洲其他部分分隔开来。

3. ［答案］B ［考点］美国历史概况。

［精析］将美国首都迁到华盛顿的是美国第三任总统Thomas Jefferson（托马斯·杰斐逊）。

4. ［答案］D ［考点］英国历史概况。

［精析］盎格鲁-撒克逊人创立的贤人会议是现今the Privy Council（英国枢密院）的基础。

5. ［答案］A ［考点］英语文学之文学流派。

［精析］在20世纪头十年间，现代主义成为国际文学趋势。

6. ［答案］B ［考点］英国文学。

［精析］*The Pilgrim's Progress*（《天路历程》）是英语文学史上最著名的宗教寓言。

7. ［答案］D ［考点］英国文学之作家作品。

［精析］*The Flea*（《跳蚤之歌》）是玄学派代表人物John Donne的作品。

8. ［答案］D ［考点］语言学基本概念。

［精析］语言学的主要分支包括：语音学、音素学、形态学、句法学、语义学和语用学，因此对语言学研究的核心主要包括上述内容，神经语言学不包含在内。

9. ［答案］A ［考点］语言学基本概念。

［精析］语用学研究的是上下文中语言的应用情况。

10. ［答案］B ［考点］语言学实例分析。

［精析］高速公路上"前方道路施工"告示牌是为了给人们提供基本的信息，获得一个事实情况。故应该是语言的信息功能（informative function）。

Model Test 17

1. ［答案］B ［考点］澳大利亚历史概况。

［精析］澳大利亚最开始是英国的殖民地，1901年，六个殖民区统一成为联邦，澳大利亚联邦成立，同时通过第一部宪法。1931年成为英联邦中的独立国家。

2. ［答案］B ［考点］英国地理概况。

［精析］克莱德河（River Clyde）是苏格兰最重要的河流。

3. ［答案］A ［考点］美国政治概况。

［精析］美国众议院的议员每两年选举一次。

4. ［答案］B ［考点］美国地理概况。

［精析］密西西比河是美国最长、最重要的河流，其流域面积达322万平方公里。

5. ［答案］A ［考点］美国文学之作家贡献。

［精析］*The Sketch Book*（《见闻札记》）标志着美国文学浪漫主义时期的开始，其作

者Washington Irving被称为Father of American Literature。

6. ［答案］C ［考点］英国文学之作家流派。
［精析］英国浪漫主义时期代表人物William Wordsworth被称为是"自然的崇拜者"。

7. ［答案］D ［考点］英国文学之作家作品。
［精析］*Romeo and Juliet*（《罗密欧与朱丽叶》）是Shakespeare戏剧作品中的正剧，而非喜剧。

8. ［答案］A ［考点］语言学实例分析。
［精析］单词构成分为合成（compound）和派生（derivation）两种。football、icy-cold和rainbow都是合成词，而unusual则属于加前缀构成的派生词。

9. ［答案］A ［考点］语言学基本概念。
［精析］句法成分为句子提供了结构。

10. ［答案］B ［考点］语言学家代表理论。
［精析］语义分析中的述谓分析（predication analysis）是由英国语言学家G. Leech提出的。

Model Test 18

1. ［答案］D ［考点］澳大利亚经济概况。
［精析］农业是澳大利亚规模最大、种类最多的产业。

2. ［答案］B ［考点］英国历史概况。
［精析］阿尔弗雷德国王因建立了强大的舰队而被称为"英国海军之父"。

3. ［答案］A ［考点］美国历史概况。
［精析］英国于1607年在美国Virginia（弗吉尼亚）建立了第一块殖民地。

4. ［答案］B ［考点］美国地理概况。
［精析］美国最大的土著部落位于科罗拉多高原。

5. ［答案］C ［考点］英国文学。
［精析］首部官方版本的《圣经》是英国国王James I于1611年修订发行的。

6. ［答案］C ［考点］英美文学基本概念。
［精析］sonnet指的是十四行诗。

7. ［答案］D ［考点］美国文学之作家流派。
［精析］Mark Twain是美国本土作家，他写了很多有关美国本土人文的作品。

8. [答案] B [考点] 语言学基本概念。

[精析] 言外行为(illocutionary act)指的是表达说话者意图的行为。

9. [答案] C [考点] 语言学基本概念。

[精析] 瑞士语言学家Saussure提出的langue和parole的差别和美国语言学家Chomsky提出的competence和performance的差别大致相同。

10. [答案] D [考点] 语言学实例分析。

[精析] 单词dozer是由bulldozer缩略而来的，而其他三个单词都属于词首字母缩略词。

Model Test 19

1. [答案] C [考点] 美国政治概况。

[精析] 美国的最高司法权力机关是最高法院。

2. [答案] B [考点] 英国历史概况。

[精析] 二战最为深远的结果之一是加速了大英帝国的瓦解。

3. [答案] A [考点] 加拿大地理概况。

[精析] 大浅滩(The Grand Banks)位于加拿大的大西洋省份，它是世界上最大的渔场。

4. [答案] C [考点] 澳大利亚地理概况。

[精析] 南澳大利亚州的首府是阿德莱德。

5. [答案] B [考点] 英国文学之作家贡献。

[精析] Francis Bacon是英国首位著名散文家，同时也是现代科学的奠基人。

6. [答案] B [考点] 美国文学之文学流派。

[精析] 美国内战之前的文学处于浪漫主义时期。

7. [答案] B [考点] 美国文学之作家作品。

[精析] Hawthorne作品中象征主义手法的运用主要体现在其著作*The Scarlet Letter*(《红字》)中。

8. [答案] A [考点] 语言学基本概念。

[精析] 语言能力(competence)指的是理想语言使用者关于语言规则的知识储备。

9. [答案] B [考点] 语言学基本概念。

[精析] 语言的随意性说明语言在意义和声音上没有确切的逻辑关联。

10. [答案] A [考点] 语言学实例分析。

[精析] 随着语言行为本身而产生的一些行为属于言外行为（an illocutionary act），故选A。言外行为是由约翰·奥斯汀（John Langshaw Austin）提出的言语行为理论（speech act theory）的三种行为中的一种。

Model Test 20

1. [答案] D　[考点] 英国政治概况。
   [精析] 英国的君主政体可以追溯到9世纪。

2. [答案] A　[考点] 美国地理概况。
   [精析] Alaska位于北美洲的西北部，与美国其他各州相分离。

3. [答案] C　[考点] 澳大利亚地理概况。
   [精析] 淘金热使得墨尔本（Melbourne）成为澳大利亚的金融中心。

4. [答案] A　[考点] 美国经济概况。
   [精析] 美国的Houston（休斯敦）被称作"世界化工之都"，是石油化工和合成橡胶中心。

5. [答案] C　[考点] 美国文学之作家作品。
   [精析] 斯蒂芬·克莱恩是美国19世纪后期的著名小说家和诗人，*The Red Badge of Courage*（《红色英勇勋章》）是以美国南北战争为历史背景写成的，奠定了他的文坛地位，故选C。

6. [答案] A　[考点] 英国文学之作家流派。
   [精析] Daniel Defoe是英国新古典主义时期的代表人物，其小说主要关注为了生存而不懈努力的不幸之人。其代表作为*Robinson Crusoe*（《鲁滨逊漂流记》）。

7. [答案] A　[考点] 英国文学之文学流派。
   [精析] 18世纪的英国文学处于浪漫主义时期。

8. [答案] A　[考点] 语言学基本概念。
   [精析] 不同语言环境中的不同音素可以代表同一个音位，这种不同的音素被称为该音位的音位变体（allophones）。

9. [答案] D　[考点] 语言学基本概念。
   [精析] 心理语言学（Psycholinguistics）主要研究儿童如何习得母语，人类运用语言时大脑如何工作，交流过程中人类如何处理接收到的信息等。

10. [答案] B　[考点] 语言学实例分析。
    [精析] 英语的句子根据语法形式（句子结构）可分为简单句、并列句和复合句。简单句（Simple Sentence）的基本形式是由一个主语加一个谓语构成。并列句

(Coordinate Sentence)是由两个或两个以上的简单句用并列连词连在一起构成的句子,并列连词有:and、but、or、so等。并列句中的各简单句意义同等重要,相互之间没有从属关系,是平行并列的关系。复合句(Complex Sentence)由一个主句(Principal Clause)和一个或一个以上的从句(Subordinate Clause)构成,主要分为定语从句、状语从句和名词性从句。题干中的例句由but这个表转折的并列连词连接,属于并列句,故选B。

Model Test 21

1. [答案]C [考点]加拿大历史概况。
   [精析]1867年的《英国北美法案》确定加拿大为自治领地。

2. [答案]C [考点]美国经济概况。
   [精析]美国是世界上最大的玉米生产国和出口国。

3. [答案]D [考点]英国历史概况。
   [精析]宪章运动是英国第一次全国范围的工人阶级运动。

4. [答案]D [考点]美国文化概况。
   [精析]爵士乐被看成是美国人对音乐的特别贡献。

5. [答案]C [考点]美国文学之作家作品。
   [精析]小说*Sister Carrie*(《嘉莉妹妹》)的作者是Theodore Dreiser,这是一个有关贫穷的乡村女孩到芝加哥追寻美国梦想的故事。

6. [答案]D [考点]英国文学之文学流派。
   [精析]英国伊丽莎白时期最盛行的文学形式是戏剧。

7. [答案]C [考点]美国文学之作家贡献。
   [精析]Ralph Waldo Emerson是美国超验主义最杰出的代表作家。

   > 要点归纳
   >
   > Ralph Waldo Emerson的代表作有:
   > - *Nature*(《论自然》)
   > - *The American Scholar*(《美国学者》)
   > - *Self-Reliance*(《论自助》)
   > - *The Transcendentalist*(《超验主义者》)

8. [答案]D [考点]语言学基本概念。
   [精析]在词典中查到的单词含义属于指示含义。

9. [答案]A [考点]语言学基本概念。
   [精析]在特定地理区域内使用的语言应该就是该地区的方言。

10. ［答案］D ［考点］语言学实例分析。

［精析］collocational synonyms意为"固定搭配的同义词"，指用在不同固定搭配中的同义词。

Model Test 22

1. ［答案］A ［考点］美国政治概况。

［精析］迄今为止，美国在位时间最长的总统是罗斯福，共在位12年。

2. ［答案］C ［考点］加拿大地理概况。

［精析］加拿大第二大城市是蒙特利尔(Montreal)。

3. ［答案］D ［考点］美国历史概况。

［精析］发现美洲新大陆的哥伦布是意大利航海家。

4. ［答案］A ［考点］澳大利亚地理概况。

［精析］澳大利亚各州中历史最悠久的是新南威尔士(New South Wales)。

5. ［答案］A ［考点］英国文学作品。

［精析］*Beowulf*(《贝奥武夫》)是盎格鲁-撒克逊时期留下的重要的古英语文学作品，它被认为是英国的民族史诗；*Sir Gawain and the Green Knight*(《高文爵士与绿衣骑士》)和*King Arthur and His Knights of the Roundtable*(《亚瑟王和他的圆桌骑士》)是中古英语时期的浪漫传奇；*The Canterbury Tale*(《坎特伯雷故事集》)是英国大诗人乔叟的一部诗体短篇小说集。

6. ［答案］D ［考点］英国文学之作家作品。

［精析］乔叟被誉为英国诗歌之父，*Troilus and Criseyde*(《特罗拉斯与克莱西德》)是他的重要作品之一。

7. ［答案］D ［考点］英国文学之作家作品。

［精析］1608-1612年被认为是莎翁的浪漫剧和和解剧的创作时期，著有四部浪漫剧与和解剧：*The Tempest*(《暴风雨》)，*Pericles, Prince of Tyre*(《泰尔亲王佩里克里斯》)，*The Winter's Tale*(《冬天的故事》)，*Cymbeline*(《辛白林》)。

8. ［答案］C ［考点］语言学基本概念。

［精析］语言习得是心理语言学研究的中心课题之一。

9. ［答案］A ［考点］语言学基本知识。

［精析］英语语言的发展历史一般分为三个阶段：古英语阶段、中世纪英语阶段和现代英语阶段。

138

10. [答案]**D** [考点]语言学实例分析。

[精析]自由词素(free morpheme)是能独立运用的词素,它有完整的意义,在句中充当一个自由的语法单位;粘着词素(bound morpheme)不能独立成词,只能依附于其他词素上以构成词或担当一定的语法功能。

Model Test 23

1. [答案]**C** [考点]美国地理概况。

[精析]世界上最大的活火山莫纳罗亚火山位于夏威夷地区。

2. [答案]**B** [考点]英国历史概况。

[精析]英国的圈地运动使农村关系中产生了新的阶级对立。

3. [答案]**C** [考点]澳大利亚地理概况。

[精析]澳大利亚的首都是堪培拉(Canberra)。

4. [答案]**A** [考点]英国历史概况。

[精析]工业革命使得英国的城镇得以迅速发展,并成为国家财富的源泉。

5. [答案]**D** [考点]英国文学之作家作品。

[精析]丹尼尔·笛福(Daniel Defoe)创作的《鲁滨逊漂流记》中的主人公鲁滨逊·克鲁索(Robinson Crusoe)有个同伴和仆人叫星期五(Friday)。

6. [答案]**C** [考点]英国文学之作家作品。

[精析]*Gulliver's Travels*(《格列佛游记》)是乔纳森·斯威夫特(Jonathan Swift)一部极具魅力的儿童故事作品,同时包含深刻的思想内容。

7. [答案]**A** [考点]英国文学之作家流派。

[精析]威廉·华兹华斯(William Wordsworth)是英国浪漫主义文学时期"湖畔派"诗人的代表人物之一。

8. [答案]**A** [考点]语言学基本概念。

[精析]考查语音学的不同分支及其研究对象。articulatory phonetics(发音语音学)研究语音的产生;acoustic phonetics(声学语音学)研究语音的物理特征;auditory phonetics(听觉语音学)研究对语音的感知;phonology(音系学)研究语音和音节的结构、分布和序列。

> **要点归纳**
>
> - Phonetics(语音学): the study of speech sounds(研究语音)
> - Phonology(音系学): the study of the rules governing the structure, distribution and sequencing of speech sounds and the shape of syllables (研究语音和音节

- Morphology（形态学）: the study of the minimal units of meaning-morphemes and word-formation processes, that is, the internal organization of words（研究意义的最小单位——语素和成词过程,也即单词的内部构造）
- Syntax（句法学）: the study of principles of forming and understanding correct English sentences（研究造句的规则）
- Semantics（语义学）: the study of how meaning is encoded in a language（研究意义如何在语言中编码）
- Pragmatics（语用学）: the study of meaning in context（研究语境中的意义）

9. ［答案］C ［考点］语言学基本知识。

［精析］考查宏观语言学的几个分支。宏观语言学(Macrolinguistics)主要包括心理语言学（psycholinguistics）、社会语言学（sociolinguistics）、人类语言学（anthropological linguistics）和计算语言学（computational linguistics）。

10. ［答案］D ［考点］语言学实例分析。

［精析］考查词汇的几种主要关系, "rain"和"reign"是典型的同音异形词。英语词汇的主要关系包括synonymy(同义关系)、polysemy(一词多义)、homonymy(同音或同形异义关系)、hyponymy(上下义关系)、antonymy(反义关系)。

Model Test 24

1. ［答案］B ［考点］美国政治概况。

［精析］美国第三任总统托马斯·杰斐逊(Thomas Jefferson)是《独立宣言》的起草者之一,该宣言明确阐述了支持美国独立战争的政治理论,而这一理论来源于英国著名哲学家约翰·洛克(John Locke)。

2. ［答案］C ［考点］英国历史概况。

［精析］艾格伯(Egbert)国王于829年统一英格兰,并建立王权,他是首位英国国王。

3. ［答案］D ［考点］加拿大地理概况。

［精析］加拿大共分为十个省和三个地区。

要点归纳

- 加拿大的十个省具体是：Alberta, British Columbia, Manitoba, New Brunswick, Newfoundland and Labrador, Nova Scotia, Ontario, Prince Edward Island, Quebec, Saskatchewan;
- 加拿大的三个地区具体是：Northwest Territories, Nunavut, Yukon Territory。

4. ［答案］**C** ［考点］美国地理概况。

［精析］休斯敦(Houston)是美国的太空城。

5. ［答案］**C** ［考点］美国文学之作家贡献。

［精析］华盛顿·欧文(Washington Irving)是首位获得国际声誉的美国作家，他被称为"美国文学之父"(Father of American Literature)。

6. ［答案］**B** ［考点］英国文学之文学流派。

［精析］威廉·华兹华斯(William Wordsworth)于1798年出版的 *Lyrical Ballads*(《抒情歌谣集》)标志着英国诗歌浪漫主义时期的开始。

7. ［答案］**C** ［考点］英国文学之作家作品。

［精析］*Paradise Lost*(《失乐园》)是John Milton的代表作。

8. ［答案］**D** ［考点］语言学概念。

［精析］语言的主要媒介是声音，这说明语言是发声系统。书面文字比口语出现得晚，这可以解释孩子们通常先学会说话，然后才学会阅读和写字。

9. ［答案］**A** ［考点］语言学实例分析。

［精析］黄色对于中国人和西方人来说含义不同，是因为黄色能给人带来不同的联想意义。

10. ［答案］**D** ［考点］语言学基本概念。

［精析］语用学主要研究：指示(deixis)、言语行为(speech acts)、间接语言(indirect language)、会话 (conversation)、礼貌 (politeness)、跨文化交际(cross-cultural communication)和前提(presupposition)。

Model Test 25

1. ［答案］**D** ［考点］美国政治概况。

［精析］美国最高法院是唯一有权解释宪法的机构。

2. ［答案］**C** ［考点］英国地理概况。

［精析］本尼维斯山是英国境内的最高峰，地处苏格兰地区。

3. ［答案］**B** ［考点］美国历史概况。

［精析］美国历史上第一批移民来自英国和荷兰。

4. ［答案］**C** ［考点］加拿大经济概况。

［精析］加拿大和美国进行的进出口贸易占到了加拿大贸易总额的三分之二。

5. [答案] D [考点] 美国文学之作家作品。

[精析] 小说*Invisible Man*(《隐形人》)是美国作家拉尔夫·埃里森(Ralph Ellison)的代表作，并不是剧作家Eugene Gladstone O'Neill的作品。

6. [答案] A [考点] 英国文学之作家流派。

[精析] William Langland(威廉·朗格兰)主要是为平民百姓写作。

7. [答案] B [考点] 美国文学之作家贡献。

[精析] 美国现实主义时期的三位主流作家是Henry James、Mark Twain和William Dean Howells。

8. [答案] A [考点] 语言学家。

[精析] Chomsky是美国著名的语言学家。

9. [答案] A [考点] 语言学基本概念。

[精析] 词缀属于粘着词素(bound morphemes)，因为它们不可独立成词。

10. [答案] D [考点] 语言学实例分析。

[精析] It is snowing. 中没有argument，因此这句话属于零向谓词(no-place predication)。

Model Test 26

1. [答案] B [考点] 美国政治概况。

[精析] Nixon(尼克松)是美国历史上第一位辞职的总统，促使其辞职的是水门事件(Watergate Scandal)。

2. [答案] C [考点] 英国文化概况。

[精析] 在英国，赛马已经成为一项重要的产业，主要分为平地赛马和越野赛马两种形式。

3. [答案] C [考点] 澳大利亚地理概况。

[精析] 墨尔本(Melbourne)是澳大利亚维多利亚州(Victoria)的首府。

4. [答案] D [考点] 美国文化概况。

[精析] 如今美国移民有80%到90%都来自亚洲和讲西班牙语的国家。

5. [答案] A [考点] 美国文学之作家作品。

[精析] Francis Scott Fitzgerald(弗朗西斯·斯科特·菲茨杰拉德)通常被看成是爵士时代美国文学的代表者。

F. Scott Fitzgerald的代表作有：

- *Tales of the Jazz Age*（《爵士时代的故事》） • *Tender Is the Night*（《夜色温柔》）
- *The Great Gatsby*（《了不起的盖茨比》）   • *The Last Tycoon*（《最后的大亨》）

6. ［答案］B ［考点］英国文学之文学流派。
   ［精析］英国文艺复兴的真正主流是伊丽莎白时期的戏剧。

7. ［答案］C ［考点］英国文学之作家生平。
   ［精析］Alfred the Great不仅是著名的散文家，同时也是一位君主。

8. ［答案］B ［考点］语言学实例分析。
   ［精析］单词desirability的词素构成是desire+able+ity，可见共有三个词素。

9. ［答案］C ［考点］语言学基本知识。
   ［精析］利用转换规则可以将深层结构转换为表层结构（surface structure），即说话人实际说出的句子。

Surface structure: it corresponds to the final syntactic form of the sentence which results from appropriate transformations.

10. ［答案］A ［考点］语言学基本概念。
    ［精析］心理语言学(Psycholinguistics)研究的是对语言的处理。

Model Test 27

1. ［答案］D ［考点］英国地理概况。
   ［精析］询问英国的四个组成部分中哪个部分总是战争不断，应该是北爱尔兰，因为他们总是想独立。

2. ［答案］D ［考点］美国地理概况。
   ［精析］美国的面积在全世界排名第四。前三名分别是俄罗斯、加拿大和中国。

3. ［答案］A ［考点］英国地理概况。
   ［精析］询问Big Ben(大本钟)在哪个城市，答案是伦敦。

伦敦著名景点：

River Thames（泰晤士河），St. Paul's Cathedral（圣保罗大教堂），Big Ben（大本钟），Whitehall（白厅，英国政府），National Gallery（国家美术馆），Westminster Abbey（威斯敏斯特教堂），Buckingham Palace（白金汉宫），Tower of London（伦敦塔）

4. ［答案］B ［考点］澳大利亚地理概况。
［精析］澳大利亚最大的城市是悉尼(Sydney)，Canberra(堪培拉)是澳大利亚的首都，Melbourne(墨尔本)是澳大利亚的第二大城市，Queensland(昆士兰州)是澳大利亚联邦的第二大州。

5. ［答案］C ［考点］英国文学之作家作品。
［精析］*Don Juan*，中文名为《唐璜》，是英国浪漫主义诗歌代表人拜伦所写的长诗。

6. ［答案］C ［考点］美国文学之作家贡献。
［精析］Henry James是美国著名小说家亨利·詹姆斯，和Mark Twain(马克·吐温)同时代。他的代表作有*The American*(《美国人》)和*The Portrait of a Lady*(《贵妇人的画像》)。

7. ［答案］A ［考点］美国文学之作家流派。
［精析］Mark Twain是美国"现实主义"的代表人。

8. ［答案］B ［考点］语言学基本概念。
［精析］Morphology(形态学)研究的是单词的内部构造。

9. ［答案］D ［考点］语言学家及其代表理论。
［精析］Competence and Performance(语言能力与语言运用)是Noam Chomsky在其代表作*Aspects of the Theory of Syntax*中提出的。

语言学中的一些重要概念的区别：

- Prescriptive and Descriptive（规定性研究与描述性研究）：前者总结语言中的标准，后者着重观察分析语言中的事实；
- Synchronic and Diachronic(共时研究与历时研究)：前者研究某个特定时期的语言，后者研究语言各个阶段的发展变化；
- Langue and Parole(语言与言语)：由Saussure提出，前者指语言系统的整体，而后者指某个个体在世界语言使用环境中说出的具体话语；
- Competence and Performance：由Chomsky提出，前者指理想语言使用者关于语言规则的知识储备，后者指真实的语言使用者在实际场景中的语言使用。

10. [答案] C [考点] 语言学概念实例分析。

[精析] 本题属于形态学的范畴, 考查词素(morpheme)的类型。toys, walks, John's都是在原有单词的基础上加上了屈折词缀（inflectional affix）, 即不改变原单词含义的后缀, 故选C。

> **要点归纳**
>
> - free morpheme（自由词素）：可以单独成词的词素, 例如：dog, nation;
> - compound（复合词）：由两个及以上的自由词素组成的单词, 例如：sunrise;
> - derivation（派生词）：由词根词缀构成的单词, 例如：nation加上派生词缀（derivational affix）-al 构成派生词national。

Model Test 28

1. [答案] B [考点] 英国地理概况。

[精析] 英国最高的山峰是本尼维斯山, 位于苏格兰, 海拔1343米。

2. [答案] D [考点] 美国地理概况。

[精析] 华盛顿和纽约都位于美国地理分区中的中部大西洋各州（the Middle Atlantic States）区。

3. [答案] A [考点] 美国历史概况。

[精析] 1974年美国总统理查德·尼克松（Richard Nixon）因水门事件而引咎辞职, 他是美国历史上首位辞职的总统。

> **要点归纳**
>
> 美国历史上几次主要战争和事件及当时在任的总统：
> - 独立战争(The War of Independence)总统George Washington
> - 美国内战(The Civil War)总统Abraham Lincoln
> - 第二次世界大战(World War II)总统Franklin Roosevelt
> - 民权运动(The Civil Rights Movement)总统John Kennedy
> - 越南战争(The Vietnam War)总统John Kennedy

4. [答案] C [考点] 加拿大文化。

[精析] 加拿大Quebec(魁北克省)在1763年以前曾是法国的殖民地, 因此该省具有浓烈的法国文化传统, 是北美地区法国文化的中心。

5. [答案] A [考点] 美国文学之作家作品。

[精析] Francis Scott Fitzgerald(弗朗西斯·斯科特·菲茨杰拉德)是美国现代主义的代表作家之一, 代表作有*The Great Gatsby*（《了不起的盖茨比》）和*Tender Is the Night*(《夜色温柔》)。

6. [答案] D [考点] 英国文学之作家流派。

[精析] 前三位作家都是19世纪英国浪漫主义的代表作家，只有James Joyce（詹姆斯·乔伊斯）活跃于20世纪。James Joyce是爱尔兰小说家，是"意识流"派（Stream of Consciousness）的奠基人，代表作有*Ulysses*（《尤利西斯》），*A Portrait of the Artist as a Young Man*（《一个青年艺术家的肖像》），*Finnegan's Wake*（《芬尼根守灵夜》）和短篇小说集*Dubliners*（《都柏林人》）。

> **要点归纳**
>
> 英国19世纪浪漫主义时期主要作家：
> - Romantic Poets of the First Generation: William Wordsworth, Samuel Taylor Coleridge;
> - Romantic Poets of the Second Generation: George Gordon Byron, Percy Bysshe Shelley, John Keats;
> - Prose Writers: Charles Lamb, William Hazlitt;
> - Novelists: Walter Scott, Jane Austen.

7. [答案] D [考点] 文学基本概念。

[精析] Irony（反讽）指使用的语言和想要表达的真实含义相反，以此来达到修辞效果。

8. [答案] B [考点] 语言学家代表理论。

[精析] 询问哪一项不属于Halliday所定义的成人语言的功能。Halliday是Systematic-functional Grammar（系统功能语法）的创始人。根据他的理论，语言有三个功能，即Ideational Function（概念功能），Interpersonal Function（交际功能）和Textual Function（文本功能）。

9. [答案] C [考点] 语言学基本概念。

[精析] Theme（主位）和Rheme（述位）是系统功能语法中的两个重要概念。

> **要点归纳**
>
> - Theme: it is known or at least in the given situation and from which the speaker proceeds.
> - Rheme: it is what the speaker starts about, or in regard to, the starting point of the utterance.

10. [答案] D [考点] 语言学概念实例分析。

[精析] smog是由smoke和fog混合而成的，属于blending word（混合词），就是将两个单词的一部分结合起来构成的一种合成词。

> **要点归纳**
>
> 特有的词汇变化：
> - Invention（新创词语）：nylon
> - Blending（混合词）：transfer + resister → transistor

- Abbreviation(缩写词)：advertisement → ad.
- Acronym(首字母缩写词)：World Trade Organization→ WTO
- Back-formation(逆构词法)：editor→ edit
- Borrowing(外来词)：Kung-fu

Model Test 29

1. ［答案］C ［考点］加拿大地理概况。
［精析］加拿大British Columbia（不列颠哥伦比亚省）最大的城市是温哥华（Vancouver），温哥华也是加拿大第三大城市。

2. ［答案］C ［考点］英国文化概况。
［精析］《华尔街日报》(*The Wall Street Journal*) 是美国的报纸，而不是英国的报纸，故选C。

要点归纳
英美主要报刊：
- 英国：*Daily Express, Daily Mail, Daily Mirror, Daily Star, Financial Times, The Guardian, The Times, The Observer;*
- 美国：*The Wall Street Journal, USA Today, The New York Times, Los Angeles Times, Washington Post, Reader's Digest, National Geography, Time.*

3. ［答案］A ［考点］美国地理概况。
［精析］美国中西部(Midwest)是美国最重要的农业区。

4. ［答案］A ［考点］美国历史概况。
［精析］1929~1933年，美国遭遇了经济大萧条(The Great Depression)，1932年罗斯福当选总统后实施"新政"，目的就是拯救美国的经济，故选A。

5. ［答案］B ［考点］英国文学之作家作品。
［精析］George Bernard Shaw（萧伯纳）是英国现代著名的戏剧家，其代表作为*Pygmalion*(《皮格马利翁》，又名《卖花女》)。

6. ［答案］B ［考点］美国文学之作家流派。
［精析］Emily Dickinson(埃米莉·迪金森)是19世纪美国著名的女诗人，是后现代主义的代表人物，和Walt Whitman（沃尔特·惠特曼）齐名，代表作有*I'm Nobody. Who Are You?*(《我是无名小卒！你是谁？》)。

7. [答案] D [考点] 美国文学之作家流派。

[精析] 华盛顿·欧文(Washington Irving)、詹姆士·芬尼莫尔·库珀(James Fenimore Cooper)和纳撒尼尔·霍桑(Nathaniel Hawthorne)都是美国浪漫时期的代表人物，赫尔曼·麦尔维尔(Herman Melville)的作品则体现出了现实主义的色彩，他的代表作是《白鲸》(*Moby Dick*)。

8. [答案] B [考点] 语言学基本概念。

[精析] Phatic Communion(交感性谈话)指的是语言的社会交际功能。例如，我们经常说一些诸如God bless you.等看似毫无意义的话语来和他人寒暄。

要点归纳

语言的功能：
- Informative(信息功能)
- Interpersonal function(人际功能)
- Performative(施为功能)
- Emotive function(情感功能)
- Phatic communion(交感性谈话，即寒暄语)
- Recreational function(娱乐功能)
- Multilingual function(多语言功能，即人类可以用语言来谈论、改变语言本身)

9. [答案] C [考点] 语言学家及代表理论。

[精析] The Cooperative Principles (合作原则) 是由美国著名语言哲学家格赖斯 (Herbert Paul Grice) 于1967年在哈佛大学的演讲中提出的，格赖斯也是语用学理论 The Theory of Conversational Implicature (会话含义理论) 的创始人；John Langshow Austin提出了言语行为理论(Speech Act Theory)。

要点归纳

The Cooperative Principles有四个具体的准则：
- Quantity Maxim(数量准则)
- Quality Maxim(质量准则)
- Relation Maxim(关系准则)
- Manner Maxim(方式准则)

10. [答案] A [考点] 语言学概念实例分析。

[精析] 句法学结构主义学派提出的组合关系(syntagmatic relation)规定，单词在句中的位置不可随意调换。

句法学结构主义学派提出的四个关键性概念具体是：

- Syntagmatic relation(组合关系)，即一个单位和同一序列中其他单位之间的关系，处于此关系的词，必须满足一些句法和语义条件，因此单词在句中的位置不可随意调换；
- Paradigmatic relation(聚合关系)，即在某个特殊的结构位置上彼此可以相互替换的成分间的关系，例如Tom和He都可以放在...is smiling.这个句子中；
- Endocentric construction(向心结构)，指有核心的结构体，例如：an old man；
- Exocentric construction(离心结构)，指没有核心的结构体，例如：on the shelf。

Model Test 30

1. [答案]D [考点]英国历史概况。
   [精析]1066年，被称为"征服者威廉"的诺曼底公爵威廉(Duke William of Normandy)攻入了英格兰，并建立了诺曼帝国。公元前55年，凯撒大帝(Julius Caesar)率领罗马人侵略英格兰；亨利八世(Henry VIII)的功绩是进行了英国宗教改革；克伦威尔(Oliver Cromwell)则是英国内战期间的实权者。

2. [答案]C [考点]澳大利亚政治概况。
   [精析]澳大利亚议会由众议院(the House of Representatives)和参议院(the Senate)组成。

   - The UK: the House of Lords and the House of Commons(上议院和下议院)。
   - The US: the Senate and the House of Representatives(参议院和众议院)。
   - Canada: the Senate and the House of Co-mons(参议院和众议院)。

3. [答案]B [考点]英国地理概况。
   [精析]英国最长的河流是the Severn(塞文河)，全长354公里。The River Thames(泰晤士河)是英国第二长河流，也是英国最为重要的河流，River Clyde(克莱德河)是苏格兰最重要的河流。

4. [答案]A [考点]美国历史概况。
   [精析]1789年，詹姆斯·麦迪逊将10条修正案加入了美国宪法，这十条修正案就是人们通常所说的 The Bill of Rights (《人权法案》)。

   The American Constitution(《美国宪法》)：
   - 起草于1787年，1789年生效，是世界上最早的成文宪法；

149

- 共有七条正文（Article I-Article VII），其中前三条分别是：the Legislative Article(立法)，the Executive Article(行政)和the Judicial Article(司法)；
- 共有二十七条修正案，前十条由James Madison提出并于1791年正式生效，总称*The Bill of Rights*（《人权法案》）。

5. [答案] B [考点] 美国文学之作家作品。
[精析] *Uncle Tom's Cabin*（《汤姆叔叔的小屋》）是一部以反抗奴隶制为主题的小说，是女作家Harriet Beecher Stowe(哈丽雅特·比彻·斯托)的成名作，林肯曾经高度评价过这部小说。

6. [答案] B [考点] 英国文学之作家贡献。
[精析] Daniel Defoe(丹尼尔·笛福)是英国现实主义小说家，被誉为"英国及欧洲小说之父"，其代表作为*Robinson Crusoe*(《鲁滨逊漂流记》)。

要点归纳

几位英国作家及其荣誉称号：
- Geoffrey Chaucer: the Father of English Poetry
- Edmund Spencer: the Poets' Poet
- William Wordsworth: Poet Laurel

7. [答案] D [考点] 英美文学基本概念。
[精析] 文学作品对历史上的或者其他文学作品中的人、地点、物的借用叫做典故(allusion)，allegory指"寓言"，archetype是"原型"，analogy意为"类比"。

8. [答案] D [考点] 语言学基本概念。
[精析] 英语中，只有nominative(主格)、accusative(宾格)和genitive(属格)，没有vocative(呼格)。

9. [答案] A [考点] 语言学家。
[精析] Saussure(索绪尔)被称为"现代语言学之父"。

10. [答案] C [考点] 语言学概念实例分析。
[精析] 美国语言学家布龙姆菲尔德（L. Bloomfield）把句法结构分为向心结构(endocentric construction)和离心结构(exocentric construction)，向心结构的句子有一定的核心和中心，且至少有一个直接成分跟整体的语法功能相同，反之则为离心结构。

Model Test 31

1. [答案] D [考点] 爱尔兰政治概况。

   [精析] 爱尔兰共和国实行的是总统共和制(republican presidential)，国家元首是总统，总统的任期是7年。

2. [答案] A [考点] 英国文化概况。

   [精析] 布鲁克林大桥(Brooklyn Bridge)是美国纽约市的著名建筑，主要连接纽约曼哈顿区和布鲁克林区。

   > 要点归纳
   >
   > 纽约市简介：
   > - 美国最大的城市，被称作Big Apple(大苹果)；
   > - 有五个区：Manhattan, Brooklyn, Queens, the Bronx, Staten Island
   > - 著名景点：The Statue of Liberty（自由女神像），Chinatown（唐人街），Broadway(百老汇), the U.N. Headquarters(联合国总部)。

3. [答案] D [考点] 澳大利亚地理概况。

   [精析] 澳大利亚的首都是堪培拉(Canberra)；悉尼(Sydney)是澳大利亚最大的城市；Melbourne（墨尔本）是澳大利亚的第二大城市；达尔文市是澳北区(Northern Territory)的首府，也是这个地区唯一一座城市。

4. [答案] C [考点] 美国文化概况。

   [精析] 哈佛大学(Harvard)成立于1636年，是美国最早的私立大学之一；耶鲁大学(Yale)创立于1701年，是美国历史上创立的第三所大学；牛津大学(Oxford)是英国世界著名的学府，创办于1167年；斯坦福大学(Stanford)成立于1885年，位于美国加利福尼亚州的斯坦福市。

5. [答案] D [考点] 英国文学之作家作品。

   [精析] Shelley(雪莱)的代表作有 *Prometheus Unbound*(《解放了的普罗米修斯》)和 *Ode to the West Wind*(《西风颂》)。

6. [答案] B [考点] 美国文学之作家贡献。

   [精析] 沃尔特·惠特曼(Walt Whitman)是第一个使用了free verse(自由诗体)形式的诗人，他的代表作是《草叶集》(*Leaves of Grass*)。

7. [答案] C [考点] 英国文学之文学流派。

   [精析] The Renaissance（文艺复兴）起源于意大利，英国文学深受这一运动的影响，该运动充满了人文主义(Humanism)的色彩，在文艺复兴的影响下，英国戏剧得到了快速的发展。

8. ［答案］D ［考点］语言学基本概念。

［精析］语义学(Semantics)研究的主要对象是语言的意义。

9. ［答案］A ［考点］语言学基本知识。

［精析］语义三角(semantic triangle)主要包括reference(概念，也可称为thought)，symbol(语言成分，如单词和短语，即form)和referent(概念的所指，即感官世界中的真实物体)。

10. ［答案］C ［考点］语言学概念实例分析。

［精析］一般情况下，一个元音就是一个音节，但是某些特定的辅音如[b][d]可以和其他辅音如[1]构成一个音节，因此middle有两个音节，虽然它只有一个元音字母发音，而题干中的syllable有两个元音字母发音，ble也构成了一个音节，因此总共有3个音节。

Model Test 32

1. ［答案］C ［考点］英国历史概况。

［精析］英国最早的居民是伊比利亚人(the Iberians)。

要点归纳

英国各时期居民：
- 英国早期居民：Iberians，其后是Celts (700 B.C.)
- 罗马统治时期：Romans (1st to 5th century)
- 盎格鲁-撒克逊时期：Anglo-Saxons (mid-5th century)
- 诺尔曼征服时期：Normans (1066 A.D.)

---

2. ［答案］B ［考点］美国历史概况。

［精析］《独立宣言》来自英国哲学家约翰·洛克(John Locke，1632~1704)的理论。约翰·洛克是英国著名哲学家和政治学家。《政府论》是他的代表作，上篇主要批评君权神授理论，下篇从自然权利和社会契约理论出发，论述了政府的起源、范围和目的。洛克在《政府论》中提出："人类天生都是自由、平等和独立的，如不得本人的同意，不能把任何人置于这种状态之外，使受制于另一个人的政治权力……他们的政治社会都起源于资源的结合和人民自由地选择他们的统治者和政府形式的相互协议。"《独立宣言》继承并发展了洛克的天赋人权学说，认为人人生而平等，"生命、自由和追求幸福的权利"是大自然所赋予的，不可剥夺。

3. ［答案］A ［考点］澳大利亚地理概况。

［精析］悉尼(Sydney)是澳大利亚新南威尔士州的首府，也是澳大利亚的最大城市，世界主要港口。

4. ［答案］A ［考点］美国历史概况。

［精析］马丁·路德·金(Martin Luther King)是美国民权运动的领袖，当时的美国总统是约翰·肯尼迪(John Kennedy)，两人先后遇刺身亡。Abraham Lincoln领导了美国的南北战争；George Washington则领导了美国的独立战争，是美国的第一届总统。

5. ［答案］C ［考点］英国文学之作家作品。

［精析］《坎特博雷故事集》是英国中世纪著名诗人杰弗里·乔叟(Geoffrey Chaucer)的作品，乔叟被称为"英国诗歌之父"和"英国小说之父"。

6. ［答案］C ［考点］美国文学之作家流派。

［精析］沃尔特·惠特曼(Walt Whitman)是美国浪漫主义时期著名诗人，代表作为《草叶集》(*Leaves of Grass*)，他是第一位使用自由体(Free Verse)的诗人。

7. ［答案］D ［考点］英国文学之作家流派。

［精析］亚历山大·波普(Alexander Pope)是英国新古典主义代表人物，代表作为*An Essay on Criticism* （《论批评》）、*The Rape of the Lock* （《夺发记》）、*Essay on Man*（《论人类》）。

┌─ 要点归纳 ─┐

18世纪英国文学流派及其代表人物：

- Neo-Classicism: Alexander Pope, Richard Steele, Samuel Johnson
- Realistic Novelists: Daniel Defoe, Jonathan Swift
- Sentimentalist Novelists: Samuel Richardson, Laurence Sterne, Oliver Goldsmith
- Poetry of Pre-Romanticism and Sentimentalism: William Blake, Robert Burns

8. ［答案］C ［考点］语言学基本概念。

［精析］心理语言学属于宏观语言学，研究人类语言和大脑的关系。

9. ［答案］B ［考点］语言学概念实例分析。

［精析］Semantically different synonyms意为"语义不同的同义词"，指语义相近但是略有不同的几个单词。

┌─ 要点归纳 ─┐

英语词汇的Synonymy(同义关系)包括：

- Dialectal synonyms(地域同义词)：指不同方言中表示同一概念的词汇，如英式英语的autumn和美式英语的fall；
- Stylistic synonyms(文体同义词)：指风格或者正式程度不同的词汇，如kid,

child, offspring;

- Synonyms that differ in their emotive or evaluative meaning（感情或评估同义词）：指含义相同，但是表示说话人的不同情感或者观点态度的词汇，如collaborator和accomplice；
- Collocational synonyms（固定搭配）：指用在不同固定搭配中的同义词，如accuse... of...和charge... with...
- Semantically different synonyms（语义不同）：指语义略有不同的单词。

10. ［答案］B ［考点］语言学家代表理论。

［精析］The Prague School（布拉格学派）主要进行共时性语言学研究（Synchronic linguistics），从功能（function）的角度研究语言。

Model Test 33

1. ［答案］D ［考点］英国历史概况。

［精析］在英国历史上，罗马人曾占领英国约有400年之久，开始于公元前55年的凯撒大帝入侵。

2. ［答案］A ［考点］美国历史概况。

［精析］1776，美军在Saratoga（萨拉托加）战胜英军，萨拉托加战役则成为独立战争的转折点。

> 要点归纳
>
> 与美国独立战争（The War of Independence）相关的重要历史事件：
> - 1774年9月：召开第一届大陆会议（the First Continental Congress），开始拒绝购买英国货物
> - 1775年4月19日：莱克星顿之役标志着战争的开始
> - 1775年：成立大陆军（Continental Army），由George Washington率领
> - 1776 年：Thomas Jefferson 起草《独立宣言》（The Declaration of Independence）
>   美军在Saratoga战胜英军，战争的转折点
> - 1783年：签署《巴黎条约》（the Treaty of Paris），英国承认美国独立
> - 1789年：成立联邦政府（the Federal Government），George Washington任第一任总统

3. ［答案］D ［考点］美国地理概况。

［精析］密西西比河是世界上最大的陆地河流之一，它被称为"Father of Waters"或者"Old Man River"，其最长的支流是密苏里河（The Missouri River）；俄亥俄河（The Ohio River）被称为"the American Ruhr"，河流沿岸矿产丰富，钢铁工业发达；哈得孙河（The Hudson River）是美国纽约州东部河流。

4. [答案]A [考点]英国历史概况。

[精析]爱德华八世是"不爱江山爱美人"的代表,为了娶一位离异的美国女子而放弃了王位。

5. [答案]B [考点]美国文学之作家作品。

[精析]《远大前程》(*Great Expectations*)是英国19世纪批判现实主义小说家查尔斯·狄更斯(Charles Dickens)的代表作品。

6. [答案]C [考点]英国文学之作家生平。

[精析]约翰·济慈(John Keats, 1795~1821)是英国第2代浪漫主义诗人代表。代表作为*Ode to a Nightingale*(《夜莺颂》),写作风格推崇"Beauty is truth, truth is beauty."。

7. [答案]D [考点]文学基本概念。

[精析]Free Verse意为"自由诗体",没有固定的韵律或者长度,完全依靠自然的韵律以及重读和非重读音节的对照成诗,代表诗人是沃尔特·惠特曼(Walt Whitman)。

8. [答案]D [考点]语言学基本知识。

[精析]语言学研究的核心内容包括:语音学(phonetics)、音素学(phonology)、形态学(morphology)、句法学(syntax)、语义学(semantics)和语用学(pragmatics)。社会语言学是语言学的一个分支,但不是语言学研究的核心内容。

9. [答案]B [考点]语言学概念实例分析。

[精析]最小对立体指除了出现在同一位置上的一个音之外其余都相同的两个语音组合,如pen[pen]和ben[ben],由此看出选项中的"bat"和"pat"、"sink"和"zinc"、"fine"和"vine"都是最小对立体,故选B。

10. [答案]C [考点]语言学基本概念。

[精析]句法学(syntax)主要研究的是句子结构及词、词组和短语组成句子的规则。

Model Test 34

1. [答案]B [考点]英国文化概况。

[精析]牛津大学(Oxford)是位于英国的世界著名学府,创办于1167年;耶鲁大学(Yale)创立于1701年,是美国历史上创立的第3所大学;哈佛大学(Harvard)成立于1636年,是美国最早的私立大学之一;斯坦福大学(Stanford)成立于1885年,位于美国加利福尼亚州的斯坦福。

2. [答案]C [考点]英国历史概况。

[精析]1337~1453年英法之间的战争断断续续地持续了一百年,称之为"英法百年战争"(Hundred Years' War)。

3. ［答案］B ［考点］加拿大地理概况。

［精析］加拿大的首都是Ottawa（渥太华）；Montreal（蒙特利尔）是加拿大第二大城市；Vancouver（温哥华）是加拿大第三大城市；Quebec（魁北克）是魁北克省的首府，是加拿大的第一座城市。

4. ［答案］A ［考点］美国历史概况。

［精析］Woodrow Wilson（伍德罗·威尔逊，1856~1924）是美国第28届总统。1918年1月8日该总统宣布关于实现世界和平的"Fourteen Point"（"十四点计划"），其内容有：各国进行公开谈判，缔结公开条约，反对秘密外交；无论战时或和平时，保障航海绝对自由；取消经济壁垒，建立贸易平等条件；裁减军备；调整对殖民地的权利要求；建立各国联盟，相互保证所有大小国家的政治独立与领土完整。所倡议建立的各国联盟即联合国的前身，1920年成立的"国际联盟"。

5. ［答案］C ［考点］英美文学之作家流派。

［精析］约瑟夫·艾迪生（Joseph Addison）、理查德·斯蒂尔（Richard Steele）和亚历山大·波普（Alexander Pope）都是英国启蒙时期文学的代表，他们从各个角度评判当时英国社会，讨论社会问题，甚至涉及道德伦理和个人生活，崇尚新古典主义，威廉·布莱克（William Blake）是浪漫主义诗人。

6. ［答案］A ［考点］英美文学之作家作品。

［精析］*Emma*（《爱玛》）是简·奥斯汀（Jane Austen）的重要作品之一，描写女主人公认识自身并逐渐抛开幻想的过程。奥斯汀刻意描绘的都是平常的人和事，但不乏对社会关系的最深入的描写。她正是通过对熟悉的人和事的描写展示了她所生活的时代英国乡绅阶层的生活景观，如财产继承、家庭问题、教育状况、妇女地位和出路以及道德与习俗等。她的作品以深刻清新和细致敏锐的特点而著称，包含了超越历史时空的对人性的透视和哲理。

7. ［答案］D ［考点］英美文学之作家贡献。

［精析］笛福（Daniel Defoe）被誉为"英国和欧洲小说之父"，乔叟（Geoffrey Chaucer）是英国诗歌之父，斯宾塞（Edmund Spenser）是"诗人中的诗人"，而弗朗西斯·培根（Francis Bacon）是英国唯物主义哲学的创始人。

8. ［答案］A ［考点］语言学基本概念。

［精析］语音学（Phonetics）是从自然的角度出发研究语言发音的语言学分支，主要关注语音的产生、传播和接受的过程，并着重考察人类语言中的单音，包括对语音的描述、分类、标示等。

9. ［答案］D ［考点］语言学家代表理论。

［精析］语言（Langue）和言语（Parole）的区别的语言学概念是由现代结构主义语言学创始人索绪尔提出。语言指语言系统的整体，"所有（语言使用）个体头脑中存储

的词语—形象之总和"，这个整体相对较为稳定；言语则指某个个体在实际语言使用环境中说出的具体话语，这是随时间和地点变化的一个动态的实体。

10. ［答案］C ［考点］语言学概念的实例分析。
   ［精析］"fall"是美国英语中的"秋天"，而"autumn"是英国英语中的"秋天"，这是两个用于不同地域的同义词，称为地域同义词(dialectal synonyms)，故选C。

Model Test 35

1. ［答案］B ［考点］英国政治概况。
   ［精析］英国议会由君主(the Sovereign)、上议院(the House of Lords)和下议院(the House of Commons) 构成，其中具有实权和立法权的是下议院，自1964年以来，上议院无权阻止下议院已经通过的立法。

2. ［答案］C ［考点］美国和加拿大地理概况。
   ［精析］北美大陆的大多数原住民都是印第安人（Indians），土著居民（Aborigines）是澳大利亚的原住民，毛利人（Maoris）是新西兰的原住民，而因纽特人（Inuits），也称爱斯摩摩人(Eskimos)是北极地区的原住民。

3. ［答案］B ［考点］英国文化概况。
   ［精析］板球(cricket)是最典型的英国体育运动，它最早出现在13世纪，板球运动被称为"贵族运动"；而足球是最受英国人欢迎的运动，因为足球于19世纪出现在英格兰，1863年足球协会(Football Association)在英格兰成立。

4. ［答案］A ［考点］加拿大地理概况。
   ［精析］加拿大的国歌是《哦！加拿大》(O Canada)，《天佑女王》(God Save The Queen)是英国的国歌和英联邦的皇室颂歌。

5. ［答案］A ［考点］英国文学之作家流派。
   ［精析］"颂"(ode) 被认为是济慈最具有代表性和最为成功的诗歌形式，他的代表作品有《夜莺颂》(Ode to a Nightingale)，《希腊古瓮颂》(Ode on a Grecian Urn)，《秋颂》(To Autumn)等。

6. ［答案］D ［考点］英国文学之作家作品。
   ［精析］萧伯纳的剧作《华伦夫人的职业》(Mrs. Warren's Profession)塑造了一个在经济重压下普通妇女的形象，该剧揭露了一个令人愤怒的事实：在资本主义社会，娼妓业也存在社会对妇女在经济上的剥削。

7. ［答案］B ［考点］英国文学之作家作品。

[精析]塞缪尔·约翰逊(Samuel Johnson)是18世纪英国人文主义文学批评的巨匠，《莎士比亚戏剧集序言》(*The Preface to Shakespeare*)和《诗人传》(*Lives of the Poets*)是他的著名的文学批评著作。

8. [答案]C [考点]语言学实例分析。
   [精析]tree意为"树"，是所有树木的总称，它是一个上义词（superordinate）；而willow意为"柳树"，是一种具体的树的名称，willow是下义词(hyponyms)，因此这两个单词属于上下义关系。

   ┌─ 要点归纳 ───
   词义关系中的上下义关系(hyponymy)主要包括：
   - 上义词 (superordinate): the upper term or the class name in the sense relation, e.g. flower;
   - 下义词 (hyponyms): the lower terms or the members, e.g. violet;
   - 并列下义词 (co-hyponyms): the members of the same class, e.g. violet, tulip.

9. [答案]D [考点]语言学概念实例分析。
   [精析]color和idea这两个单词都是自由词素(free morpheme)，自由词素是能独立运用的词素，它有完整的意义，在句中充当一个自由的语法单位。

10. [答案]A [考点]语言学基本概念。
    [精析]对人类语言进行研究的是语音学（Phonetics），它从自然的角度出发研究语音的产生、传播和接受的过程，主要分为三个领域：发声语音学（articulatory phonetics）、声学语音学（acoustic phonetics）和听觉语音学（auditory phonetics）。

Model Test 36

1. [答案]A [考点]英国政治概况。
   [精析]英国议会中最古老的部分是上议院（the House of Lords），它是由国王咨询会议(Great Council)发展而来的。

2. [答案]A [考点]英国文化概况。
   [精析]英国全国发行的报纸可以分为两类，一类是全国性日报，另一类是全国性星期天报纸。

3. [答案]D [考点]加拿大地理概况。
   [精析]温哥华(Vancouver)位于加拿大西岸地区，是加拿大的第3大城市，也是北美第三大海港，冬季不结冰，享有"不冻港"之美誉。

4. [答案]B [考点]美国历史政治概况。

[**精析**]亚伯拉罕·林肯(Abraham Lincoln)是美国第16届总统,带领美国人走过美国内战,颁布了《解放黑人奴隶宣言》,维护了美国联邦的统一,但是在战争结束不到一周就被暗杀了。

5. [**答案**]B [**考点**]英国文学之作家作品。
[**精析**]《指环与书》(*The Ring and the Book*)是英国维多利亚时代著名诗人罗伯特·勃朗宁(Robert Browning)晚年时的代表诗作。

6. [**答案**]A [**考点**]英国文学之作家作品。
[**精析**]《多佛海滩》(*Dover Beach*)是英国作家马修·阿诺德(Matthew Arnold)诗歌中的名篇之一,反映了19世纪西方社会中的宗教信仰在新知识的冲击下普遍沦丧的时代风貌。

7. [**答案**]C [**考点**]英国文学之作家作品。
[**精析**]《黑暗的心》(*Heart of Darkness*)和《吉姆老爷》(*Lord Jim*)都是出生于波兰的英语小说家约瑟夫·康拉德(Joseph Conrad, 1857~1924)最富盛誉的小说。

8. [**答案**]B [**考点**]语言学基本概念。
[**精析**]历时语言学(diachronic linguistics)主要研究语言在一定的时间跨度内的发展情况;与之对应的是共时语言学(synchronic linguistics),它研究的是语言在某一特定时期的状态和发展。

9. [**答案**]B [**考点**]语言学概念实例分析。
[**精析**]"-ness"这对字母组合在weakness和darkness中作的都是名词后缀。前缀(prefix)、中缀(infix)和后缀(suffix)都属于词缀(affix),它们不能单独使用,只能添加到其他的词根或词干上使用,因此它们也是粘着词素(bound morpheme)。

10. [**答案**]C [**考点**]语言学基本理论。
[**精析**]命名论(naming theory)又叫命名说,是柏拉图首先提出来的。命名论认为,词由词形和词义构成,是用来指称客观事物或者给客观事物起名的,词与客观事物之间存在着指称与被指称、命名与被命名的关系,词义实质上就是把词与客观事物联结起来的所指关系和命名关系,命名论属于语义学范畴的概念。

Model Test 37

1. [**答案**]D [**考点**]美国文化概况。
[**精析**]伯克利(Berkeley),是美国加利福尼亚大学分院,位于美国加利福尼亚州西部。新英格兰地区(New England)包括美国的东北部的六个州,由北至南分别

为：缅因州、新罕布什尔州、佛蒙特州、马萨诸塞州、罗德岛州、康涅狄格州，耶鲁大学(Yale)就在康涅狄格州，哈佛大学(Harvard)和麻省理工大学(MIT)都在马萨诸塞州。

2. [答案]C [考点]英国文学之作家作品。
[精析]《呼啸山庄》(Wuthering Heights)是Emily Bronte的代表作。

3 [答案]C [考点]英国文化概况。
[精析]《观察家报》(The Observer)创刊于1791年，是英国创刊最早的星期日报纸。

4 [答案]B [考点]美国历史概况。
[精析]美国的"镀金时代"指的是从南北战争结束到20世纪初的那一段美国历史，这一名词来自马克·吐温的小说《镀金时代》。在这一时期，南北战争为美国资本主义发展扫清了道路，加上不断涌入的移民和西部新发现的矿藏，这一切使得美国的工业化极速发展，国家财富迅速增长，到20世纪初，美国已经是世界上最强的工业国了。

5. [答案]A [考点]英国文学之作家流派。
[精析]华兹华斯是英国浪漫主义时期"湖畔派"诗人的代表人物，他创作的诗歌按主题可分为两大类：一类是关于大自然的；另一类是关于人类生活的。

6. [答案]D [考点]美国文学之作家作品。
[精析]詹姆士·芬尼莫尔·库珀(James Fenimore Cooper)是美国浪漫主义时期的著名作家，《皮袜子故事集》(Leather Stocking Tales)是他的著名系列小说，其中包含5本著作：《拓荒者》(The Pioneers)、《最后的莫西干人》(The Last of the Mohicans)、《大草原》(The Prairie)、《探路人》(The Pathfinder)、《杀鹿者》(The Deerslayer)。

7. [答案]A [考点]美国文学之文学流派。
[精析]华盛顿·欧文《见闻札记》(The Sketch Book)的出版标志着美国浪漫主义的开始，而惠特曼创作的《草叶集》(Leaves of Grass)的出版则标志着美国浪漫主义的结束。

8. [答案]B [考点]语言学基本概念。
[精析]词素(morpheme)是最小的意义单位，也是语言中最小的构词单位。

9. [答案]A [考点]语言学概念实例分析。
[精析]长和短都是相对的，没有绝对的标准，因此long和short属于等级反义关系(gradable antonymy)。

> **要点归纳**
> - 词义关系中的反义关系(antonymy)主要包括：
> - 等级反义关系(gradable antonymy): the commonest type of antonymy, e.g. good & bad;
> - 互补反义关系 (complementary antonymy): the members of a pair complementary to each other, e.g. male & female;
> - 逆向反义关系 (converse antonymy): pairs of words co-exist, e.g. lend & borrow.

10. [答案] B [考点] 语言学基本概念。
[精析] 对个体而言的语言称之为"个人习语"(idiolect)，它是某些基本语言的变体，与之对应的是共同体共同使用的语言，称之为"社会语"。

Model Test 38

1. [答案] B [考点] 英国历史概况。
[精析] 英国《大宪章》(*The Great Charter*)，是1215年英国国王约翰(King John)在以兰顿(Langton)为首的贵族和教士们的压力下签署的重要政治法律文件，该宪章主要内容为保障贵族利益，限制王权，大宪章被认为是维护公民权利不受王权侵犯的重要文件，为英国的宪法奠定了基础。

2. [答案] D [考点] 英国地理概况。
[精析] 北爱尔兰的首府是贝尔法斯特(Belfast)，加的夫(Cardiff)是威尔士(Wales)的首府。

3. [答案] C [考点] 加拿大地理概况。
[精析] 加拿大第一大城市是多伦多(Toronto)，第二大城市是蒙特利尔(Montreal)，第三大城市是温哥华(Vancouver)，渥太华(Ottawa)是加拿大的首府，也是加拿大的第四大城市，故选C。

4. [答案] B [考点] 美国文学政治概况。
[精析] 托马斯·杰斐逊(Thomas Jefferson)，美国第3届总统(1801~1809)，是《独立宣言》(*The Declaration of Independence*)的主要起草者，也是第一位在首都华盛顿宣誓就职的总统。

5. [答案] D [考点] 英国文学之作家作品。
[精析] 莎士比亚的四大喜剧主要有：《仲夏夜之梦》(*A Midsummer Night's Dream*)、《威尼斯商人》(*The Merchant of Venice*)、《第十二夜》(*Twelfth Night*)、《皆大欢喜》(*As You Like It*)，《暴风雨》(*The Tempest*)是正剧与喜剧的结合体。

161

6. [答案] B [考点] 美国文学之作家作品。

[精析]《睡谷的传说》(*The Legend of Sleepy Hollow*) 是美国作家华盛顿·欧文 (Washington Irving)创作的著名短篇小说，被收藏在他的著名散文集《见闻札记》中。

7. [答案] D [考点] 英国文学之作家贡献。

[精析] 理查德·谢里登(Richard B. Sheridan, 1751~1816)被认为是18世纪英国最有成就的剧作家，他的代表作是《造谣学校》(*The School for Scandal*)。

8. [答案] C [考点] 语言学之实例分析。

[精析] 题干中的句子意为"水在0℃时开始结冰"，这叙述的是一个简单的事实或真理，语言的这种功能叫做信息功能，它是语言最重要的一个功能。

9. [答案] B [考点] 语言学基本概念。

[精析] 根据言语行为理论（Speech Act Theory），说话者说话时可能同时实施三种行为：言内行为（locutionary act），言外行为（illocutionary act）和言后行为（perlocutionary act），表达说话者意图的行为被称为言外行为。

10. [答案] D [考点] 语言学家代表理论。

[精析] 转换生成语法是美国语言学家乔姆斯基(Noam Chomsky)提出的一个描述语法的术语。

Model Test 39

1. [答案] B [考点] 美国地理概况。

[精析] 阿拉斯加州位于美国西北太平洋东岸，是美国最大的州，1867年美国从俄国手中购得，是第49个加入美国的州。

2. [答案] A [考点] 爱尔兰地理概况。

[精析] 爱尔兰共和国的首都是都柏林(Dublin)。

3. [答案] A [考点] 美国政治概况。

[精析] 美国联邦最高法院(The Supreme Court)是拥有美国宪法最终解释权的唯一司法机构。

4. [答案] B [考点] 英国地理概况。

[精析] 英国国旗为红白蓝三色的米字旗，分别由原英格兰的白地红色正十旗、苏格兰的蓝地白色交叉十字旗和北爱尔兰的白地红色交叉十字旗重叠而成，故英国米字旗由3个十字交叉而成。

5. [答案] B [考点] 英国文学之作家贡献。

[精析] 英国唯物主义哲学之父是弗朗西斯·培根(Francis Bacon)。

6. ［答案］C ［考点］美国文学之作家贡献。

［精析］埃兹拉·庞德（Ezra Pound）是美国诗歌革命的重要代表，他曾创立意象派（Imagism）诗歌，虽然后来脱离意象派，但他的诗歌理论冲击了陈旧的诗歌传统，为美国诗歌的发展开辟了道路。

7. ［答案］D ［考点］美国文学之作家作品。

［精析］Harriet Beecher Stowe是美国现实主义时期的代表人物，其代表作为*Uncle Tom's Cabin*（《汤姆叔叔的小屋》）。

8. ［答案］B ［考点］语言学基本概念。

［精析］以语言在一定时间跨度内的发展情况为研究对象的语言学被称为历时语言学（diachronic linguistic）。

9. ［答案］C ［考点］语言学基本概念。

［精析］根据声音从产生到接收的过程将语音学划分为三个部分：发音语音学（articulatory phonetics）、声学语音学（acoustic phonetics）和听觉语音学（auditory phonetics），其中发展最完善的是发音语音学。

10. ［答案］D ［考点］语言学概念实例分析。

［精析］push加上"es"表示的是push这个动词的第三人称单数形式，像这种表示词汇语法变化的词素叫做"屈折词素"（inflectional morpheme），它只限于后缀，不改变词的词性；而派生词素（derivational morpheme）则可以附着于其他词素而构成新的词汇。

Model Test 40

1. ［答案］D ［考点］英国地理概况。

［精析］英格兰的象征是玫瑰，被誉为英国的国花；蓟（Thistle）是苏格兰的象征，用作苏格兰的国徽；三叶草（Shamrock）为爱尔兰的国花；黄水仙花（Daffodil）是威尔士的国花。

2. ［答案］A ［考点］澳大利亚地理概况。

［精析］澳大利亚的第二大城市是墨尔本（Melbourne），它也是加拿大维多利亚州的首府；布里斯班（Brisbane）是昆士兰州的首府，澳大利亚的第三大城市，全国最大的海港，位于澳大利亚的东部沿海地区；堪培拉（Canberra）是澳大利亚的首都；阿德莱德（Adelaide）是南澳大利亚州的首府。

3. ［答案］A ［考点］英国历史概况。

［精析］英国最早的居民是伊比利亚人，后来依次遭到了凯尔特人（Celts）、罗马人（Roman）和盎格鲁-撒克逊人（Anglo-Saxons）的入侵，朱特人（Jutes）后来被统称为盎格鲁-撒克逊人。

4. ［答案］D ［考点］美国历史概况。

［精析］1620年，为了躲避宗教迫害，102名清教徒搭乘"五月花号"轮船来到北美，在普利茅斯登陆，并建立了普利茅斯殖民地。

5. ［答案］B ［考点］英国文学之作家贡献。

［精析］菲茨杰拉德(F. Scott Fitzgerald)是爵士时代的代言人，他的小说真实地反映了爵士时代上层社会人们醉生梦死的空虚精神状态。

6. ［答案］C ［考点］美国文学之作家作品。

［精析］《八月之光》(Light in August)是美国杰出的现实主义小说家威廉·福克纳(William Faulkner)的作品，其他三部《嘉莉妹妹》(Sister Carrie)、《巨人》(The Titan)和《珍妮姑娘》(Jennie Gerhardt)都是德莱赛的代表作品。

7. ［答案］D ［考点］英国文学之作家作品。

［精析］威廉·布莱克(William Blake)是英国第一位重要的浪漫主义诗人，《诗歌素描》(Poetical Sketches)、《天真之歌》(Songs of Innocence)和《天堂和地狱的婚姻》(The Marriage of Heaven and Hell)都是他重要的代表诗集。

8. ［答案］C ［考点］语言学家代表理论。

［精析］系统功能语法(SF Grammar)是韩礼德在弗斯理论的基础上发展起来的。

9. ［答案］C ［考点］语言学基本概念。

［精析］成分分析法(componential analysis)是结构语意学家提出分析词意(lexical meaning)的一种方法，而述谓分析法(predication analysis)是由Leech提出的一种分析句子语义(sentence meaning)的方法。

10. ［答案］D ［考点］语言学概念实例分析。

［精析］poultry意为"家禽"，属于表示概括性含义的上义词(superordinate)，duck意为"鸭子"表示的是一种具体的家禽动物，duck属于表示具体事物的下义词(hyponym)，因此"poultry"和"duck"这两个词属于上下义关系(hyponymy)。

第二部分

改错

第一节 真题自测

The passage contains TEN errors. Each indicated line contains a maximum of ONE error. In each case, only ONE word is involved. You should proof-read the passage and correct it in the following way:

For a <u>wrong</u> word,   underline the wrong word and write the correct one in the blank provided at the end of the line.

For a <u>missing</u> word,   mark the position of the missing word with a "∧" sign and write the word you believe to be missing in the blank provided at the end of the line.

For an <u>unnecessary</u> word,   cross the unnecessary word with a slash "/" and put the word in the blank provided at the end of the line.

EXAMPLE

When ∧ art museum wants a new exhibit,   (1) <u>an</u>

it never buys things in finished form and hangs   (2) <u>never</u>

them on the wall. When a natural history museum

wants an <u>exhibition</u>, it must often build it.   (3) <u>exhibit</u>

    Psycholinguistics is the name given to the study of the psychological processes involved in language. Psycholinguists study understanding, production, and remembering language, and hence are concerned with   41. _____

listening, reading, speaking, writing, and memory for language.

    One reason why we take the language for granted is that it usually   42. _____

happens so effortlessly, and, most of time, so accurately.   43. _____

Indeed, when you listen to someone speaking, or looking at this page,   44. _____

you normally cannot help but understand it. It is only in exceptional

circumstances we might become aware of the complexity   45. _____

involved: if we are searching for a word but cannot remember it;

if a relative or colleague has had a stroke which has influenced   46. _____

their language; if we observe a child acquire language; if

we try to learn a second language ourselves as an adult; or

if we are visually impaired or hearing-impaired or if we meet

anyone else who is. As we shall see, all these examples

of what might be called "language in exceptional circumstances"

reveal a great deal about the processes evolved in speaking,

listening, writing, and reading. But given that language processes

were normally so automatic, we also need to carry out careful

experiments to get at what is happening.

47. _____

48. _____

49. _____

50. _____

第二节 真题点评

篇章结构分析

第一段对"心理语言学"这一概念进行了解释。

第二段阐述语言心理通常是难以捕捉的，其中一个原因是：对于人们来说，说出话语和理解话语往往是自然而然发生的事情，只有在某些特殊情况下，人们才会意识到语言的复杂性。文章最后总结道：即使语言机制经常是自动运作的，我们也有必要通过实验仔细研究人类思维处理语言的过程。

试题详解

41. ［答案］production → producing　　　　［考点］本题考查动词形态的一致性。
　　［精析］study后面接的第一个宾语是understanding（language），第三个宾语是remembering language，production的位置上应该是study的第二个宾语，属于平行结构的一部分，因此要用动名词producing来保持动词形式的一致。此处意为：心理语言学研究的是人们如何理解、生成和记住语言。

42. ［答案］去掉the　　　　　　　　　　　　［考点］本题考查冠词。
　　［精析］通过阅读上下文可知，此处的language并没有特指某一种语言，只是泛指"语言"这一抽象意义，故不需定冠词the。take language for granted意为"认为语言是一件自然而然（或想当然）的事情"。

43. ［答案］在time前加the　　　　　　　　　［考点］本题考查固定搭配。
　　［精析］此处表示"绝大部分时间里"，正确的表达应该是most of the time。

44. ［答案］looking → look　　　　　　　　　［考点］本题考查动词形态的一致性。
　　［精析］此处的looking和前面的listen是由or连接的两个并列的谓语动词，所以looking应改为look，和listen在形式上保持一致。

45. ［答案］we前面加that　　　　　　　　　　［考点］本题考查固定搭配。
　　［精析］此处是一个强调句：It is＋被强调的状语部分（in exceptional circumstances）＋that从句，意为"只有在某些特殊情况下，人们才会意识到语言的复杂性。"强调句中的that不可以省略。

46. ［答案］去掉colleague后面的has　　　　　［考点］本题考查时态。
　　［精析］本句描述的是过去的事实（中风）对现在的影响（影响到语言功能），后面

168

的which引导的定语从句用现在完成时态表影响，因而此处应该用过去时态表事实。

47. [**答案**] their → his　　　　　　　　[**考点**] 本题考查物主代词与主语一致。
[**精析**] 本句的主语是a relative or colleague，意为"一个亲戚或同事"，显然是一个单数概念，因此物主代词不能用表达复数的their，而要改成his。

48. [**答案**] anyone → someone　　　　　[**考点**] 本题考查不定代词的用法。
[**精析**] anyone表示"任何人"，通常用在否定句和疑问句中；someone表示"某人"，通常用在肯定句中。本句意为"如果我们的视力或听力受到了损伤，或者我们遇到的其他人是这种情况的话……"因此应该用someone else表示"(某些)其他人"这一概念。

49. [**答案**] evolved → involved　　　　[**考点**] 本题考查形近词的辨析。
[**精析**] evolve是指生物方面的"进化，演变"，也可表示"发展"；而involve 是指"牵涉，涉及"。本句中需要的显然是后者，表示"涉及说、听、写、读的一些过程"，所以用involved。

50. [**答案**] were → are　　　　　　　　[**考点**] 本题考查时态。
[**精析**] 该句中由given引导一个条件状语从句，主句时态是一般现在时，所以从句中的were应该改为are，与主句时态保持一致。

第三节 TEM-8考试大纲对改错测试的要求

1 测试要求

《高校英语专业八级考试大纲》(2004年新版,以下简称《大纲》)规定:专八改错要求考生能运用语法、词汇、修辞等语言知识识别所给短文内的语病并提出改正方法。

2 测试形式

本部分为主观试题,由一篇250词左右的短文构成,短文中有10行标有题号,该10行均含有一处错误,要求学生使用"增添"、"删去"或"改变其中的某一单词或短语"三种方法中的一种,改正错误。考试时间为15分钟,满分为10分,占考试总分的10%。

3 测试目的

专八改错从词、句、篇三个不同的层次考查考生综合运用语言知识的能力。

第二章
历年真题与技巧点拨

第一节 真题分析

一、题目构成

经过我们对历年专八改错题目的研究，我们发现改错的题目均由Direction和试题两部分组成，且每年的Direction部分表述基本一致，即：

The passage contains TEN errors. Each indicated line contains a maximum of ONE error. In each case, only ONE word is involved. You should proofread the passage and correct it in the following way:

For a <u>wrong</u> word,	underline the wrong word and write the correct one in the blank provided at the end of the line.
For a <u>missing</u> word,	mark the position of the missing word with a "∧"sign and write the word you believe to be missing in the blank provided at the end of the line.
For an <u>unnecessary</u> word,	cross the unnecessary word with a slash "/" and put the word in the blank provided at the end of the line.

EXAMPLE

When∧art museum wants a new exhibit,	(1)	an
It never buys things in finished form and hangs	(2)	never
them on the wall. When a natural history museum		
wants an <u>exhibition</u>, it must often build it.	(3)	exhibit

通过阅读**Direction**我们了解到，改错的文章中有10行标有题号，代表着这10行中均有错误，且每行中有且仅有一处错误，要求考生根据下面的答题方式作答：

对于错误的单词，要在此单词下划线，并将正确的词写在空格处；

对于需要增补的单词，要在需要增补处划"∧"号，并在空格处填入需要填补的词；

对于删减的词，要在此词上划"/"号，以示删掉，并将要删减的词写在空格处。

考生在复习时要充分理解**Direction**部分，以免因使用了错误的答题方式而丢分。

二、命题范围

《大纲》中明确规定专八改错由一篇250词左右的短文构成。我们对专八改错真题从主要内容、题材、体裁及词数等方面进行了全面的剖析。

年份	主要内容	题材	体裁	词数	句数
2013	语言心理学	语言	议论文	203	7
2012	翻译的直译和意译	语言	议论文	191	9
2011	我是如何开始写作的	文化	议论文	237	8
2010	每种语言都具备同样的水平来表达其使用者想表达的内容	语言	说明文	228	9
2009	校园歌谣和儿童歌谣的区别	文化	说明文	198	4
2008	人类总是想用一种独特的语言来展示他们与其他民族的不同	语言	说明文	185	7
2007	人类语言的起源	语言	说明文	210	6
2006	语言是人与人交流的主要工具	语言	议论文	202	5
2005	论证大学学费大幅上涨的原因	教育	议论文	281	9
2004	美国国会具有的一项重要的非立法功能	政治	说明文	194	9
2003	二战后美国人倾向于早结婚、多要孩子，当时离婚率也有所下降	社会	议论文	201	7
2002	人类普遍使用同一个发音标准有很大的障碍	语言	议论文	207	6
2001	小麦是加拿大西部经济的晴雨表	经济	议论文	232	12
2000	语法词和实词在很大程度上有着显著的区别	语言	说明文	221	7
1999	以狩猎和采集为生的部落的饮食结构	社会	说明文	212	9
1998	婴儿与新生动物不同，他们离不开其他人的照料	科普	说明文	290	9

由上表可以看出，专八改错的题材非常广泛，曾经出现过有关语言、社会、文化、教育、政治、经济和科普方面的文章。内容基本上都在广大考生所熟悉的范畴之内。所涉及的题材中，语言类的有8篇，社会类的有2篇，文化类的有2篇，其他如教育、政治、经济和科普类各有1篇，也就是说改错文章的题材以语言类的为主，且自从2006年以来，题材均是语言类和文化类。

从体裁上看，主要出现了两种体裁：说明文和议论文。其中说明文和议论文各出现了8篇。

文章的词数与句数在某种程度上体现了文章的难易度，所以此处我们特意对词数和句数进行了分析。由上表中我们可以看出，改错文章词数的范围在180词到290词之间，句数在4句到12句之间，具体的词数和句数的分布情况通过下面两个表我们会看得更加清晰：

词数分布情况

词数区间	180-	190-	200-	210-	220-	230-	280-	290-
出现篇数	1	3	4	2	2	2	1	1
平均词数	218							

句数分布情况

句数	4	5	6	7	8	9	12
出现篇数	1	1	2	4	1	6	1
平均句数	8						

由以上两表可以看出，改错文章的词数主要集中在190词到230词之间，较少的180词偶尔出现一次，240词以上的文章出现次数也不多，平均词数大约是218词。从每篇文章的句数上看，9句文章的篇数最多，出现了6次，其他依次是7句、6句，最少的4句和最多的12句均出现了1次，平均句数是8句。我们再用平均词数218除以平均句数8，大概得出每句平均词数是27.25，也就是说改错文章每句话平均都在28词左右，这显然是改错很难的原因之一。以2010年的真题为例：

1. So far as we can tell, all human languages are equally complete and perfect as instruments of communication: that is, every language appears to be well equipped as any other to say the things their speakers want to say. **40**

2. There may or may not be appropriate to talk about primitive peoples or cultures, but that is another matter. **20**

3. Certainly, not all groups of people are equally competent in nuclear physics or psychology or the cultivation of rice or the engraving of Benares brass. **26**

4. Whereas this is not the fault of their language. **10**

5. The Eskimos can speak about snow with further more precision and subtlety than we can in English, but this is not because the Eskimo language （one of those sometimes miscalled "primitive"）is inherently more precise and subtle than English. **40**

6. This example does not come to light a defect in English, a show of unexpected "primitiveness". **17**

7. The position is simply and obviously that the Eskimos and the English live in similar environments. **17**

8. The English language will be just as rich in terms for different kinds of snow, presumably, if the environments in which English was habitually used made such distinction as important. **31**

9. Similarly, we have no reason to doubt that the Eskimo language could be as precise and

subtle on the subject of motor manufacture or cricket if these topics formed the part of the Eskimos' life. **36**

整篇文章共9句话，超过30词的句子就有4句（标有下画线的句子）。长句本身理解起来就有难度，加之这其中还可能有1~2处错误（阴影标识处为错误），这就更增加了做题的难度。

三、考点分析

① 改错题形式分析

下表我们对专八改错真题的改错形式进行了分析：

	2013	2012	2011	2010	2009	2008	2007	2006	2005	2004	2003	2002	2001	2000	1999	1998
增添	2	4	3	1	1	2	1	2	3	3	1	1	1	1	2	2
删减	2	2	1	2	2	1	2	2	1	1	2	2	1	2	2	1
改错	6	4	6	7	7	7	6	6	6	6	7	7	8	7	7	7

由上表得知，2007年以前增添、删减和改错的题数每年都有所变化，但2007年到2010年，改错的题数保持在7道题，而2011年以后又出现了增添、删减和改错题目不规律的变化。我们在具体分析这些增添和删减的考题时发现，这些增添或删减的词大多数是固定搭配中缺失的介词、副词、冠词等，另外还包括不定式符号to、助动词be、代词、副词等的增添或删减，以及语义重复词的删减。

② 考点分析

改错的考查类型无外乎三种：词法错误、句法错误和逻辑错误。其中词法错误包括冠词、名词、动词、代词、介词、形容词副词本身的使用错误以及固定搭配错误等；句法错误包括时态语态错误、主谓不一致错误、并列不一致错误、语义重复、定语从句和同位语从句连词使用错误、非谓语动词使用错误、it使用错误以及固定句型使用错误等；逻辑错误是针对于篇章而言的，主要是指上下文的逻辑衔接错误以及篇章语义错误。

下面我们分别对专八改错真题的考点分布（表I）及比例（表II）进行分析：

	年份	13	12	11	10	09	08	07	06	05	04	03	02	01	00	99	98	总
词法错误 句法错误	固定搭配	1	4	2	2	2	3	3	1	3	3	1	2	2	5	1	3	38
	形容词、副词			3	1	2	2	1	2			2	2	3	2		1	21
	代词	2			1	2	2	1	2	1	1	1				1	2	16
	动词	1		1	1			1		1	1		1	1		1	1	10
	冠词	1	2		1			1				1		1	1	1		10
	介词													1	1	2		4
	名词			1			1				1	1						4
	非谓语动词							1	1	1	1		1		1			6
	定语从句			1				1		1	1	1		1				6
	it 用法				1					1			1					3
	固定句型		1			1				1	1							4
	并列一致	2				1				1								4
	时态	2	1		1									1				5
	语义重复													1	1			2
	语态						1											1
	同位语从句			1						1								2
	主谓一致															1		1
	强调句	1																1
逻辑错误	逻辑衔接		1	1	1	1		2	1		1	2	1	1	1	3		16
	篇章语义			1	1		1		1			2						6

由表I可得出表II的数据分析：

（表Ⅱ）

年份	13	12	11	10	09	08	07	06	05	04	03	02	01	00	99	98	比例
词法错误	5	6	7	6	6	8	7	5	5	6	6	5	7	9	6	9	64.4%
句法错误	5	3	1	2	3	1	1	3	5	3	0	4	2	0	1	1	21.8%
逻辑错误	0	1	2	2	1	1	2	2	0	1	4	1	1	1	3	0	13.8%

由表II我们了解到，改错侧重于考查词法错误，句法错误和逻辑错误考查比重差不多。再从表I的考点分布来看，词法错误依次重点考查了固定搭配、形容词副词、代词、

动词、冠词、介词以及名词；句法错误依次重点考查了非谓语动词、定语从句、it用法、固定句型、并列一致、时态、语义重复以及仅出现过1次的语态、同位语从句和主谓一致；逻辑错误只有逻辑衔接和篇章语义两种考点，偏重对逻辑衔接的考查。

另外对表I进行横向分析。有以下几点值得考生注意：

- 对固定搭配的考查是改错的必考项，每年都不落，最多的2000甚至考查了5个，不过近几年一直保持在2~3个的状态；
- 2003年到2013年，除了2011年和2012年外，其他年份都对代词进行了考查；
- 单独考查介词意义的辨析和用法只有在2001年、2000年和1999年出现过，而近几年对介词的考查一般都出现在固定搭配中；
- 对it用法的考查主要是对it作形式主语和指代作用的考查；
- 对语义重复的考查也只在2002年和2001年出现过2次；
- 同位语从句考查过2次。
- 2013年考查了强调句。

了解了上述对于改错的题材、体裁、词数、考点等的全面分析，考生在复习时就可以更好地抓住复习重点，比如多阅读语言类题材的文章，多积累有用的固定搭配，牢牢掌握代词、冠词等的用法等。不过，编者在此郑重地提示各位考生，虽然有些考点在历年的真题中没有出现过，比如强调句、倒装句、虚拟语气等，但并不代表这些考点在以后不会出现，所以最科学最有效的复习方法是全面而有所侧重的复习。

第二节 高分改错技巧点拨

从上一节的考点分析中我们了解到，改错的错误类型有三种：词法错误、句法错误和逻辑错误。本节我们将结合真题实例讲解解答这三类错误的应试技巧。

一、词法错误

从对历年改错真题的分析中我们了解到，词法错误包括冠词、名词、动词、代词、介词、形容词副词本身的使用错误、以及固定搭配错误等，主要测试考生对常用词汇的词性、含义、搭配和用法等的掌握。

① 固定搭配

固定搭配错误主要体现在介词的搭配错误、实词的搭配错误、词组的用法错误上。下表列举了改错真题中出现的所有固定搭配错误：

年份	题	原文	改正	错误点
2013	43	most of time	most of the time	冠词缺失
2012	41	The argument has been going	The argument has been going on	副词缺失
	43	the message rather the form	the message rather than the form	介词缺失
	45	in the turn of 19th century	at the turn of 19th century	介词错误
	49	This view culminated the statement	This view culminated in the statement	介词缺失
2011	41	when I grew	when I grew up	副词缺失
	43	soon or later	sooner or later	副词错误
2010	41	be well equipped as any other	be as well equipped as any other	副词缺失
	46	come to light a defect	bring to light a defect	动词错误
2009	46	in the general	in general	冠词冗余
	50	to let alone	let alone	用法错误
2008	47	stick on to	stick to	介词冗余
	48	at the end	in the end	介词错误
	49	carry with	carry on with	介词缺失
2007	46	in other grounds	on other grounds	介词错误
	47	in return to	in response to	名词错误
	49	to large extent	to a large extent	冠词缺失

年份	题	原文	改正	错误点
2006	43	in his disposal	at his disposal	介词错误
2005	42	irrespective	irrespective of	介词缺失
	45	in the school	in school	冠词冗余
	50	give discounts on... customers	give discounts to... customers	介词错误
2004	43	in rare occasions	on rare occasions	介词错误
	45	make out detailed studies of issues	make detailed studies of issues	副词冗余
	47	public	the public	冠词缺失
2003	50	in the same extent	to the same extent	介词错误
2002	43	speak out	speak	副词冗余
	49	holding a community	holding a community together	副词缺失
2001	46	ask	ask for	介词缺失
	48	life costs	living costs	名词错误
2000	43	as opposed in	as opposed to	介词错误
	45	far away from	far from	副词冗余
	47	differ as	differ in	介词错误
	48	by no mean	by no means	名词错误
	50	a great number of	a great deal/amount of	名词错误
1999	44	in average	on average	介词错误
1998	43	pay attention to	draw attention to	动词错误
	44	get on one's feet	get to one's feet	介词错误
	45	in risk	at risk	介词错误

　　由上表可以看出，固定搭配的错误点中，有18题错在介词的缺失、冗余和搭配错误上，有8题错在副词的缺失或冗余上，有5题错在冠词的缺失或冗余上，有4题错在名词的搭配错误上，有2题错在动词的搭配错误上，还有1题错在词组本身的用法错误上。总的来说，考生在做改错时，要根据上下文将重点放在固定搭配中的介词、副词和冠词上，同时还要注意固定搭配中名词或动词是否符合上下文的语境。为了方便考生备考，本书总结了一些专八常考固定搭配，供大家记忆：

a fraction of 一小部分，一点儿

abide by 忠于；遵守

absence of mind 心不在焉

access to 能接近；进入；了解

accomplish a task 完成一项任务

accomplish one's purpose 达成目的

account for 解释，说明

acquaint sb. / oneself with 使认识，使了解，使熟悉

act for 代理

act on 奉行，按照……行动

adhere to = conform to = comply with = insist on = persist in 坚持；遵循

adjust a policy 调整政策

adjust a watch 调表

adjust expenses to income 量入为出

admit of 有……的可能，留有……的余地

agree on 双方就某事达成一致

agree to 同意（建议、安排、计划等）

agree with 赞同（某人意见）

ahead of 在……之前，先于

ahead of schedule 提前

allow for 考虑到，顾及

amount to 总计，等于

answer for 对……负责

answer to 适合，符合

apply to 与……有关，适用

appoint to 任命，委任

approve of = consent to = be in favor of 赞成

arise from 由……引起

assure sb. of sth. 向……保证，使……确信

at one's convenience 在某人方便时

at one's own risk 自行负责

at the expense of 以……为代价；由……付费，由……负担费用

attend to 注意；照顾

attribute...to 把……归因于

be absent from 缺席，没参加

be absorbed in 全神贯注于

be abundant in 富于，富有

be accustomed to doing 习惯于

be acquainted with 了解

be ashamed of 以……为羞耻

be at odds（with）（与）不一致；争执

be at one's back 支持，维护

be aware of 意识到；知道

be capable of 能够，有能力

be cautious of 谨防

be certain of 有把握，一定

be complementary to 补充的，辅助的

be concentrated on 全神贯注于

be exhausted from 因……而十分疲乏

be inferior to 比……差

be on one's back 卧床不起

be scheduled for 定在某时（进行）

be well supplied with 富于，富有

be / caught in a dilemma 处于（或陷于）进退两难的境地

beat...at 在……运动项目上打赢

behind schedule 落后于计划进度；晚于规定时间，晚点

blame sb. for sth. = blame sth. on sb. 指责，把……归咎于

boast of / about 吹嘘

bring a halt to（使）停止，终止；制止

browse through 浏览，翻阅

but for 要不是（表示假设）

by accident 偶然地，意外

by all means 无论如何，必定

by instinct 凭本能

by means of 借助于，用

by no means 决不，无论如何不

call a halt（命令）停止；途中休息

cater for sb. / sth. 迎合

center one's attention on 把某人的注意力集中在……上

come in handy 有用，派得上用场

come / bring to a halt 停止，停住

confer sth. upon / on sb. 把……授予某人

confer with 商谈，商议

conform to 适合，符合

cooperate with 合作，协助

deduce from 推断

depart from 背离；违反；离开

deviate from 背离，偏离

dispose of 处理，处置

divert sb.'s attention from sth. 转移某人对于某事的注意力

dwell on / upon 细想，凝思；详述

embark on / upon 从事，着手；开始工作

endow with 给予，赋予

excel in / at 在……方面超过

excel oneself 表现出色；超水平发挥

exert oneself to do sth. 努力；尽力

exert sth. on / over 对……施加……

for sure 肯定地，有把握地

for the benefit of 为了……的利益

for the better 好转

get the better of 打败，胜过

grasp at 攫取，抓住

have an advantage over 胜过

have the advantage of sb. 知道某人所不知道的事

have the advantage of 由于……处于有利条件

immerse in 沉浸在，使专心于

in accord with 与……一致

in accordance with 依照，根据

in addition to 除……外

in addition 此外，又，加之

in advance 预告，事先

in any case = for love or money = at any rate = at any price = at any cost = whatever happens 无论如何

in brief 简言之

in case of = in the event of 如果发生……，万一

in case 万一

in haste 匆忙地；草率地

in no case 在任何情况下都不

in principle 原则上，大体上 // on principle 根据原则

in prospect of 预期，期望

in succession 连续地

in the air 不肯定，不具体；在流传中

in the case of 至于，就……而言

in the last (final) analysis 归根结底，总而言之

in the process of 在……的过程中

in the process 在进行中

make allowance(s) for 考虑到，顾及；体谅，照顾

make an attempt at doing sth. (to do sth.) 试图做

modify one's approach 改变方法

obtain a degree 获得学位

occupy oneself with / in 忙于(某事)

of one's own accord 自愿地，主动地

on account of 因为

on average 平均

on behalf of 以……的名义

on business 出差办事

on one's own account 为自身利益；依靠自己，自行负责

on one's own initiative 主动地

on schedule 按预定时间，按时，准时

on the basis of 根据，在……基础上

out of one's accord with 同……不一致

participate in 参与，参加

peer at 仔细看

peer into 朝……里面看

persist in 坚持，固执；坚持不懈

pose a challenge 挑战

pose a question 提问

pose a threat to 对……造成威胁

pose as 假装，摆出……的样子

postpone doing sth. 推迟做某事

prompt to 敏捷的，动作迅速的

pursue a career 从事……职业

pursue a degree 攻读学位

pursue a goal / aim 追逐目标

recommend sb. sth. 向某人推荐某物

senior to 比……年长

shirk one's responsibility 逃避责任

sketch out 简略地概述

skim through 浏览，略读

take after 与……相像

take attendance 点名

take the initiative 带头, 倡导, 发起

take up the attention of 吸引……的注意力

take... for granted 想当然, 认为理所当然

take... into account 考虑, 顾及

target sth. at / on sb. / sth. 把……作为……的目标

turn one's back on sb. 不理睬(某人); 背弃, 抛弃

undertake responsibility 承担责任

withstand financial risks 抵御金融风险

② 形容词、副词

形容词副词错误大体上包括四类错误: 一是形容词词义辨析错误, 二是副词的词义、用法辨析错误, 三是形容词、副词的比较级用法错误, 四是形容词、副词的意义、用法混淆错误。

首先以2011年真题的46题为例:

...I had the lonely
child's habit of making up stories and holding conversations with imaginative (46) _____
persons, and I think from the very start my literal ambitions were mixed up (47) _____
with the feeling of being isolated and undervalued...

46题应该将imaginative改为imaginary, 考查形容词辨析。imaginative 表示"(人)富有想象力的, 有创造力的"。根据上下文, 此处意为"我养成了孤僻的小孩子惯有的习惯: 编造故事和与想象中的人交谈", 故将imaginative改为imaginary, 意为 "想象中的, 虚构的, 幻想的"。

针对此类考点, 特为考生提供一些常见的形容词辨析供考生学习:

historic 历史上著名的, 可名垂青史的; 有历史意义的
historical 有关历史的, 有关历史研究的

electric 用电的, 带电的, 有电的
electrical 电器的, 电气科学的

economic 经济的, 经济上的
economical 经济的, 节俭的

industrial 工业的
industrious 勤奋的

considerable 相当多(或大)的
considerate 体谅的, 体贴的, 周到的

sensible 实用的; 明智的
sensitive 敏感的

continual 连续的；一再重复的
continuous 连续不断，不间断的

respectable 值得尊敬的，有名望的
respectful 尊敬人的，有礼貌的
respective 分别的，各自的

imaginable 可想象的
imaginary 想象中的，虚构的，幻想的
imaginative 富有想象力的，有创造力的

intelligent 有才智的，聪明的
intelligible 易了解的，易领悟的
intellectual 知识的，智力的

alternate 轮流的，交替的
alternative 选择的，两者选一的

comparable 可比较的，有类似之处的
comparative 比较而言的，相当的

beneficial 有益的
beneficent 多多行善的

official 官方的
officious 多管闲事的

confident 有信心的，自信的
confidential 机密的

momentary 瞬间的，短暂的
momentous 重大的

memorable 值得记忆的，不能忘却的
memorial 纪念的

social 社会的
sociable 善于社交的

childish 幼稚的
childlike 孩子般的

distinct 明显的，清晰的
distinctive 独特的，有区别的

classic 一流的；典型的；经典著作
classical 古典的

182

earthly 人间的，尘世的
earthy 泥土的，像泥土的

effective 有效的
efficient 有效率的
effectual（事物）奏效的

fatal 致命的
fateful 决定性的

impractical 不切合实际的
impracticable 无法使用的

notable 著名的（指事）
noted 著名的（指人）

practical 实际的
practicable 可行的，行得通的

regretful 感到遗憾的（指人）
regrettable 令人遗憾的（指事）

healthy 健康的
healthful 有益于健康的

likely 可能的
likable 可爱的

再以2002年真题的44题为例：

Large numbers of us, in fact, remain throughout our lives	
quite unconscious with what our speech sounds like when we	（42）_____
speak out, and it often comes as a shock when we	（43）_____
firstly hear a recording of ourselves. It is not a voice...	（44）_____

44题应将firstly改为first，本题考查副词辨析。firstly意为"第一，首先"，通常用于表示顺序中的第一。first则表示时间上的"第一次，首次"，与原文想表述的"第一次听到自己的录音"相符，因此把firstly改为first。

此处为考生归纳总结一下英语-ly副词与其同源副词的用法比较：

英语中有一些表示方式、程度的副词具有两种形式，如late, lately; high, highly; slow, slowly等等。在这些词当中，两种不同形式的词所表达的含义有的完全不同，有的很相似，而有的却完全一致。这就给考生造成了很大的困惑。

①诸如hard, hardly; late, lately; most, mostly等等，这两种副词形式、含义完全不同，所以，使用时不易引起混淆。例如：

He works **hard** all day. 他整天都在努力地工作。

He **hardly** works at all. 他很少工作。

You have come too **late**. 你来得太晚了。

Have you seen him **lately**? 你最近见到过他吗?

The person who talks **most** is often the one who does least. 说得最多的人常常干得最少。

The audience consisted **mostly** of women. 观众大部分是女的。

The next flight dose not go **direct** to Tokyo; it goes by way of Shanghai.

下趟航班不直飞东京, 而是绕道上海。

He will be here **directly**. 他马上就来。

The rider pulled his horse up **short**. 骑手突然一下把马勒住。

Make a right turn **shortly** beyond the village. 在过村子不远处右拐。

②诸如wide, widely; close, closely; high, highly等等, 这两种副词形式不同, 含义也有差别, 但是没有上一类的区别明显, 而且翻译成汉语时用词也很接近。所以使用时很容易混淆。这类词义及用法上的主要特点是: 不带-ly的副词表示具体的行为和动作, 这些动作或状况具有可测量性和可见性; 而以-ly结尾的同源副词所表达的常常是抽象性的行为和状况。这时, 这些词大都具有greatly和extremely的含义。试比较下面的句子:

Do you see that butterfly flying **high** above the street?

你看见那只在街道上方高高飞舞的蝴蝶了吗?(表示可见的高度)

The distinguished guests were **highly** praised.

贵宾们受到了高度赞扬。(表示赞扬的程度)

He flung the door **wide** open. 他猛地把门大敞开。(表示可见的宽度)

We were **widely** different on many questions.

我们在许多问题上分歧很大。(表示分歧的程度)

She stood **close** against the wall. 她紧挨着墙站着。(表示距离很近)

The police were watching him **closely**. 警察密切监视着他。(表示监视的程度)

They had to dig **deep** to reach water. 要挖到水他们得挖得很深。(表示可见的深度)

You have offended him **deeply**. 你冒犯他可不轻。(表示冒犯的程度)

③在固定词组中或修饰与其固定搭配的动词时, 倾向于使用不带-ly的副词形式, 例如:

Take it **easy**. 不要紧张。

Stand **firm** and hold it **tight**. 站稳抓牢。

He often plays **high**. 他赌注常下得很大。

They were drinking **deep** in the fort **deep** into the night. 他们在堡垒中痛饮到深夜。

再以2007年真题的45题为例：

It is often said, of course, that the language originated in cries of	(43) _____
anger, fear, pain and pleasure, and the necessary evidence is	(44) _____
entirely lacking: there are no remote tribes, no ancient records,	
providing evidence of a language with a large proportion of such	(45) _____
cries than we find in English...	

45题应将large改为larger，此处考查形容词的比较级。根据后文的than可知这里是将其他语言和英语进行比较，故要用比较级。

为了便于考生学习，本书对形容词副词比较级用法的一些重要结构进行了归纳，供考生复习巩固：

①as + adj. / adv. + as或not so / as + adj. / adv. + as。前者表示"和……一样……"，后者表示"不像……那样……"。例如：

My computer is not so / as expensive as yours. 我的电脑不如你的贵重。

②主语 + 比较级 + than any other...。表示主语所描述的事物比其他任何一个都……，比较级形式表示最高级含义。例如：

Li Ming is much cleverer than any other student in the class.

李明是他们班上最聪明的学生。

注意：若比较范围不同，than后应该用"any + 可数名词单数"的结构。例如：

China is larger than any country in Africa. 中国比非洲的任何国家都大。

③诸如never之类的否定词与形容词或副词的比较级连用，表示最高级含义，意为"再没有比……更……的了"。例如：

I have never heard such an interesting story. 我从来没有听过比这更有趣的故事。

④"adj. + to"结构也可表示比较含义。例如：

This kind of car is superior in quality to that. 这种汽车的质量比那一种好得多。（superior to意为"优于；胜过"）

Li ping is three years senior to Liu Gang. 李平比刘刚大三岁。（senior to意为"年长于；资格老于；地位高于"）

⑤"no + 比较级 + than"结构表示对两个比较对象都进行否定。（可由neither...nor...结构来改写）例如：

I'm no taller than you. 我们俩都不高。（相当于Neither I nor you is tall.）

⑥"not more + 比较级 + than"结构表示在程度上前者不如后者。例如：

This book is not more interesting than that one. 这本书不如那本书有趣。(相当于This book is less interesting than that one.)

⑦"形容词比较级 + than + adj.", 意为"与其说……倒不如说……"。例如：

Jack is much harder than clever. 与其说杰克聪明, 倒不如说他学习用功。

⑧would rather...than, prefer...to..., prefer to do...rather than...这三个句型表示"宁愿……而不愿……; 喜欢……胜过……; 宁愿做……而不愿做……"。虽无比较级形式, 但表示比较级含义。例如：

She would rather die than give in. 她宁死不屈。

He preferred to go out rather than stay home. 他宁愿出去也不愿待在家里。

⑨"The + 比较级, the + 比较级"结构意为"越……越……"。例如：

The more difficult the questions are, the less likely he is able to answer them.

问题越难, 他回答出来的可能性就越小。

最后以2009年真题的47题为例：

...If, therefore, a playground rhyme can be shown to has been currently for a hundred years, or even just for fifty, it follows that it has been retransmitted over and over, very possibly it has passed along a chain of two or three hundred young hearers and tellers, ...	(47) _____ (48) _____

47题将currently改为current, 此处考查形容词副词的区别用法。分析句子结构, 主干是If a playground rhyme has been currently for..., 句子缺少谓语, 应该将currently改为current作be的表语。be current意思是"流行, 盛行"。

要记住形容词修饰名词、代词, 而副词修饰动词、形容词以及整个句子这一规律。平时背单词的过程中注意形容词和副词的词性及其用法, 在做题时认真分析句子结构, 此类错误是很容易发现并改正的。

③ 代词

代词类错误主要体现在指代错误和代词辨析错误上。

以2009年真题的43、44题为例：

...In nursery lore a verse, learnt in early childhood, is not usually passed on again when the little listener has grown up, and has children of their own, or even grandchildren. The period between learning a nursery rhyme and transmitting it may be something from 20 to 70 years...	(42) _____ (43) _____ (44) _____

43题是代词的指代错误, 答案是将their改为his。根据文章得知their指的应该是the

186

little listener, 故应该用单数his。意思是"有了他自己的孩子甚至是孙子"。

44题是代词的辨析错误，答案是将something改为anything, something指的是特定的某个事物（如：The right answer should be something from 0 to 11. 指其中的一个）。而anything指的是任何事物，是泛指。这里应该是指20年到70年间的任何一段时间，故改为anything。

下面为考生总结一下需要注意的几组代词辨析：

①代词one(s)与the ones的用法区别

- ones主要用于替代复数名词，表泛指；若需特指，则用the ones。例如：

If you haven't got a big plate, two small ones will do.

如果没有大盘子，两个小盘子也行。

We still have shortcomings, and very big ones too.

我们仍有缺点，而且是很大的缺点。

Do you know the ones who moved here recently?

你认识最近搬到这里来的那些人吗？

- 复数形式的ones之前一般不直接用名词所有格、物主代词、数词以及 some, any, both, several, dozen, own 等词修饰。例如：

Have you got any drawing-pins? Can I borrow some please? （不能说：...some ones?）

你有图钉吗？我能借一些吗？

—Do you have any new diaries? —We don't have any at the moment. （不能说：... any ones）

——有新的日记本吗？——我们现在一本也没有了。

- 当一个名词被另一个名词修饰时，通常不宜用one(s)来替代。但若一个名词被表示材料的名词修饰，可用one(s)替代。例如：

Do you need coffee cups or tea cups? （不能说：...or tea ones?）

你们需要咖啡杯还是茶杯？

We can lend you plastic chairs or metal ones.

我们可以借给你塑料椅子或者金属椅子。

- 当替代词one / ones 紧跟在形容词最高级、序数词以及this, that, these, those, which, either, neither, another等限定词之后时，通常可以省略。例如：

I think my dog's the fastest (one). 我想我的狗是跑得最快的(一只)。

Either (one) will suit me. (这两个当中)哪一个对我来说都合适。

②代词one与the one的用法区别

- one 主要用于替代"a + 单数可数名词"，表泛指；若需特指，则用 the one。例如：

A high speed train is one that goes fast. 高速列车是一种快速行驶的火车。

The accident was similar to the one that happened in 2008.

这起事故与发生在2008年的那起事故类似。

Open the drawer on the left, the one with a key in it.

打开左边的抽屉，上面有钥匙的那个。

Here are six rings. Pick out the one you like best.

这里有六枚戒指，选出你最喜欢的一枚。

I want very much to see these films, especially the one you mentioned.

我很想看这些电影，特别是你提到的那一部。

- the one与that均可表特指，the one只用于替代单数可数名词，that则可用于替代可数或不可数名词。

③one's own的用法

特别强调所有关系时，可以在任何所有格形容词（而不是代词）后面加上own。这样构成的词组可以起所有格形容词（如my own room）或所有格代词（如it is my own）的作用。我们还经常用a / an + 名词 + of one's own来代替one's own + 名词。例如：

I want to have my own room / a room of my own. 我想要有一个自己的房间。

我们可以说one's own room或者a room of one's own，但我们不能在one's own之后加上one。例如：

别用我的梳子，用你自己的。

正：Don't use my comb. Use your own.

误：Don't use my comb. Use your own one.

④代词it, one, that和those用法说明

为了避免重复出现前面已经出现的名词，常用it, one, that, those来替代。这几个替代词是考试中的一个常考点。现将各个替代词的用法归纳如下：

- it和that都可替代"the + 单数名词（可数或不可数）"，都是特指，都可替代可数和不可数名词，但it指前面提到的"同一个"事物，而that是指前面提到的"同类"事物。例如：

I can't find my hat. I think I must buy one.

我找不到我的帽子了。我想我该去买一顶。（不定）

The hat you bought is bigger than that I bought.

你买的那顶帽子比我买的大。（同类但不同个）

I can't find my hat. I don't know where I put it.

我找不到我的帽子。我不知道把它放在哪了。（同一物）

- one替代"a + 单数可数名词"，表示泛指；其复数形式ones替代泛指的复数名词。特指的the one相当于that，替代"the + 单数名词"；the one的复数形式the ones，替代"the + 复数名词"，在口语中也常用those代替。当后面有of短语时，多用that或those；当有前置修饰语时，只能用one(s)。另外，one(s), the one(s), those都只能替代可数名词。例如：

Radios are useful for me to learn English. I'd like to buy one.

收音机对我学英语很有用，我想买一台。（one替代a radio，是泛指收音机这类东西中的一台）

We still have shortcomings, and they are very big ones too.

我们仍有缺点，而且是很大的缺点。（ones替代shortcomings）

We kept seats for those who might arrive late.

我们给可能来晚的人留了座位。(those = the ones, 替代the persons)

Waves of red light are about twice as long as those of blue light.

红色光线的波长约为蓝色波长的两倍。(those替代the waves)

The population of Scotland was eight times as large as that of Cornwall.

苏格兰的人口是康沃尔人口的八倍。(that替代不可数名词the population, 不能用the one)

⑤other, the other, another与others, else, the rest 表示"另外的"不定代词

这些不定代词不仅在含义上有单复数之分, 而且在用法上有泛指(无the)和特指(有the)之别。其用法区别可归纳如下:

• 指单数时的区别: 若泛指, 用another; 若特指, 用the other。例如:

Give me another (one). 给我另外一个。

Shut the other eye, please. 请把另一只眼睛也闭上。

• 指复数时的区别: 若泛指, 用other(后接复数名词); 若特指, 用the other(后接复数名词)。例如:

There are other ways of doing it. 做这事还有其他的办法。

Where have the other students gone? 其他学生都到哪里去了?

• others的用法: 它永远表示复数意义 (且其后不能再接名词)。其用法相当于"other + 复数名词"。同样地, the others 相当于"the other + 复数名词"。例如:

Other people [Others] may not think that way. 别的人可能不这样想。

He is cleverer than the others [the other students] in her class.

他比班上其他学生更聪明。

• another的用法: 一般只能表单数, 且其后接名词也只能接单数名词。但是如果其后有数词或few修饰时, 也可接复数名词。例如:

We need another few chairs. 我们还需要几把椅子。

In another two weeks it'll be finished. 再过两个星期就可做完了。

• else只能放在复合不定代词或者疑问词后, 其所有格形式是else's。例如:

Is there anything else you want? 你还想要些别的什么吗?

• the rest 既可代替可数名词, 也可代替不可数名词。而 another, others, the other(s) 只能代替可数名词。例如:

The rest of the milk has gone bad. 其余的牛奶都变质了。

John's Scottish and the rest of us are Welsh.

我们当中, 约翰是苏格兰人, 其余的是威尔士人。

④ 动词

动词类错误主要考查动词的用法(及物动词、不及物动词、使役动词)和动词辨析。

以2010年真题的49题为例：

> The English language will be just as rich in terms for　　　　(48) _____
> different kinds of snow, presumably, if the environments in which English
> was habitually used made such distinction as important.　　　(49) _____

49题答案是去掉as。本题考查make的使役用法。make作使役动词接形容词作宾补的结构为make + sth. / sb. adj.。这里应该是make such distinctions important，故去掉as。

英语中有一些"小"动词，如take, turn, wear, come, make, get, go等，虽然是初中词汇，却依然是专八考试的重点。因为它们"个头"虽小，但能量巨大，它们不仅本身具有很多含义和用法，而且还能与其他名词、介词、副词等构成众多搭配，使用频率相当高。在此我们就为考生总结一下这些词的易混搭配：

① take词组

take a bath / walk / rest / trip 洗澡／散步／休息／旅行

take a day off 休一天假

take a deep breath 深呼吸

take a look at 看

take a photo 照相

take a photograph of 给……拍照

take along 带着，带在身边

take aim at 瞄准

take away 拿走

take back 带回，收回(话)

take down 拿下；记录下

take...for 把……误当做

take hold of 抓住

take interest 对……发生兴趣

take it easy 别紧张；别过累

take medicine 吃药

take measures 采取措施

take notes 做笔记

take notice of 注意

take off 脱下(衣、鞋、帽)；(飞机)起飞

take office 就职

take on workers 雇用工人

take one's place 坐某人的座位，代替某人的职位

take one's / a seat 坐下，坐好

take one's temperature 量体温

take one's time 从容行事，慢慢来

take out 取出

take part in 参加(活动)

take place 发生

take pride in 为……而骄傲

take the lead 带头

take the place of 代替，取代

take the side of 支持某人，支持某方

take trouble 费劲，费力

take turns 轮流

take up 开始；拿起

② make词组

make a clean breast of 坦白，招认(错事)

make a fool of sb. 愚弄，使……出丑

make a fool of oneself (自己)做蠢事

make a point of 重视

make a thing of 对……小题大做

make allowance(s) for 考虑到；体谅

make an example of sb. 杀一儆百

make an exhibition of 出洋相，当众出丑

make for 促进，有助于

make one's hair stand on end 令人毛骨悚然

make history 创造历史

make it (尤指在困难情况下)做到，成功；
及时到达

make off 匆忙离开；仓皇出逃

make oneself scarce 躲开，回避；溜走

make peace 言和，和解

make sb. / sth. out 看清；听清；辨认清楚；
弄懂

make sense 有道理，合乎情理的

make sth. of sb. / sth. 领会；理解

make sure 确保，设法保证

make the best of sth. 尽可能做好……

make the most of sth. 充分利用

make up 形成，构成

make up for 补偿，弥补

make up one's mind 下定决心，打定主意

make use of 利用(以获私利)

make way 让路；腾出地方或位置

make one's way 去，前往

③ turn词组

turn a blind eye to 熟视无睹

turn a deaf ear to 置若罔闻

turn about 转身；向后转

turn against 转而反对；与……反目

turn around 转向；改变(意见)

turn away 把……打发走；驱逐

turn back 折回，往回走

turn down 调低速度、音量

turn into (使)变成

turn left / right 向左 / 右转

turn off 关闭，停止

turn on 打开，开启

turn one's back on sb. 避开某人；背弃某人

turn out 结果是，证明是

turn over 翻转；移交；营业额达

turn over a new leaf 重新开始

turn one's blood cold 使人毛骨悚然

turn sb. out (of) 把……撵出去

turn sth. over in one's mind 反复考虑

turn the tables 反败为胜

turn the tide 扭转局势

turn the corner 好转，转危为安

turn thumbs down 表示反对，表示不满

turn to sb. 求助于，转向

turn up 调高音量；出现

turn up one's nose at 对……嗤之以鼻

④ come词组

come about 发生

come across 遇见

come after 追逐；跟随

come along 随同

come and go 来来去去

come apart 破碎

come around 到来；苏醒

come at sb. 袭击某人

come at sth. 发现(事实、真相等)

come back 回来

come before 优先于

come by 走过

come down 下降；(雨、雪等)落下

come forward 挺身而出

come in 进来；流行起来

come into 进入；得到

come into being 形成，产生

come into effect 开始生效

come into fashion 开始风行

come into power 当权，执政

come off 从……掉落

come out 出来；出版；开花

come out of 出自

come through 安然度过

come up 上升

come to 达到；苏醒

come together 聚会，相见

come to a close 临近结束

come to a conclusion 得出结论

come to a stop 停止

come to an agreement 达成协议

come up with 想出；提出(想法)

⑤ get词组

get a commitment to 奉献

get a name 成名

get a raise 得到加薪

get about / around 四处走动

get across (使)通过；(使)被理解

get air 传播，宣扬出去

get along with sb. 与某人相处

get away from 逃离

get back 回来；恢复

get down 下来；取下，拿下

get down to doing sth. 开始做某事

get in 进入；到达；收获

get in the way 妨碍

get in touch with 和……取得联系

get in trouble 惹上麻烦

get into debt 负债

get off 下车；出发

get on 上车

get on in years 年老，上年纪

get on the air 开始广播

get out 出去；离开；出版

get out of 逃避；避免

get over 克服；恢复

get ready for 为……做好准备

get rid of 摆脱；除去

get there 到达那里；实现目标

get through 用完；通过(考试)

get to 到达；接触到

get up 起床；筹备

⑥ wear词组

wear and tear 磨损

wear away 磨损；消磨

wear down 磨损；使疲劳

wear off 磨损；逐渐消逝

wear on 穿戴

wear one's heart on one's sleeve 把情感表露出来

wear out 磨损；耗尽；使筋疲力尽

wear through 将(衣服)穿破

wear through the day 好歹过了一天

⑦ go词组

go aboard 上船或飞机等
go across 走过；穿过
go after 追逐；追求
go against 反对；违反；不利于
go against the stream 反潮流
go all lengths 竭尽全力
go all out 全力以赴
go along with 支持，赞同
go astray 步入歧途
go broke 破产
go by 从……旁走过
go by the rules 照章办事，按规矩行事
go current 流行，通用
go down 下降；传下去
go from bad to worse 每况愈下
go halfway 妥协，向……让步

go halves 平分
go in for 参加；追求；从事
go into 进入；加入
go into business 从事商业
go into details 详述，逐一细说
go into effect 生效
go off 离开；去世
go out 出去；熄灭；过时；罢工
go out of date 过时
go out of one's mind 发疯
go out of service 停止使用
go over 转变；(对……进行)仔细检查；复习
go round 到处走动；顺便去
go to extremes 走极端
go up 上升；增长
go with 伴随；与……相配；和(异性)交朋友

⑧ have词组

have a class / lesson 上课
have a drink 喝一杯
have a fever 发烧
have a good time 过得愉快
have a headache 头痛
have a lecture 听讲座
have a look (at) 看一看
have a rest / break 休息一会儿
have a saying 有句名言
have a talk 谈话
have a try 试一试
have access to 可以接近；可以使用
have an eye on 注视；监视
have business with 与……有关
have full assurance of 完全相信

have fun 玩得开心，过得愉快
have little mind to do sth. 没有心思做某事
have no acquaintance with 不了解
have no idea 不清楚
have nothing to do with 与……无关
have ones foot in the grave 风烛残年
have pity on sb. 怜悯某人
have sth. done 让人做某事
have sth. to do with 与……有关系
have sports 进行体育活动
have sth. back 要回，收回
have sth. in mind 记住
have sth. on 穿着，戴着
have (got) to 不得不

⑨ give词组

give sb. a hand 帮助某人
give a talk 做报告，做讲演

give an opinion on 对……发表意见
give away 把……赠送给某人；泄露(秘密)

give back 归还

give birth to 生小孩

give ear to 倾听，听取意见

give expression to 反映

give full play to 充分发挥

give lessons to 给……上课

give off 发出

give one's mind to 专心于

give oneself over to 沉溺于（恶习）

give oneself airs 摆架子

give oneself up 自首；放弃

give out 分发

give rise to 引发

give up 停止；放弃

give voice to 表达

give way 让路；撤退

再以2005年真题的49题为例：

...Just as business

firms sometimes collude to shorten the rigors of competition, universities   (49) _____

collude to minimize the cost to them of the athletes whom they recruit in

order to stimulate alumni donations, so the best athletes now often bypass

higher education in order to obtain salaries earlier from professional teams.

49题是将shorten改为reduce或weaken。此处考查动词的辨析。shorten意为"缩短，使变短"，无法与the rigors of competition(竞争的残酷)相搭配，因此应将shorten改为reduce（减少）或weaken（削弱）。

专八易考易混动词辨析：

used to do sth. 过去常常做某事	例如：I used to get up at 5.
be used to doing sth. 习惯做某事	例如：I'm used to getting up late.
be used to do sth. 被用来做某事	例如：Pens are used to write.
divide 把整体"划分"为若干份	例如：The island is divided into two parts.
separate 把连在一起或靠近的"分隔开"	例如：The Taiwan Straits separates Taiwan from Fujian.
hurt 普通用语，多指精神上的伤害	例如：He felt hurt at your words.
injure 较正式，多指身体上的伤害	例如：A bullet injured his left leg.
harm "对……有害"，多用于抽象事物	例如：Don't harm your health by smoking.
wound 指刀伤、枪伤等严重的伤	例如：The thief wounded him with a knife.
look for "寻找"的过程	例如：I'm looking for my wallet.
find "寻找"的结果	例如：I didn't find my wallet.
receive （客观地）收到（某物）	例如：I received a letter from my sister.
accept （主观地）乐意接受	例如：I accepted his advice.

| rise 上升（不及物动词） | 例如：The river is rising after the rain. |
| raise 提升，提高（及物动词） | 例如：She raises her head. |

| acquire 获得 | 例如：She has acquired a good knowledge of English. |
| inquire 询问，打听 | 例如：Go and inquire about the flight to Tokyo. |

| affect 影响；感动 | 例如：The climate affected his health. |
| effect 产生，引起 | 例如：The war effected changes all over the world. |

需要注意的是专八改错考查的动词辨析往往都是通过上下文语境、搭配来判断该用哪个动词，不要生硬地记下这些词的辨析。

再以1998年真题的48题为例：

> ...For this reason, biologists now suggest that
> language be "species specific" to the human race, that is to say,　　　（48）_____
> they consider the human infant to be genetic programmed　　　（49）_____
> in such way that it can acquire language.

48题将be改为is，此处考查suggest的用法。此处的suggest意为"认为，提出某观点"，而非"建议"，其宾语从句无需采用虚拟语气，因此把be改为is。

与suggest用法相似的词还有insist。insist在表示"坚持认为或坚持说"时，宾语从句不用虚拟语气，而当insist意为"坚决要求"时，宾语从句就要用虚拟语气，例如：

I insist that he is innocent. 我坚决认为他是无辜的。（不用虚拟语气）

I insist that he should come with us. 我坚决要求他跟我们一块儿来。（用虚拟语气）

另外，表示建议、命令、要求等含义的动词所接的宾语从句一般用虚拟语气，虚拟语气由"should + 动词原形"构成，should 可省略。有类似用法的动词还包括：advise（建议），demand（要求），desire（要求），order（命令），propose（建议），recommend（建议），require（要求），request（要求）。

5 冠词

冠词错误主要考查冠词的用法。

以2010年真题的50题为例：

> Similarly, we have no reason to doubt that the Eskimo language
> could be as precise and subtle on the subject of motor manufacture
> or cricket if these topics formed the part of the Eskimos' life.　　　（50）_____

50题去掉第一个the或将第一个the改为a，此处考查冠词的用法。文中"汽车制造或板球成为爱斯基摩人生活的一部分"中的"生活的一部分"是泛指，且在文章中第一次出现，故应用不定冠词。"生活的一部分"也可以不用冠词，故the可去掉或改为a。

对于冠词有以下几点需要注意：

①不定冠词用于形容词最高级前无比较含义，表示"非常……"。例如：

It is a most useful book. 这是本非常有用的书。（most不表最高级）

It is the most useful book. 这是一本最有用的书。（most表最高级）

②不定冠词用在序数词前不表顺序，意为"另一个"。例如：

I want to read this book for a second time. 我想再看一遍这本书。（second表示再一次）

I read this book for the second time. 我是第二次看这本书了。（second表示第二次）

③定冠词用于形容词前表示一类人。例如：

the rich 富人　　　　　the poor 穷人　　　the old 老人　　　the young 年轻人

the injured 伤员　　　the impossible 不可能的事　　　the unknown 未知世界

④表示演奏某种乐器时要用定冠词，而表示进行球类运动时不用冠词。例如：

play the violin 拉小提琴　　　　　play the piano 弹钢琴

play basketball 打篮球　　　　　play football 踢足球

⑤注意冠词在某些固定搭配中的用法。例如：

at the same time 同时　　　by the way 顺便问一句　　　in the long run 从长远来看

as a result 因此　　　　　as a rule 通常　　　　as a whole 总体上说

on foot 步行　　　　　one by one 一个接一个　　　heart and soul 全心全意

⑥ 介词

此处的介词错误指的是介词本身的意义、用法的辨析错误，近年来没有考查过。

以1999年真题的41题为例：

The hunter-gatherer tribes that today live as our prehistoric	(41) _____
human ancestors consume primarily a vegetable diet supplementing	(42) _____
with animal foods...	

41题将as改为like，此处考查介词的辨析。as意为"作为……"，而原文想要表达的是"像史前人类祖先那样生活"，因此将as改成意为"像……"的like。

⑦ 名词

名词类错误主要考查的是名词的词性、词义的辨析。

以2011年真题的42题为例：

> ...Between the ages of about seventeen and (41) _____
> twenty-four I tried to abandon this idea, but I did so with the conscience (42) _____
> that I was outraging my true nature and ...

42题答案将conscience改为consciousness，此处考查名词词义辨析。此处要表达的是："……我努力放弃这种想法，但是我这么做时仍意识到这违背了我的本性……"conscience意为"良知，良心"，而consciousness才意为"意识，知觉，觉悟"。with the consciousness that意为"意识到"。

二、句法错误

句法错误包括非谓语动词使用错误、定语从句的关系连词使用错误、it用法错误、固定句型搭配错误、主谓不一致和并列不一致错误、语义重复、时态语态错误以及同位语从句的连词错误。其中重点考查非谓语动词、定语从句、it用法和固定句型，而对同位语从句和语义重复的考查均出现过2次，对语态的考查仅在2009年出现过1次，对主谓一致的考查只在1998年出现过1次，对强调句的考查仅在2013年出现过1次。

① 非谓语动词

非谓语动词错误主要体现在现在分词、过去分词和动词原形的用法混淆上，此类错误往往可通过句子的结构分析来判断。

以2005年真题的41题为例：

> A number of colleges and universities have announced steep
> tuition increases for next year—much steeper than the current, very
> low rate of inflation. They say the increases are needed because of a
> loss in value of university endowments heavily investing in common (41) _____
> stock. I am skeptical...

41题将investing改为invested，此处考查非谓语动词。 heavily investing... 为university endowments的后置定语，而两者显然为被动关系，因此应将investing改为过去分词形式invested。

对于非谓语动词有如下几点需要注意：
①有些及物动词后必须加不定式作宾语，例如：manage（设法），offer（提供），promise（承诺），pretend（假装），intend（打算），decide（决定），learn（学习），desire（渴望），agree（同意）等，例如：

I want to be with you forever. 我想和你永远在一起。

They planed to have a picnic this Sunday. 他们计划周末去野餐。

He desires to win her back. 他想把她赢回来。

②有些及物动词后必须加动名词作宾语, 如: avoid（避免）, finish（完成）, suggest（建议）, mind（介意）, enjoy（喜欢）, require（要求）, delay（延迟）, practice（练习）, consider（考虑）, miss（想念）, imagine（想象）, give up（放弃）, can't help（忍不住）等, 例如:

She can't help laughing when she heard the news. 当听到这个消息时, 她忍不住笑了。

He managed to avoid being punished. 他设法逃脱了惩罚。

Can you imagine living with such a boring man?

你能想象和这么无聊的人住在一起是什么样的吗?

③有些动词既可以接不定式作宾语也可以接动名词作宾语, 但它们有一定的区别。例如:

stop { to do 停下来去做某事 / doing 停下正在做的事

mean { to do 打算做某事 / doing 意味着……

like { to do 想要做某事 / doing 喜欢做某事

try { to do 努力做某事 / doing 试图做某事

need { to do 需要做某事 / doing 某事需要被做

go on { to do 继续做另一件事 / doing 继续做同一件事

want { to do 想要做某事 / doing 某事想要被做

forget { to do 忘记做某事 / doing 忘记做过某事

remember { to do 记住做某事 / doing 记住做过某事

④使役动词和感官动词接动词不定式作宾语补足语, 要省去to。使役动词主要有make, get, let, have 等, 感官动词主要有smell, taste, hear, see等, 例如:

I made the door open. 我把门打开了。

I saw him go upstairs. 我看见他上了楼。

注意: 使役动词和感官动词后也可接现在分词作宾语补足语。不定式作宾语补足语与现在分词作宾语补足语的区别是, 不定式表示动作的结果或已经发生的动作, 而现在分词表动作正在进行或动作发生的全过程, 例如:

I heard her sing. 我听见了她唱歌。

I heard her singing. 我听见她正在唱歌。

⑤分词作后置定语相当于定语从句, 现在分词表主动和进行, 过去分词表过去和被动。例如:

the boy standing by the table: the boy who is standing by the table / the boy stands by the table 站在桌边的男孩

work done on time: work which is done on time 按时完成的工作

198

⑥分词作状语时，分词的逻辑主语与主句主语一致。例如：

Arriving at the railway station, they missed the train. = When they arrived at the railway station, they missed the train. 当他们到达火车站时，他们错过了火车。

主语不一致时用分词的独立结构"名词/代词＋分词"。例如：

All done, we went. = When all is done, we went. 所有的事做完后，我们走了。

2 定语从句

定语从句错误主要体现在关系代词、关系副词、介词、从句中谓语动词以及先行词的使用错误上。

以2008年真题的44题为例：

At the time the United States split off from Britain, for example,	(44) _____
there were proposals that independence should be linguistically accepted	(45) _____
by the use of a different language from those of Britain.	(46) _____

44题在time后加上when，此处考查定语从句的关系副词。the United States split off from Britain是the time的定语从句，the time为先行词，关系副词when不可省。

再以2006年真题的44题为例：

...the English speaker has in his disposal a vocabulary and a	(43) _____
set of grammatical rules which enables him to communicate his	(44) _____
thoughts and feelings, in a variety of styles, to the other English	(45) _____
speakers...	

44题将enables改为enable，此处考查定语从句的谓语动词。关系代词which引导的定语从句，其先行词为a vocabulary and a set of grammatical rules，因此从句谓语动词应为动词原形enable。

再以2005年真题的47题为例：

The ways which universities make themselves attractive to students	(47) _____
include soft majors, student evaluations of teachers, giving students a	
governance role, and eliminate required courses...	

47题在which之前加in，此处考查定语从句中介词的用法。介词in通常与名词ways搭配，表示"通过……方法"，因此应在which之前加上介词in，引导以ways为先行词的定语从句。

再以2004年真题的50题为例：

Congressional committees also have the power to compel testimony from
unwilling witnesses, and to cite for contempt of Congress witnesses
who refuse to testify and for perjury these who give false testimony. （50）_____

50题将these改为those，此处考查定语从句的先行词。these应为who引导的定语从句的先行词，但these不能用作先行词，因此应将其改为those，同时指代之前的witnesses。

再以2002年真题的45题为例：

...It is not a voice（44）_____
we recognize at once, whereas our own handwriting is
something which we almost always know. We begin the "natural"... （45）_____

45题将which改为that，此处考查定语从句的关系代词。如果先行词是something，定语从句的关系代词只能用that。

定语从句有几点注意事项：
①定语从句中关系代词的选择。具体是：
who用于指人，在从句中作主语；
whom用于指人，在从句中作宾语，可省略；
whose可用于指人，也可以指物，在从句中作定语；
which 用于指物，在从句中作主语或宾语；
that既可指人也可指物，在从句中作主语或宾语，作宾语时可省略；
when用于指时间，在从句中作状语；
where用于指地点，在从句中作状语；
why用于指原因，在句中作状语，先行词一般为reason。
②that和which引导定语从句时的区别。具体有以下几点：
1）非限制性定语从句只能用which引导，不能用that，例如：
We don't want to enter the house, which is very cold. 我们不想进这个冰冷的房间。
2）介词后的定语从句只能用which引导，不能用that，例如：
The chair in which you are sitting is made of iron. 你坐的椅子是铁制的。
3）当不定代词作先行词且由only、形容词最高级和序数词修饰时，或先行词同时出现人和物时，定语从句只能用that引导，例如：
That is the only thing that I want to know. 那是我唯一想知道的事情。
All that you need is help. 你所需要的是帮助。
The first lesson that I learned will never be forgotten.
我永远都不会忘记我的第一堂课。

They talked of things and persons that they remembered in the school. 他们谈到了他们能记起的学校里的人和事。

3 it用法

it用法错误主要体现在it作形式主语和指代的错误。

以2010年真题的43题为例：

There may or may not be appropriate to talk about primitive peoples or cultures, but that is another matter.	(43) _____

43题将There改为It，此处考查it作形式主语。这里it作的是形式主语，真正的主语是to talk about primitive peoples or cultures。如果用there，该句就缺少主语，故将there改为it。

再以2006年真题的48题为例：

We take it for granted the two most common forms of transmission—by means of sounds produced by our vocal organs（speech）or by visual signs（writing）.	(48) _____

48题去掉take之后的it，此处考查it的指代用法。take...for granted意为"认为……是理所应当的"，句中被认为是理所应当的是the two most common forms of transmission，因此应去掉指代关系不明确的it。

在此我们对it的用法简单地总结一下：
①it指时间、距离、天气或自然现象，例如：
It is 5 o'clock. 现在五点。
It is about four kilometers long. 大概有四公里长。
It's sunny outside. 外面天气晴朗。
②it可作形式主语或形式宾语，例如：
It is necessary to forecast weather. 预报天气很有必要。
I found it necessary to forecast weather. 我觉得预报天气很有必要。（it代替to forecast weather作宾语，necessary作宾语补足语）
③it用于强调句中，基本结构是"It + be + 被强调部分 + 人（who）/ 物（that）+ 其他成分"，它的特点是拆掉强调结构it is...that / who，句子也成立，例如：
It was yesterday that he met Li Ping. = Yesterday he met Li Ping.（强调状语）
It is from the sun that we get light and heat. = We get light and heat from the sun.（强调状语）

④ 固定句型

固定句型错误主要体现在搭配错误上。

以2009年真题的42题为例：

> ...In nursery lore a verse, learnt
>
> in early childhood, is not usually passed on again when the little listener （42）_____
>
> has grown up, and has children of their own, or even grandchildren. （43）_____

42题将when 改为until, 此处考查not...until...句型。根据上下文意思"在童年听到的童谣直到听童谣的人长大才会再传下去……"可知这里应用not...until...这个句型。故将when改为until。

在此列举一些专八可能会考到的常见固定句型。

①either...or... 意为"不是……就是……，要么……要么……"，谓语动词采用就近原则，例如：

Either you or he is right. 不是你对，就是他对。

②neither...nor... 意为"既不……也不……，两者都不……"，谓语动词也采用就近原则，例如：

Neither he nor I have ever read this book. 我和他都没有读过这本书。

③get + 形容词比较级 + and + 形容词比较级，意为"变得越来越……"，例如：

It gets warmer and warmer. 天气越来越暖和了。

④The + 形容词比较级..., the + 形容词比较级..., 意为"越……越……"，例如：

The colder it is, the more people wear. 天气越冷，人们穿得就越多。

⑤had better (not) do sth. 意为"最好(不)做某事"，例如：

You'd better wear more. 你最好多穿点。

⑥It is + adj. (+ for sb. / sth.) + to do sth. 意为"对(某人)来说，做某事……"，例如：

It is necessary to change your job. 你很有必要换工作。

⑦It is + adj. + of sb. + to do sth. 常用于描述人的品质，例如：

It is very kind of you to invite me. 能邀请我，你真是太好了。

⑧It is (high) time that sb. did sth. 意为"某人现在该做某事了"，例如：

It is high time that we went home. 我们该回家了。

⑨find / think / feel + it + adj. (for sb.) to do sth. 意为"发现 / 认为 / 觉得做某事如何"，例如：

More and more people have found it unhealthy to eat too many hamburgers.

越来越多的人发现吃太多汉堡包不利于健康。

A lot of students have found it very hard to make friends at college.

很多大学生发现在大学中交友很难。

202

并列一致指的是由and连接的两个成分应保持时态和形式上的一致。

以2009年真题的41题为例：

> The previous section has shown how quickly a rhyme passes
> from one schoolchild to the next and illustrates the further difference   (41) _____
> between school lore and nursery lore. In nursery lore a verse, learnt
> in early childhood, is not usually passed on again when the little listener   (42) _____
> has grown up, and has children of their own, or even grandchildren.

41题将illustrates改为illustrated，此处考查并列一致原则。本句的主谓结构是The previous section has shown...and illustrates，and连接的两个并列成分应该保持时态和形式上的一致。and前面是完成时has shown，因此后面的illustrates应改为过去分词illustrated。

6 时态

在专八改错中时态错误出现过5次。

以2002年真题的46题为例：

> ...We begin the "natural"   (45) _____
> learning of pronunciation long before we start learning to read or write,
> and in our early years we went on unconsciously imitating and   (46) _____
> practicing the pronunciation of those around us for many more hours per
> every day than we ever have to spend learning even our difficult   (47) _____

46题将went改为go，此处考查时态。本文通篇用的都是一般现在时，所以此处也应用一般现在时，故将went改为go。

7 语义重复

汉语是允许语义重复的，但在英语中语义重复是错误的。专八改错中在2002年和2001年出现过此类考点。

以2002年真题的47题为例：

> ...We begin the "natural"   (45) _____
> learning of pronunciation long before we start learning to read or write,
> and in our early years we went on unconsciously imitating and   (46) _____
> practicing the pronunciation of those around us for many more hours
> per every day than we ever have to spend learning even our difficult   (47) _____

47题去掉per或every。per和every都是"每"的意思，表意重复，因此应删去其中的一个。

⑧ 语态

专八改错中单独考查语态的只有1次，即2009年真题的48题：

...If, therefore, a playground	
rhyme can be shown to has been currently for a hundred years, or	(47) _____
even just for fifty, it follows that it has been retransmitted over	
and over, very possibly it has passed along a chain of two or three	(48) _____
hundred young hearers and tellers, and the wonder is that it remains live	(49) _____
after so much handling, to let alone that it bears resemblance to the	(50) _____
original wording.	

48题在has后面加上been，此处考查语态。句中的主语it指代的是a playground rhyme，校园歌谣不能自己主动流传，应是被流传，故用被动语态。

⑨ 同位语从句

专八改错考试中，考查同位语从句的有2次，以2005年真题的44题为例：

...The rise in tuitions	(43) _____
may reflect the fact economic uncertainty increases the demand for	(44) _____
education...	

44题在fact之后加that，此处考查同位语从句。economic uncertainty...是对fact的具体说明，是其同位语从句，而关系词that在同位语从句中是不可省略的，因此应在从句前加上that。

⑩ 主谓一致

主谓一致错误在专八改错中出现过1次，即1998真题的42题：

When a human infant is born into any community in any part of the	
world it has two things in common with any infant, provided neither of them	(41) _____
have been damaged in any way either before or during birth. Firstly, and...	(42) _____

42题将have改为has，此处考查主谓一致原则。neither作主语时，谓语动词应用单数。

三、逻辑错误

逻辑错误是专八改错考查的重点，主要有逻辑衔接和篇章语义两种错误，这两种错误中更偏重于对前者的考查。

① 逻辑衔接

句子间的逻辑关系通常通过连词表现出来，纵观历年专八改错真题中含有逻辑衔接错误的句子，连词的前后两个部分一般具有因果关系、并列关系、让步关系、条件关系、转折关系、对比关系、递进关系和选择关系等。连词的使用错误往往要通过上下文来判断。此类错误主要考查考生对上下文的理解。下表列举了改错真题中出现的所有逻辑衔接错误的答案：

年份	题号	答案	逻辑关系转换
2012	50	and → but	并列关系 → 转折关系
2011	50	Therefore → Nevertheless	因果关系 → 转折关系
2010	44	whereas → but	对比关系 → 转折关系
2009	45	therefore → however	因果关系 → 转折关系
2007	41	and → or	并列关系 → 选择关系
	44	第二个 and → but	并列关系 → 转折关系
2006	49	or → and	选择关系 → 并列关系
2004	48	nevertheless → therefore / thus	转折关系 → 因果关系
2003	47	nevertheless → also 或去掉 nevertheless	转折关系 → 递进关系
	49	Since → Although / While	因果关系 → 让步关系
2002	41	and → while / whereas	并列关系 → 转折关系
2001	43	so → but	因果关系 → 转折关系
2000	42	but → and	转折关系 → 并列关系
1999	43	and → or	并列关系 → 选择关系
	45	as → whereas / while	因果关系 → 让步关系
	49	if → although	条件关系 → 让步关系

由上表可以看出，逻辑衔接错误主要涉及转折、并列、因果、选择、让步关系，而对比、条件关系则偶尔出现。考生在做题时要特别注意and、but、whereas、while、although、or等连词。

此处为考生按关系类别归纳了专八改错常考的逻辑衔接词：

①表次序关系

above all 首先，最重要的是
eventually 最后
finally 最后
first(ly) / first of all 首先
in the end 最后

last but not least 最后但同样重要的是
lastly 最后，最后一点
second(ly) / in the second place 其次
to conclude 总而言之，最后

②表举例关系

a case in point 一个很好的例子是
as an illustration 作为例证
as follows 如下所述
for example 例如

for instance 例如
including 包括……在内
such as 例如；……等；像……

③表并列关系

and 而且
both...and 既……又……

as well as 和

④表转折关系

at the same time 同时；然而，不过
but 但是
however 然而
on the contrary 与此相反，恰恰相反

otherwise 否则，不然
still 还是，不过
yet 还

⑤表让步关系

although 虽然
despite 尽管，不管
even so 尽管如此
even though 尽管，虽然
in spite of 不管

nevertheless 尽管如此，不过，然而
notwithstanding 虽然，尽管
regardless of 不管
though 虽然，尽管，即使
while 虽然，尽管，然而

⑥表递进关系

additionally 同时，此外
also 也，还
as well 也，同样

besides 除……之外（还）
equally important 同样重要的是
furthermore 此外

in addition 另外
in other words 换句话说
likewise 还，亦，而且
moreover 而且

not only...but also 不仅……而且……
that is to say 也就是说
what's more 而且

⑦表因果关系

accordingly 因此，所以
as a result 结果……
as a result of 由于
because(of) 因为
consequently 因此，所以
due to 由于
hence 因此，由此
now that 既然如此
on account of 由于，因为

owing to 由于
since 因为，由于
so 所以
so long as 只要
so that 所以
thanks to 多亏了
therefore 因此
thus 因此，从而，所以

⑧表比较关系

equally 同样地
in comparison（with）与……相比
in contrast with / to 与……相比
in / by contrast 相比之下

instead 代替，反而，却
on the contrary 与此相反
while 然而

⑨表选择关系

alternatively 要不，或者
either...or 不是……就是……
instead of 代替
neither...nor 既不……也不……

not...but 不是……而是……
rather than 而不是
whether...or 不是……就是……

(2) 篇章语义

篇章语义错误主要体现在两点：一是错误之处表达了与上下文相反的含义，二是错误之处与前后文意义搭配不当。

首先以2010年真题的47题为例：

...The position
is simply and obviously that the Eskimos
and the English live in similar   (47)
environments...

47题将similar改为different，本题就是错误之处表达了与上下文相反的含义。根据文章和常识可知，爱斯基摩人和英国人应该是生活在不同的环境中，故将similar改为different。

再以2008年真题的45题为例：

At the time the United States split off from Britain, for example,	(44) _____
there were proposals that independence should be linguistically accepted	(45) _____
by the use of a different language from those of Britain.	(46) _____

45题将accepted改为realized，本题的错误之处与前后文意义搭配不当。accepted的对象是independence，"接受独立"从意义上讲不通，应该是"实现独立"，故将accepted改为realized。

Test 1

The central problem of translating has always been whether to translate
literally or freely. The argument has been going since at least the first   (41) _____
century BC. Up to the beginning of the 19th century, many writers
favoured certain kind of 'free' translation: the spirit, not the letter; the   (42) _____
sense not the word; the message rather the form; the matter not   (43) _____
the manner. This is the often revolutionary slogan of writers who   (44) _____
wanted the truth to be read and understood. Then in the turn of 19th   (45) _____
century, when the study of cultural anthropology suggested that
the linguistic barriers were insuperable and that the language   (46) _____
was entirely the product of culture, the view translation was impossible   (47) _____
gained some currency, and with it that, if was attempted at all, it must be as   (48) _____
literal as possible. This view culminated the statement of the   (49) _____
extreme 'literalists' Walter Benjamin and Vladimir Nabokov.

The argument was theoretical: the purpose of the translation, the
nature of the readership, the type of text, was not discussed. Too
often, writer, translator and reader were implicitly identified with
each other. Now, the context has changed, and the basic problem remains.   (50) _____

真题点评

结构分析

第一段首先提出翻译的核心问题：直译与意译之争。这个问题可以追溯到公元前一世纪。直到19世纪初，很多作者都喜欢意译。然而到了19世纪和20世纪之交，直译又开始盛行。

第二段指出事实上二者的争论一直停留在理论阶段，并没有考虑很多实质性问题。现在时过境迁，但问题却依然存在。

41. [答案] going后加on [考点] 本题考查固定搭配。
[精析] go意为"前进；出发；运转"，而go on意为"继续；持续"，此处要表达"持续"的含义，且本句为现在完成进行时，表示从过去某时开始一直持续到现在的动作，并且还将持续下去，所以应改为has been going on。

42. [答案] certain前加a [考点] 本题考查冠词。
[精析] a certain kind of表示"某种"，前面的不定冠词a不能省略，故在certain前加a。

43. [答案] rather后加than或rather→not [考点] 本题考查固定搭配。
[精析] 根据上下文，分号隔开的并列部分表达的意思都是"是……而不是……"，因此这里表示的应该是"而不是"，需要用固定搭配rather than或将rather改为not。

44. [答案] is→was [考点] 本题考查时态。
[精析] 此处陈述的是过去的事实，且本句中的定语从句也用了过去时，所以主句也要改为过去时。

45. [答案] in→at [考点] 本题考查固定搭配。
[精析] 此处表示"在19世纪和20世纪之交"，正确用法是at the turn of 19th century。

46. [答案] 去掉第二个the [考点] 本题考查冠词。
[精析] 根据上下文，此处的language并没有特指某种语言，只是泛指语言，故不需定冠词the。

47. [答案] the view后加that [考点] 本题考查同位语从句。
[精析] 分析句子结构可知，该句的主句是the view gained some currency，其中translation was impossible是view的同位语从句，引导同位语从句的that不能省略，故在the view后加that。

48. [答案] 去掉was [考点] 本题考查省略结构。
[精析] 在句子...and with it that, if was attempted at all, it must be as literal as possible中，if条件句中显然缺少主语，再分析句子可以发现，从句主语即为主句中的it，如果从句的主语和主句的主语一致或主语是it时，从句中的"主语+系动词"均要省略，故去掉was。

49. [答案] culminated后加in [考点] 本题考查固定搭配。
[精析] culminate作及物动词时，表示"使达到最高点；使结束"，其主语应是某种"结果"，如：Their marriage culminated their long friendship. (他俩是很多年的朋友，最后终成眷属。)这句的主语Their marriage就是"结果"。 culminate作不及物动词时

常与in搭配，culminate in意为"以……达到最高点，以……而告终"，这里"结果"应作其宾语。题目中此处要表达的是"这种观点以极端直译主义者沃尔特·本杰明和弗拉基米尔·纳博科夫的言论而达到顶峰"，此处的宾语"极端直译主义者沃尔特·本杰明和弗拉基米尔·纳博科夫的言论"是"结果"，故在culminate后加 in。

50. ［答案］and→but　　　　　　　　　［考点］本题考查逻辑关系。
［精析］根据句意，这里表示"……改变了，但是……仍然存在"，因此使用表示转折关系的but。

Test 2

From a very early age, perhaps the age of five or six, I knew that
when I grew I should be a writer. Between the ages of about seventeen and　41. _____
twenty-four I tried to abandon this idea, but I did so with the conscience　42. _____
that I was outraging my true nature and that soon or later I should have to　43. _____
settle down and write books.

I was the child of three, but there was a gap of five years on either　44. _____
side, and I barely saw my father before I was eight. For this and other
reasons I was somewhat lonely, and I soon developed disagreeing mannerisms　45. _____
which made me unpopular throughout my schooldays. I had the lonely
child's habit of making up stories and holding conversations with imaginative　46. _____
persons, and I think from the very start my literal ambitions were mixed up　47. _____
with the feeling of being isolated and undervalued. I knew that I had a facility
with words and a power of facing in unpleasant facts, and I felt that this　48. _____
created a sort of private world which I could get my own back for my failure　49. _____
in everyday life. Therefore the volume of serious—i.e. seriously intended　50. _____
—writing which I produced all through my childhood and boyhood would
not amount to half a dozen pages. I wrote my first poem at the age of four or five,
my mother taking it down to dictation.

真题点评

结构分析

　第一段作者叙述从小就知道将来应该成为一名作家，虽然曾经一度尝试放弃，但深知自己将来一定还会从事写作。
　第二段作者叙述了由于家庭环境等客观因素使自己具有了写作天赋。

41. [答案] 在grew后加up   [考点] 本题考查固定搭配。

[精析] grow强调"长"的过程,意为"成长,发育",而grow up强调"长"的结果,意为"长大",此处要表达的是"长大",故应为grow up。

42. [答案] conscience → consciousness   [考点] 本题考查词义辨析。

[精析] 此处要表达的是"……我尝试放弃这种想法,但是我这么做时仍意识到这违背了我的本性……"conscience意为"良知,良心",而consciousness意为"意识,知觉,觉悟"。with the consciousness that意为"意识到"。

43. [答案] soon → sooner   [考点] 本题考查固定搭配。

[精析] sooner or later为固定搭配,意为"迟早"。

44. [答案] 在the后加middle   [考点] 本题考查语义理解。

[精析] 根据下文可知,作者是三个孩子中的老二,因此用middle修饰child,此句意为"我是三个孩子中的老二,老大和老三分别与我相隔五岁"。

45. [答案] disagreeing → disagreeable   [考点] 本题考查词义辨析。

[精析] 此处的mannerism意为"言谈举止",disagreeing是disagree的现在分词,不能用来修饰mannerism,而disagreeable意为"难相处的;脾气坏的",可以用来修饰mannerism。

46. [答案] imaginative → imaginary   [考点] 本题考查词义辨析。

[精析] imaginative表示"(人)富有想象力的;有创造力的"。根据上下文,此处意为"我养成了孤僻小孩子惯有的习惯:编造故事和与想象中的人交谈",故将imaginative改为imaginary,意为"想象的;虚构的;假想的"。

47. [答案] literal → literary   [考点] 本题考查词义辨析。

[精析] literal意为"文字的",而根据上下文,此处要表达的是"我的文学抱负",故将literal改为literary,意为"文学的"。

48. [答案] 去掉in   [考点] 本题考查动词用法。

[精析] face用作及物动词,表示"面对",后面可以直接跟名词。

49. [答案] which前加 in   [考点] 本题考查定语从句连接词。

[精析] 此处要表达的是"我感觉这样就创造了一个私人世界,在那里我可以为我每天的挫败找到支持",此处要用关系副词where或in which来引导定语从句,修饰先行词a sort of private world。

50. **[答案]** Therefore → Nevertheless   **[考点]** 本题考查逻辑关系。
    [精析] 上文提到"我感觉这样就创造了一个私人世界，在那里我可以为我每天的挫败找到支持"。后文提到"我整个童年和少年时代创作的严肃作品都不到六页"，前后为转折关系，而非因果关系。

Test 3

So far as we can tell, all human languages are equally
complete and perfect as instruments of communication: that is,
every language appears to be well equipped as any other to   (41) _____
say the things their speakers want to say.   (42) _____

　　There may or may not be appropriate to talk about primitive   (43) _____
peoples or cultures, but that is another matter. Certainly, not all
groups of people are equally competent in nuclear physics or
psychology or the cultivation of rice or the engraving of Benares
brass. Whereas this is not the fault of their language. The Eskimos can   (44) _____
speak about snow with further more precision and subtlety than   (45) _____
we can in English, but this is not because the Eskimo language
(one of those sometimes miscalled "primitive") is inherently more
precise and subtle than English. This example does not come to light   (46) _____
a defect in English, a show of unexpected "primitiveness". The position
is simply and obviously that the Eskimos and the English live in similar   (47) _____
environments. The English language will be just as rich in terms for   (48) _____
different kinds of snow, presumably, if the environments in which English
was habitually used made such distinction as important.   (49) _____

　　Similarly, we have no reason to doubt that the Eskimo language
could be as precise and subtle on the subject of motor manufacture
or cricket if these topics formed the part of the Eskimos' life.   (50) _____

真题点评

结构分析

　　第一段提出，每种语言都具备同样的水平来表达其使用者想表达的意思。
　　第二段以爱斯基摩人对于雪的丰富表达为例，阐述了不同地区的环境差异对语言的影响。
　　最后一段重申地区环境差异影响语言表达的观点。

41. [答案] **在well前加上as**   [考点] 本题考查固定搭配。
    [精析] 根据后文的as判断,这里应该是as...as...结构。文章中"as well equipped as"指"每种语言都同样具备……"。

42. [答案] their → its   [考点] 本题考查代词。
    [精析] speakers前的代词指代的应该是every language,应该用单数,故改为its。

43. [答案] There → It   [考点] 本题考查代词。
    [精析] 这里it作的是形式主语。真正的主语是to talk about primitive people or cultures,故改为it。

44. [答案] Whereas → But   [考点] 本题考查连词的使用。
    [精析] whereas有"然而,但是,反之"的意思,引导表示对立、相反的状语从句,一般用于法律法规等较正式的文体中。but表示句意的转折。根据上下文,此处应表示转折,故改为but。

45. [答案] further → far / much   [考点] 本题考查形容词比较级的修饰语。
    [精析] further不可以修饰形容词的比较级。a bit, a little, rather, much, far等可以修饰形容词的比较级。

46. [答案] come → bring   [考点] 本题考查固定短语。
    [精析] come to light意思是"真相大白,为人所知",后面不能再接宾语。bring to light意思是"发现,揭露",后面可以接宾语,故改为bring。译为:这个例子并不是要揭露英语的缺点。

47. [答案] similar → different   [考点] 本题考查篇章的理解。
    [精析] 根据文章和常识,爱斯基摩人和英国人应该是生活在不同的环境中,故改为different。

48. [答案] will → would   [考点] 本题考查时态。
    [精析] 该句是一个条件状语从句,从句部分用的是一般过去时,主句应该用相应的过去将来时,故改为would。

49. [答案] **去掉as**   [考点] 本题考查make作使役动词的用法。
    [精析] make作使役动词接形容词作宾补的结构为make sth./sb. + *adj*。这里应该是make such distinctions important,故去掉as。

50. [答案] **去掉第一个the或第一个the → a** [考点] 本题考查冠词。
    [精析] 文中"汽车制造或板球成为爱斯摩人生活的一部分"中的"生活的一部分"是泛指,且在文章中第一次出现,故应用不定冠词。"生活的一部分"也可以不用冠词,故第一个the可去掉或改为a。

Test 4

The previous section has shown how quickly a rhyme passes

from one schoolchild to the next and illustrates the further difference   (41) _____

between school lore and nursery lore. In nursery lore a verse, learnt

in early childhood, is not usually passed on again when the little listener   (42) _____

has grown up, and has children of their own, or even grandchildren.   (43) _____

The period between learning a nursery rhyme and transmitting

it may be something from 20 to 70 years. With the playground   (44) _____

lore, therefore, a rhyme may be excitedly passed on within the very hour   (45) _____

it is learnt; and, in the general, it passes between children of the   (46) _____

same age, or nearly so, since it is uncommon for the difference in age

between playmates to be more than five years. If, therefore, a playground

rhyme can be shown to has been currently for a hundred years, or   (47) _____

even just for fifty, it follows that it has been retransmitted over

and over, very possibly it has passed along a chain of two or three   (48) _____

hundred young hearers and tellers, and the wonder is that it remains live   (49) _____

after so much handling, to let alone that it bears resemblance to the   (50) _____

original wording.

真题点评

结构分析

第一句指出校园歌曲流传速度快，并解释了校园歌谣和儿童歌谣的区别。

第二句和第三句指出儿童歌谣要得到流传必须要等听童谣的人长大后，其间大致要经过20到70年。

第四句和第五句说校园歌谣能即学即传，并且由于玩伴之间的年龄差距通常不超过五岁，因此一首已经盛行100年的歌谣可能已经拥有200个甚至300个听众或传诵者。令人称奇的是它仍然存在，更不用说它保持着与原有歌谣相似的用词。

试题详解

41. [答案] illustrates → illustrated   [考点] 本题考查并列一致原则。
[精析] 本句的主谓结构是The previous section has shown...and illustrates, and连接的两个并列成分应该保持时态和形式上的一致。and前面是完成时has shown，因此后面的illustrates应改为过去分词illustrated。

42. [答案] when → until   [考点] 本题考查固定句型。

[精析] 根据上下文的意思"在童年听到的童谣通常直到听到童谣的人长大才会再传下去……"可知这里应用not...until...这个句型。

43. [答案] their → his   [考点] 本题考查代词指代一致。

[精析] 根据文章得知their指的应该是the little listener, 故应该用单数his。意思是有了他自己的孩子甚至是孙子。

44. [答案] something → anything   [考点] 本题考查词义的辨析。

[精析] something指的是特定的某个事物(如: The right answer should be something from 0 to 11. 指其中的一个)。而anything指的是任何事物, 是泛指。这里应该是指20年到70年间的任何一段时间, 故改为anything。

45. [答案] therefore → however   [考点] 本题考查上下文逻辑关系。

[精析] 上文讲的是童谣流传需要20到70年, 之后讲到校园歌谣能即学即传, 两者之间的流传时间形成对比, 故改为however。

46. [答案] 去掉in the general中的the   [考点] 本题考查固定搭配。

[精析] in general是固定搭配, 意为"一般, 通常", 中间不加任何冠词, 故去掉the。

47. [答案] currently → current   [考点] 本题考查句子结构。

[精析] 分析句子结构可知, 本句主干是If a playground rhyme has been currently for..., 句子缺少谓语, 将currently改为current, 作be的表语。be current 意思是 "流行, 盛行"。

48. [答案] 在has后面加上been   [考点] 本题考查语态。

[精析] 句中的主语it指代的是a playground rhyme, 校园歌谣不能自己主动流传, 应是被流传, 故用被动语态。

49. [答案] live → alive   [考点] 本题考查形近词辨析。

[精析] live作形容词是"活的, 生动的"的意思, 一般作定语。alive和live意思差别不大, 但常作表语。remain"保持"是系动词, 后接表语。故改为alive。

50. [答案] 去掉to let alone中的to   [考点] 本题考查固定搭配。

[精析] let alone是固定搭配, 意思是"更别提, 更不用说"。它没有时态、语态和单复数变化, 在任何情况下都用原形。

Test 5

The desire to use language as a sign of national identity
is a very natural one, and in result language has played a   (41) _____
prominent part in national moves. Men have often felt the   (42) _____
need to cultivate a given language to show that they are
distinctive from another race whose hegemony they resent.   (43) _____
At the time the United States split off from Britain, for example,   (44) _____
there were proposals that independence should be linguistically accepted   (45) _____
by the use of a different language from those of Britain.   (46) _____
There was even one proposal that Americans should adopt
Hebrew. Others favoured the adoption of Greek, though,
as one man put it, things would certainly be simpler for Americans
if they stuck on to English and made the British learn Greek.   (47) _____
At the end, as everyone knows, the two countries adopted   (48) _____
the practical and satisfactory solution of carrying with   (49) _____
the same language as before.

Since nearly two hundred years now, they have shown the   (50) _____
world that political independence and national identity can be complete
without sacrificing the enormous mutual advantages of a common language.

真题点评

结构分析

第一句和第二句指出，人类总是想用一种独特的语言来展示他们与其他民族的不同。

第三句到第五句主要介绍美国试图采用与英国不同的语言来实现他们语言上的独立，以此来证明前两句的观点。

最后两句指出，美国最终采用了与英国一样的语言体现出两个国家语言的异同与他们政治独立和民族特征没有多大关联。

试题详解

41. [答案] one → thing   [考点] 本题考查代词。
    [精析] 本句的主干是the desire...is a very natural...，意思是"对……的渴望是一种很自然的……"，one只是代词，而前文没有可指代的东西，首次提到的事物应该用名词，故改为thing。

42. [答案] moves → movements　　　　[考点] 本题考查形近名词词义辨析。

[精析] moves作名词时是"移动"的意思，而这里应该是说"语言在民族运动中产生了重要作用"，故改为movements。

43. [答案] distinctive → distinct / different　　[考点] 本题考查形近形容词词义辨析。

[精析] distinctive是"特色的，显著的"的意思，而这里要表达的应该是"人类都认为有必要培养一门语言来显示他们与其他民族的不同"，且distinct / different...from构成固定搭配，是"与……不同"的意思，故改为distinct / different。

44. [答案] 在time后加上when　　　　[考点] 本题考查定语从句的关系副词。

[精析] the United States split off from Britain是the time的定语从句，the time为先行词，关系副词when不可省。

45. [答案] accepted → realized　　　　[考点] 本题考查句意理解。

[精析] accepted的对象是independence，"接受独立"从意义上讲不通，应该是"实现独立"，故改为realized。

46. [答案] those → that　　　　[考点] 本题考查代词。

[精析] ...a different language from those of Britain中的those指代的应该是language，而language是不可数名词，故应由单数指示代词that来指代，指代对象是复数时用those。

47. [答案] 去掉on　　　　[考点] 本题考查固定搭配。

[精析] 没有stick on to这个短语，只有stick on(粘在……上)和stick to(坚持)，这里明显应该是"坚持用英语"，故去掉on。

48. [答案] At → In　　　　[考点] 本题考查固定搭配。

[精析] 表达 "最后，最终" 一般用in the end。at the end 不可单独用，一般用at the end of...，故改为in。

49. [答案] carrying后加on　　　　[考点] 本题考查固定搭配。

[精析] carry with是"携带；进行"的意思，carry on with是"继续"的意思。原文应该是指"美国和英国继续使用相同的语言"，故加上on。

50. [答案] now → ago　　　　[考点] 本题考查词义理解。

[精析] 原文意为"自从两百年前"，而不是"自从两百年现在"，故改为ago。

Test 6

From what has been said, it must be clear that no one can make
very positive statements about how language originated. There is
no material in any language today and in the earliest records of   (41) _____
ancient languages show us language in a new and emerging state.   (42) _____
It is often said, of course, that the language originated in cries of   (43) _____
anger, fear, pain and pleasure, and the necessary evidence is   (44) _____
entirely lacking: there are no remote tribes, no ancient records,
providing evidence of a language with a large proportion of such   (45) _____
cries than we find in English. It is true that the absence of such
evidence does not disprove the theory, but in other grounds too the   (46) _____
theory is not very attractive. People of all races and languages
make rather similar noises in return to pain or pleasure. The fact   (47) _____
that such noises are similar on the lips of Frenchmen and
Malaysians whose languages are utterly different, serves to
emphasize on the fundamental difference between these noises and   (48) _____
language proper. We may say that the cries of pain or chortles of
amusement are largely reflex actions, instinctive to large extent,   (49) _____
whereas language proper does not consist of signs but of these that   (50) _____
have to be learnt and that are wholly conventional.

真题点评

结构分析

　　第一句和第二句指出没有相关的明确肯定的资料能够证明人类语言的起源。

　　第三句指出，一种理论认为人类的语言源于人类愤怒、恐惧、疼痛和喜悦时发出的声音，但是也缺乏相关的证据。

　　第四到第六句对第三句提到的理论进行分析，指出这一理论不仅缺乏证据也不合理。

　　最后一句话总结指出，对疼痛的呻吟声和咯咯的笑声都是人类的条件反射，但是语言是人类所学到的东西的载体，也是约定俗成的。

试题详解

41. ［答案］and → or　　　　　　　　　［考点］本题考查连词。

　　［精析］根据语义可知，该句是表达否定的含义，意为"在如今的语言中没有，在对

于古老语言最早的纪录中也没有"。并列结构中，or通常用于否定句，and通常用于肯定句。

42. [答案] show → showing　　　　　　[考点] 本题考查非谓语动词。
[精析] 本句结构是There is no material...show us..., 出现了两个谓语，应该用There be sth. + 分词句型。show的逻辑主语是material, 所以show应该用现在分词形式。

43. [答案] 去掉the　　　　　　　　　　[考点] 本题考查冠词。
[精析] 此处的language是泛指所有的语言，并不表示特指，因此不用定冠词，而language是不可数名词，也不用a, an修饰，故去掉the。

44. [答案] 第二个and → but　　　　　　[考点] 本题考查连词的运用。
[精析] and表示并列，but表示转折。前文提到语言可能源于人类在愤怒、恐惧、疼痛和喜悦时发出的声音，后文说缺乏必要的证据。显然，这里是转折关系，而不是并列关系，故改为but。

45. [答案] large → larger　　　　　　　[考点] 本题考查形容词的比较级。
[精析] 根据后文的than可知这里是将其他语言和英语进行比较，故要用比较级。

46. [答案] in → on　　　　　　　　　　[考点] 本题考查介词短语的搭配。
[精析] on other grounds意思是"根据其他理由"，介词不能用in。该句意思是"有其他理由也可以表明这一理论并不吸引人"。

47. [答案] return → response　　　　　　[考点] 本题考查固定短语的意思。
[精析] 原文大意为，各个民族、讲各种语言的人在对疼痛或者愉悦做出反应而发出的声音非常相似，由此可知in return to应该是"反应，回应"的意思，但没有in return to这个短语，只有in return for, 意思是"以……作为回报"。in response to才是"对……做出回应"的意思，故改为response。

48. [答案] 去掉on　　　　　　　　　　[考点] 本题考查动词。
[精析] emphasize是及物动词，后面可以直接接宾语，不用on，只有在emphasize的名词emphasis后面才用on，如：He concluded with emphasis on the environmental protection.

49. [答案] to后面加a　　　　　　　　　[考点] 本题考查固定搭配。
[精析] to a large extent意思是"在很大程度上"，a不可省略。

50. [答案] these → those　　　　　　　[考点] 本题考查并列一致原则。
[精析] 根据文章得知此处that引导了定语从句，而定语从句中作先行词的复数代词只能用those。

Test 7

We use language primarily as a means of communication with
other human beings. Each of us shares with the community in which we
live a store of words and meanings as well as agreeing conventions as   (41) _____
to the way in which words should be arranged to convey a particular   (42) _____
message; the English speaker has in his disposal a vocabulary and a   (43) _____
set of grammatical rules which enables him to communicate his   (44) _____
thoughts and feelings, in a variety of styles, to the other English   (45) _____
speakers. His vocabulary, in particular, both that which he uses actively
and that which he recognizes, increases in size as he grows
old, as a result of education and experience.   (46) _____

But, whether the language store is relatively small or large, the system
remains no more than a psychological reality for the individual, unless
he has a means of expressing it in terms able to be seen by another   (47) _____
member of his linguistic community; he has to give the system a
concrete transmission form. We take it for granted the two most   (48) _____
common forms of transmission—by means of sounds produced by our
vocal organs (speech) or by visual signs (writing). And these are   (49) _____
among most striking of human achievements.   (50) _____

真题点评

结构分析

　　第一段指出语言是人与人之间进行交流的工具，同一生活团体享有共同的词语和表达方式。随着人们教育程度和阅历的不断增加，他们的单词量也会增加。

　　第二段指出无论语言知识储备多少，人们传递情感的最主要方式就是说和写。这也是人类最引人注目的两大成就。

试题详解

41. ［答案］agreeing → agreed　　　　　　［考点］本题考查非谓语动词的用法。
　　［精析］as well as连接的是words and meanings和agreeing conventions，共同作介词of的宾语。agreeing应改为过去分词形式agreed作conventions的定语，表示"一致的，得到大家认定的习俗"。

42. ［答案］在words之前加the或those　　　［考点］本题考查限定词。
　　［精析］句中的words应该是指前文中的a store of words，因此应用the或those加以限定，以示强调。

221

43. [答案] in → at 　　　　　　　　　[考点] 本题考查固定搭配。
[精析] at one's disposal为固定搭配，意为"由某人支配"，与原文意思相符。

44. [答案] enables → enable 　　　　　　[考点] 本题考查主谓一致。
[精析] 关系代词which引导的定语从句，其先行词为a vocabulary and a set of grammatical rules，因此从句谓语动词应为动词原形enable。

45. [答案] 去掉other之前的the 　　　　　　[考点] 本题考查the other和other的区别。
[精析] the other后常接单数名词，特指两者中的"另一个"，因此此处应去掉the，直接用泛指的other(其他的)限定English speakers即可。

46. [答案] old → older 　　　　　　　　　[考点] 本题考查语义的理解。
[精析] 原句意为"他的词汇量……随着他年龄的增长而增加"，而年龄的增长是相对于过去而言的，暗含比较意味，因此应将old改为older。grow old意为"变老"，与原文不符。

47. [答案] seen → understood 　　　　　　[考点] 本题考查语篇的理解。
[精析] able to...为修饰terms(术语)的后置定语。用术语所表述的内容应该是被理解的，而不是被看到的，因此应将seen改为understood，也可改成perceived或comprehended。

48. [答案] 去掉take之后的it 　　　　　　　[考点] 本题考查代词的指代。
[精析] take...for granted意为"认为……是理所应当的"，句中被认为是理所应当的是the two most common forms of transmission，因此应去掉指代关系不明确的it。

49. [答案] or → and 　　　　　　　　　　[考点] 本题考查连词的意思。
[精析] or表选择关系，二者选其一；and则表并列，两者全选。原文句中提到两种最常见的表达形式，即说和写，因此应将or改为and。

50. [答案] 在most之前加the 　　　　　　　[考点] 本题考查形容词最高级的用法。
[精析] 形容词最高级前应用定冠词the加以限定，此处意为"人类成就中最为显著的"。

第一节 标准模拟题

语言类

【高分演练1】

Tracing missing persons can take much patient detective work. But
a special kind of "private eye" can trace the missing ancestors of whole
peoples by studying the clues buried by words. These philologists,
such as the language detectives are called, have traced the word trail
back from peoples in Europe, India, South Africa, the Americas, and the
Pacific islands in a tiny nameless, and forgotten tribe that roamed central
Eurasia 5,000 to 6,000 years ago, before the dawn of writing history.
Since a long time scholars puzzled over the striking difference of
words in different languages. In Dutch, vader; in Latin, pater; in old Irish,
athir; in Persian, pidar; in the Sanskrit of distant India, itr. These words
all sounded likely and meant the same thing—"father". Where did it
happen that widely separated peoples used such close related sound
symbols? The problem baffled linguists for years. The more so because
"father" was but one of a host of such coincidences. Towards the end
of the 18th century it dawned on scholars that perhaps all these words
stemmed from some common language.

(1) _____
(2) _____
(3) _____
(4) _____
(5) _____
(6) _____
(7) _____

(8) _____

(9) _____
(10) _____

【高分演练2】

Pronouncing a language is a skill. Every normal person is expert
with the skill of pronouncing his own language, but few people are even
moderately proficient at pronouncing foreign languages. There are many
reasons this, some obvious, some perhaps not so obvious. But I suggest
that the fundamental reason which people in general do not speak
foreign languages very much better than they do are that they never
fail grasp the true nature of the problem of learning to pronounce,

(1) _____

(2) _____
(3) _____
(4) _____
(5) _____

223

and consequently never set to tackling it in the right way. Far (6) _____
too many people fail to realize that pronouncing a foreign language
is a skill—one needs careless training of a special kind, (7) _____
and one that cannot be acquired by just leaving it to take care of
itself. I think even teachers of language, while recognizing the
importance of a good accent, tend to neglect, in their practical
teaching, the branch of study concerning with (8) _____
speaking the language. So the first point which I want to make is (9) _____
that English pronunciation must be taught; the teacher
should be prepared to devote some of the lesson time to this,
and by his whole attitude to the subject should get the student
to feel that here is a matter worthy receiving his close attention. (10) _____

【高分演练3】

I think it is true to saying that, in general, language teachers (1) _____
have paid little attention to the way sentences are used in combination
to form stretches of disconnected discourse. They have tended to take (2) _____
their cue from the grammarian and have concentrated to the teaching (3) _____
of sentences as self-contained units. It is true that these are often
represented in "contexts" and strung together in dialogues and
reading passages, but these are essentially setting to make the (4) _____
formal properties of the sentences stand out more clearly, properties
which are then established in the learner's brain by means of practice (5) _____
drill and exercises. Basically, the language teaching unit is the (6) _____
sentence as a formal linguistic object. The language teachers' view of
what that constitutes knowledge of a language is essentially the same (7) _____
as Chomsky's knowledge of a syntactic structure of sentences, (8) _____
and of the transformational relations which hold them. Sentences
are seen as paradigmatically rather than syntagmatically related.
Such a knowledge "provides the basis for the actual use of language
by the speaker-hearer". The assumption that the language appears to (9) _____
make is that once this basis is provided, then the learner will have no
difficulty in the dealing with the actual use of language. (10) _____

【高分演练4】

The changes in language will continue forever, but no one knows   (1) _____

sure who does the changing. One possibility is that children are

responsible. A professor of linguistic at the University of Hawaii,   (2) _____

explores this in one of his recent books. Sometimes around 1880, a   (3) _____

language catastrophe occurred in Hawaii when thousands of emigrant   (4) _____

workers were brought to the islands to work for the new sugar

industry. These people speaking different languages were unable to

communicate with each other or with the native Hawaiians or the

dominant English-speaking owners of the plantations. So they first

spoke in Pidgin English—the sort of thing such mixed language   (5) _____

populations have always done. A pidgin is not really a language at all.

It is more like a set of verbal signals used to name objects and   (6) _____

without the grammatical rules needed for expressing thought and

ideas. And then, within a single generation, the whole mass of mixed

people began speaking a totally new tongue: Hawaiian Creole. The   (7) _____

new speech was contained ready-made words borrowed from all the   (8) _____

original tongues, but beared little or no resemblance to the   (9) _____

predecessors in the rules used for stringing the words together.

Although generally regarded as primitive language, Hawaiian Creole   (10) _____

had a highly sophisticated grammar.

【高分演练5】

Scientific and learned English is not merely international

in using international words. English is frequently used nationally

for these purposes, as was pointed out in the previous chapter.

A scholar in Denmark or Poland or even a vast country as Russia   (1) _____

will today often write or at any rate publish in English, because his   (2) _____

work will thereby reach for a wider public. This does not mean that   (3) _____

such a scholar has a native-like knowledge of English. In fact, the

preface will usually acknowledge the help of someone who has

corrected and checked the English or even does a good deal of   (4) _____

translation. The scholar himself may be very poorly equipped to

speak English or even to write it, esp. on any subject than his own   (5) _____

field of interest. This is that is today called having a "restricted" or   (6) _____

"specialized" knowledge of English, and we have come to recognize
increasingly this limited degree of linguistic ability. Few people   (7) _____
have the time that is required to master a "full" knowledge of
a foreign language and few still would be to make the much   (8) _____
practical use of such a language. Indeed, as has already been
implied, even as native speakers we vary greatly in the amount   (9) _____
and variety of fields of discourse in where we feel at home.   (10) _____

【高分演练6】

Everyone knows that human language can be a superb means
of communication. Therefore, it can be damnably misleading   (1) _____
a barrier to people's understanding with each other, and never   (2) _____
more so than when names given for the ease of classification   (3) _____
are taken to mean more than they do. If, for instance, they say
that this man is white and that man coloured, we say no more
than truth as long as we understand that we are speaking only of
the colour of the skin. We can also make neutral and honest comments (4) _____
such as that "A" is above average height, has little than the average (5) _____
intelligence, is red-haired, is born in the north, and is left-handed.
The danger raises when we find other men who are white or coloured,   (6) _____
who are tall, stupid, red-haired, northerners, or sinister. It is
then we begin to correlate one fact with another and to make assumptions (7) _____
about other characteristics, which we believe are linked to the   (8) _____
features we first observe. So that when we talk about the white   (9) _____
or the coloured, we are apt to imply and believe that each adjective
tells us more about the person in the question than it can. We   (10) _____
are making them into portmanteau words into which we have
packed our hopes, our wishes, our prejudices and our fears.

【高分演练7】

How men first learnt to invent words is unknown; in other words,
the origin of language is a mystery. All we really know is that men,
unlike animals, somehow invented certain sound to express thought   (1) _____
and feelings, actions and things, so that they could communicate with
each other; and that later they agreed upon certain signs, calling letters, (2) _____
which could be combined to represent those sounds, and which could

be written. Those sounds, whether spoken or written in letters, we

call words. The power of words, then, lies in their associations—the

things they take up before our minds. Words become filled with meaning (4) _____

for us by experience; and the better we live, the more certain words recall (5) _____

to us the glad and sad events of our past; and the more we read and learn,

the more the number of words that mean something to us increase. Great (6) _____

writers are those who not only have great thoughts but also express these

thoughts in words which appeal powerfully for our minds and emotions. (7) _____

This charming use of words is what we call literary style. After all, the (8) _____

real poet is a master of words. He can convey his meaning in words which

sing like music, and which by their position and association can move

men with tears. We should therefore learn to choose our words carefully and (9) _____

use them accurately, or they will make our speech silly and dully. (10) _____

(3) _____

【高分演练8】

There is agreement among linguists who have considered the

situation over half of the world's languages are moribund, (1) _____

i.e. effectively being passed on to the next generation. We and our (2) _____

children, then, are living in the point in human history where, (3) _____

within perhaps two generations, most languages in the world will die out.

This mass extinction of languages may not appear immediate (4) _____

life-threatening. Some will feel that a reduction in numbers of languages

will ease communication, and perhaps helps build nations, even global (5) _____

solidarity. But there has been well pointed out that the success of humanity (6) _____

in colonizing the planet has been due to our ability to develop

cultures suit for survival in a variety of environments. These (7) _____

cultures have everywhere transmitted by languages, in oral (8) _____

traditions and latter in written literatures. So when language (9) _____

transmission itself breaks down, especially before the advent of

literacy in a culture, there is always a large loss of inherited knowledge.

Valued or not, that knowledge is lost, but humanity is the poorer. Along (10) _____

with it may go a large part of the pride and self-identity of the community

of former speakers.

【高分演练9】

After the year 1600, the British Empire began to spread English
around the world. That process was given a huge boost in the 20th century
through the business, technology and post-war re-construction effects   (1) _____
of the US. Beyond this, there were a number of quite extraordinary
trends in culture, science and the arts that were reinforced these developments. (2) _____
Many of these were spontaneous, but others were high deliberate—the   (3) _____
work of the British Council, for example. Either way, English now
stands challenged as the world's international language.   (4) _____

But the English language also has some inherent qualities that
enabled this process even far. English is a "mongrel language"   (5) _____
that has always borrowed heavily from the other languages. This has
allowed to grow quickly, flexibly, and efficiently. It has developed   (6) _____
spontaneously without an Academie Francaise to restrict it, for example, so   (7) _____
it has intended towards a simplification—from a more highly inflected   (8) _____
language towards becoming a less highly inflected one.

Therefore, almost every educated person in the entire world knows   (9) _____
some English. Very few people anywhere would not consider it essential   (10) _____
part of an education in science, art, business, etc. There's a pretty clear
dynamic at work here.

【高分演练10】

All of us have different styles of communicating with other people.
Our style depends on a lot of things: our educational background, our age,
and it also can depend on our gender.

The styles that men and women used to communicate have been described (1) _____
as "debate vs. relate", "report vs. rapport", or "competitive vs. cooperative".
Men often seek straightforward solutions with problems and useful advice   (2) _____
therefore women tend to try and establish intimacy by discussing problems   (3) _____
and show concern and empathy in order to reinforce relationships.   (4) _____

Jennifer Coates, in her book *Women, Men and Language,* studied
men-only and women-only discussion groups and found women   (5) _____
talk to each other they reveal a lot about their private lives. They also
stick on to one topic for a long time, let all speakers finish their sentences   (6) _____
and try to have everyone participate. Men, on the other hand, merely   (7) _____

228

talked about their personal relationships and feelings but compete to (8) _____

prove them better informed about current affairs, travel, sport, etc. (9) _____

The topics changed often and the men tried to, over time, establish

a reasonably stable hierarchy, with some men dominating

conversation and the others talking very little. (10) _____

【高分演练11】

Nonverbal communication is a process which communicators (1) _____

use the natural features of their bodies to deliver information

and express specific meaning instinctive to the other communicator. (2) _____

The study of nonverbal communication covers three major parts:

Proxemics, Kinesics and Body Language, and Paralanguage. (3) _____

Proxemics refers that people keep a certain space with each other (4) _____

when they communicate and the meaning it suggests. For example,

Arabians like to keep close while Englishmen like to keep a

certain distance. It is fun to see they are in conversation. (5) _____

Arabians will come closer and closer but Englishmen will

withdraw further and further. When they finish the conversation,

they are far from the place they stood. Kinesics is also called (6) _____

body language, that studies the meanings of the movement of (7) _____

all parts of body and it includes many nonverbal behavior such like (8) _____

eye language, gestures, postures, facial expressions, touch and

so on. Paralanguage refers to all kinds of sound signs made by (9) _____

mouth, which can express certain emotions and ideas. Paralanguage

is not the phrases and sentences with clear meanings. It is to transform

information by sound, such as "Ouch". Except this, the pitch of tone (10) _____

and loudness or quietness of voice also belongs to paralanguage.

And some researchers believe that clothing belongs to paralanguage, too.

【高分演练12】

Language change inevitably leads to variation, and variation

within a speech community often leads to social valuation of

particular features as "good" or "bad". "Good" variants are typically

believed to be characterized logical superiority or venerability, (1) _____

or either; "bad" variants must then be illogical and/or recent inventions (2) _____

by the vulgar.

But neither logic nor great age play a significant role in the　　　(3)＿＿＿＿
labeling of variants. Consider "ain't", which may be the English word
most is despised by schoolteachers and pundits. Far from being　　　(4)＿＿＿＿
logical or recent, "ain't" is a legitimate phonological descendant　　　(5)＿＿＿＿
of "amn't", which was the original contraction of "am not". It
isn't clear how "ain't" fell in disrepute, but once there, it left an　　　(6)＿＿＿＿
awkward gap in the system of negative contractions: We have
"You're going, aren't you?", "She's going, isn't she?", and so on,
but sure no real person actually says "I'm going, am I not?".　　　(7)＿＿＿＿
Instead, people say "I'm going, aren't I?", in the part because they　　　(8)＿＿＿＿
have been taught to avoid "ain't" like the plague; and here logic
shudders, because while "You are going, She is going," etc., are fine,
"I are going" is possible for native speakers of English. The point　　　(9)＿＿＿＿
of this example is not to urge rehabilitation of ain't—legislating
language change is generally a losing proposition—but to illustrating　　　(10)＿＿＿＿
the linguistically arbitrary nature of social valuation of the results
of language change.

【高分演练13】

Although China has one of the most ancient lexicographical
traditions, we know much about the etymology of the more recent　　　(1)＿＿＿＿
Chinese words. My goal in undertaking this study was therefore
to establish the entity and characteristic of lexical events　　　(2)＿＿＿＿
between 1840 and 1898, and show that Modern Chinese lexicon is
not simple the fruit of the linguistic experiments that took place　　　(3)＿＿＿＿
in context of the literary movements of the early 20th century　　　(4)＿＿＿＿
but in fact developed thanks both to its traditional base and to the
contribution of lexical inventions of the 19th century. With
the starting assumption that languages react external stimuli, I　　　(5)＿＿＿＿
drew particular attention to the impact on Chinese lexicon of　　　(6)＿＿＿＿
those works written by Chinese either by foreigners or by Chinese　　　(7)＿＿＿＿
in contact with foreigners, either in China or abroad. The impact
of western language on Chinese lexicon could only be direct,　　　(8)＿＿＿＿
and take place via the formation of semantic loans and
loan-translations, since Chinese has great difficulty absorb　　　(9)＿＿＿＿
phonemic loans. The impact of Japanese was far greater. Because　　　(10)＿＿＿＿

different in structural terms, to some extent Japanese and Chinese
share the same writing form.

【高分演练14】

Some people complain about the imprecise use of language.
If human language won't suffice for code information in the future   (1) _____
due to information density and speed and of course due to misunderstandings
(ambiguity) then the analogue language we have now might make away   (2) _____
for a digital language. Nowadays, everything is becoming digital.
Why not human language? Of course, I don't mean to changing human   (3) _____
language by prescription but by convention. Once human language
is digitized or replaced a digital language whether prescribed or   (4) _____
agreed on, not only ambiguity ends but also beauty and mysticism and
culture of human heritage. This means there will definite be   (5) _____
advantages of density, speed and clarity so I am afraid a lot of   (6) _____
disadvantages as I already mentioned will ensue. Foremost among
that is reduction. Digital data is compressed or zipped. Compression   (7) _____
means losing part of the information which is beyond human
perception. Furthermore, digitalization means reducing human language to   (8) _____
two modes, there is current or no current, a duality of yes and no
like vending machines or computers. It is always a win/lose situation.
This is an economic principle. Although I spend two hours on reading at home   (9) _____
I might lose two hours of conversation with my friends.
We have to make decision and set priorities.   (10) _____

社会类

【高分演练15】

In a competitive and fast-paced modern society, busy
business executives are so engrossing in their work   (1) _____
that they hardly know what the word "leisure" means.
The higher an executive's position is on the business ladder,
the more hours he spends on his work. With a view to gaining   (2) _____

greater corporate standing or a big pay rise, he, as a rule, far (3) _____
exceeds over the 40-hour working week. The additional stress (4) _____
and tension as well as the shortage of suitable rest and recreation
very often have a disastrous effect on his health. Few such executives
realize that unless they learn how to relax, they will soon run of stream (5) _____
before they get to the top of the executive ladder. A noted American
authority on leisure has said that "The key to relaxation to busy
executives is to avoid the types of activities that are part and parcel
of their daily work and to devote themselves totally to have recreational (6) _____
pursuits for at least a part of each day, even it is only for half an (7) _____
hour. Those jobs require a great deal of contact with others can (8) _____
engage in activities that are quiet and peaceful—far from the (9) _____
madding crowd, far from client and business associates." (10) _____

【高分演练16】

When John answered the doorbell recently, he was rather
astonished to see what he had purchased on the Internet only
two days before sitting on his doorstep. "I never expected to get (1) _____
my books so quickly," he told *Business Weekly*.

Tommy shared John's experience. He said online shopping
was very good and always offered comparatively lower prices than
ordinary retailer stores. Along with the rapidly developing (2) _____
IT industry, online shopping is attracting the interest of more
and more people.

The general manager of the Electronic Business Department
of Federal Software Co. Ltd., said online shopping had tremendous
market potential giving the large population. The company established (3) _____
an online shopping center for Internet surfers. More than 14,000 kinds
of goods are available, including computers, software, books and
daily necessity. Daily visitors to the site surged from10,000 in March (4) _____
to 30,000 in June, and that figure is likely to multiple. (5) _____

Industry experts say that because of the lack of appropriate payment
tools, online shopping is still at a primitive stage. The application of
online payment marks up a milestone for the development of the online (6) _____
industry. However, problems such as a limited pot of Internet users, (7) _____

comparatively high charges on Internet surfing and traditional views （8）_____
on shopping have hindered the development of online shopping.
Federal Software Co. Ltd. plans to invest U.S. $24 million on its （9）_____
shopping website. They are going to seek cooperation with domestic
and oversea companies to extend the variety of online products. （10）_____

【高分演练17】

　　The worst thing about television and radio is that it save us （1）_____
the trouble of entertaining ourselves. A hundred of years ago, before all （2）_____
these devices were invented, if a person wanted to entertain himself
by a song or a piece of music, he would have to do the singing （3）_____
himself or pick up a violin and play it. Now, all he has to do is turn （4）_____
the radio or TV. Today, we sing songs to our children until they are
about two; we read simple books to them till they are about five, so once （5）_____
they have learnt to read themselves, we become deaf. We're alive only
with the sound of the TV and the stereo. （6）_____

　　Before TV became so common, to keep children entertained, mothers had
to do a good number of singing and tell children endless tales. People spoke （7）_____
a language; they sang it; they recited it; it is something they could feel. （8）_____

　　Professional actors' performance is extraordinarily revealing, but I
still prefer my own reading, because it's mine. For the same reason, people
find karaoke liberated. It is almost the only electronic thing that gives them （9）_____
back their own voice. Even their voices are hopelessly out of tune, at least （10）_____
it is meaningful self-entertainment.

【高分演练18】

　　Office jobs are among the positions hardest hit by computation.
Word processors and typists will lose about 93,000 jobs the next （1）_____
few years, while 57,000 secretarial jobs will vanish. Today, many
executives type their own memos and carry their "secretaries" in the
palms of their hands. But not anyone who loses a job will end up （2）_____
in the unemployment line. Many will shift to grown positions （3）_____
within their own companies. When new technologies shook up the

telecom business, telephone operator Judy Dougherty pursued
retraining. She is now communications technician, earning about   (4) _____
$ 64,000 per year.

    To succeed in the new job market, you must be able to handle
complex problem. Indeed, all but one of the 50 highest-paying   (5) _____
occupations—air-traffic controller—demands at least a bachelor's degree.   (6) _____

    For those with just a high school diploma, it's going to get tougher
to find a well-paying job. Since less factory and clerical jobs will be   (7) _____
available, what's left will be the jobs that computation can't kill: computers
can't clean offices, or care Alzheimer's patients. But, since most people   (8) _____
have the skills to fill those positions, the wages stay painfully low, means   (9) _____
computation could drive an even deeper wedge between the rich and poor.
The best advice now: never stop learning, and keep with new technology.   (10) _____

【高分演练19】

    Thirty-one million Americans are over 60 years of age, and
twenty-nine million of them are health, busy, productive citizens.   (1) _____
By the year 2030, one of every five people in the United States will   (2) _____
be over 60. Older people are members of the fastest-growing majority   (3) _____
in this country. Many call this the "graying of America". In 1973, a
group called the "Gray Panthers" was organized. This group is made   (4) _____
of young and old citizens. They are trying to treat with the special   (5) _____
problems of growing old in America. The Gray Panthers know that
many elderly people have healthy problems: some cannot walk well; others   (6) _____
cannot see or hear well; some have financial problems—prices are going
up fast that the elderly can't afford the food, clothing, and housing they   (7) _____
need. Some old people are afraid and have safety problems. Others have
emotional problems. Many elderly are lonely because of the death of a
husband and a wife. The Gray Panthers know another fact, too. Elderly   (8) _____
people want to be as independent as possible. So, the Gray Panthers are
looking at ways to solve the special problems of the elderly. They   (9) _____
want to help elders to stay youthfully at heart.   (10) _____

【高分演练20】

    In a family where the roles of men and women are not sharply

234

separated and where many household tasks are shared in a greater or   (1) _____
lesser extent, notions of male superiority are hard to maintain. The
pattern of sharing in tasks and in decisions make for equality, and   (2) _____
this in turn leads to less sharing. If the process goes too far, man's   (3) _____
role will be regarded as less important—and that has happened in some
case. It is time to reassess the role of the man in the American family.   (4) _____
That we need is the recognition that bringing up children involves a   (5) _____
partnership of equals. There are signs that psychiatrists, psychologists,
social workers, and specialists of the family are becoming more aware   (6) _____
of the part men play and they have decided that women should not   (7) _____
receive all the credit—not all the blame. We have almost given up saying
that a woman's place is the home. We are beginning, therefore, to analyze   (8) _____
men's place in the home and to insist that he does have a place in it. The
family is a cooperative enterprise for which it is difficult to lay up   (9) _____
rules, because each family needs to work its own ways for solving its   (10) _____
own problems.

【高分演练21】

    The girls in this sixth grade class in East Palo Alto, California,
all have the same access to computers with boys, but researchers say,   (1) _____
by the time they get to high school, they are victims of what the
researchers call major new gender gap in technology. Janice   (2) _____
Weinman of the American Association of University Women says,
"Girls tend to be more comfortable than boys with the computer.   (3) _____
They use it more for word processing rather than for problem solving,
rather than to discover new ways which to understand information."   (4) _____
After re-examining a thousand studies, the American Association
of University Women researchers found that girls make up only a small
percentage of students in computer science classes. Girls consistent   (5) _____
rate themselves significantly lower than boys in their ability and
confidence in using computers. And they use computers often than   (6) _____
boys outside the classroom. An instructor of a computer lab says
he's already noticed some differences. Charles Cheadle of Cesar Chavez
School says, "Boys are not so afraid they might do something what   (7) _____
will harm the computer, whereas girls are afraid they might break it

anyhow." Six years ago, the software company Purple Moon noticed (8) _____
that girls' computer usage was falling after boys. Karen Gould says, (9) _____
"One reason girls told us they don't like computer games is not that
they're too violent, or too competitive. Girls just said they're incredible (10) _____
boring."

文化教育类

【高分演练22】

It may look like just another playgroup, and a unique (1) _____
educational center in Manhattan is really giving babies something
to talk about. "It's a school to teach languages to babies and
young children by games, songs—some of the classes also have (2) _____
arts and crafts," said Francois Thibaut, the founder of the Language
Workshop for Children, a place babies become bilingual. (3) _____

Children as young as few months are exposed to French and
Spanish after many of them can even speak English. Educators use (4) _____
special songs and visual aids to ensure that when a child is ready to
talking, the languages will not be so foreign. "Children have a unique (5) _____
capacity to learn many languages at the same time," said Thibaut.
"Already at nine months, a child can say the differences between (6) _____
the sounds he or she has heard since birth and the sounds he or she
never heard yet." Thibaut says the best time to expose children (7) _____
to language is from birth to 3 years old. For the last 30 years, the
school has been using what it calls the Thibaut Technique, a system
that combines language lessons to child's play. (8) _____

Depending on the age group, classes run from 45 minutes up to
2 hours. Even when students are not in class, the program is designed
to make sure the learning continue at home. Tapes and books are (9) _____
including so kids can practice on their own. (10) _____

【高分演练23】

Although all the arts are essentially autonomous, owing to
the different materials and techniques which they employ with, there (1) _____
is clearly a kind of bond between them. We speak of the "architecture"

of a symphony, and call architecture, in return, "frozen music".　　(2)＿＿＿＿＿

Again, we say that certain writing has a "sculptural" quality,

and sometime describe a piece of sculpture as "a poem in stone".　　(3)＿＿＿＿＿

　　Admittedly, much of the phraseology which traffic between　　(4)＿＿＿＿＿

the arts is pure metaphorical, being concerned only with the　　(5)＿＿＿＿＿

effect of a work of art. Thus, in calling a statue "a poem in stone",

we merely indicate that its effect on us is that impalpable kind we　　(6)＿＿＿＿＿

normally receive from poetry; we do not make an objective statement

about the sculptor's intention or technical procedure. Such a metaphor,

while useful descriptive purposes, cannot help us to gain a deeper　　(7)＿＿＿＿＿

understanding of the nature of art.

　　On the other hand, comparison between one art and another cannot　　(8)＿＿＿＿＿

help towards this end, when the comparison is not metaphorical, but

analogical, being concerned with the artist's intention and technical

procedure. Thus, when we speak of the "architecture" of a fugue, we are

taking an objective statement that its composer has constructed it by methods　　(9)＿＿＿＿＿

analogous to those of the Architect—that he has grouped masses of

non-representational material (tone instead of stone) into significant

form, governing by the principles of proportion, balance, and symmetry;　　(10)＿＿＿＿＿

and this throws some light on a particular type of music.

【高分演练24】

　　Parkour is a physical activity that is difficult to categorize.

It is often mis-categorized as a sport and an extreme sport; however,　　(1)＿＿＿＿＿

parkour has no set of rules, team work, formal hierarchy, or

competitiveness. Most experienced practitioners think of parkour a　　(2)＿＿＿＿＿

discipline closer to martial arts. According to David Belle, "the

physical aspect of parkour is going over all the obstacles in　　(3)＿＿＿＿＿

your path as you would be in an emergence. You want to move in　　(4)＿＿＿＿＿

such a way, with any movement, as to help you gain the most

ground on someone or something, whether escaping from it or

chasing toward it." Thus, when faced with a hostile confrontation

with a person, one will be able to speak, fight, or flee. As if martial arts　　(5)＿＿＿＿＿

are a form of training for the fight, parkour is a form of training

for the flight. Because of its uniquely nature, it is often said that parkour　　(6)＿＿＿＿＿

is in its own category.

　　A characteristic of parkour is efficiency. Practitioners move not only as rapidly as they can, but also in the most direct and effective way (7) _____

possible; a characteristic that distinguishes from the similar practice (8) _____

of free running, which places more emphasis in freedom of movement, (9) _____

such as acrobatics. Efficiency also involves avoid injuries, short and (10) _____

long-term, part of why parkour's unofficial motto is to be and to last.

【高分演练25】

In social situations, the classic Intention Movement is "the
chair-grasp". Host and guest have been talking for some time,

but now the host has an appointment to keep and can get away. (1) _____

His urge to go is held in check by his desire not be rude to his (2) _____

guest, if he did not care of his guest's feelings he would simply (3) _____

get up out of his chair and to announce his departure. This is (4) _____

what his body wants to do, therefore his politeness glues his body (5) _____

to the chair and refuses to let him raise. It is at this point that he (6) _____

performs the chair-grasp Intention Movement. He continues to
talk to the guest and listen to him, but leans forward and grasps

the arms of the chair as about to push himself upwards. This is (7) _____

the first act he would make if he were rising . If he were not (8) _____

hesitating, it would only last the fraction of the second. He would (9) _____

lean, push, rise, and be up. But now, instead, it lasts much longer.

He holds his "readiness-to-rise" post and keeps on holding it. It is (10) _____

as if his body had frozen at the get-ready moment.

【高分演练26】

Gestures aren't the only area in which the unwary traveler can

get tripped up. Foreign cultures adhere different business customs (1) _____

and behavior. For example: Caffeine junkies should restrain them (2) _____

in the Middle East. "Three cups of tea or coffee is usually the polite

limit in offices and during social calls," counsel "Travel Pak," a (3) _____

free publication of Alia, the Royal Jordanian Airline. "And if your host (4) _____

keeps going, you also may continue sipping. If you've had your fill,
give your empty cup a quick twist—a sort of wiggle—as you hand it
back. That means "No more, thank you."

Middle East visitors also should be surprised "if others barge (5) _____

right into the office in the middle of your conversation with the

person you are seeing," notes "Travel Pak." An old Arab custom
calls for keeping an "open office."

The British, however, consider it impolite to interrupt into a visitor,   (6) _____
even after all business has been transacted. The commercial caller
is expected to be sensible to this point, know when to stop, and initiate   (7) _____
his or her own departure.

In Japan certain guests at evening business gatherings will
leave early. They should be allowed to leave with effusive good-   (8) _____
byes. The Japanese consider formal departures to be disruptive in
such cases and disturbing to remain guests.   (9) _____

In the Arab world, the word "no" must be mentioned three
times before it is accepted. On contrast, it is considered good business   (10) _____
manners to make many and long efforts to pick up the check.

【高分演练27】

Normally a student must attend a certain number of courses
in order to graduate, and each course which he attends and gives him a   (1) _____
credit which he may count towards a degree. In many American universities
the total work for a degree consists of thirty-six courses each lasts for   (2) _____
one semester. A typical course consists of three classes per week for fifteen
weeks; while attend a university, a student will probably attend four or   (3) _____
five courses during each semester. Normally a student would expect to
take four years attending two semesters each year. It is possible to spread
the period of work for the degree over a long period. It is also possible   (4) _____
for a student to move between one university and another during his degree
course, though this is not in fact done for a regular practice.   (5) _____

For every course that he follows a student is given a grade, which is
recorded, and the record is available for the student to show to prospective
employers. All this imposes a constant pressure and strain of work, and   (6) _____
in spite of this some students still find time for great activity in student
affairs. Elections to positions in student organizations arise much enthusiasm.   (7) _____
The efficient word of maintaining discipline is usually performed by students   (8) _____
who advise the academic authorities. Any student who is thought to
have broken the rules, for example, by cheating, have to appear before   (9) _____
a student court. With the enormous numbers of students, the operation
of the system does involve a certain number of activity. A student   (10) _____

who has held one of these positions of authority is much respected and it will be of benefit to him later in his career.

【高分演练28】

Whenever you see the old film, even one made as early (1) _____
as ten years ago, you can't help be stuck by the appearance (2) _____
of the woman taking part. Their hair-styles and make-up look dated;
their shirts look either too long nor too short; their general appearance is, (3) _____
in, fact, slightly ludicrous. The men taking part in the film, on the other hand, are
clearly recognizable. There is something about their appearance to suggest (4) _____
that they belong to an entirely different age. This illusion is created by changed (5) _____
fashions. Over the years, the great majority of men has successfully resisted (6) _____
all attempts to make them to change their style of dress. The same cannot (7) _____
be said for women. Each year a few so-call "top designers" in Paris and (8) _____
London lay down on the law and women over the whole world run to (9) _____
obey. The decrees of the designers are unpredictable and dictatorial.
This year, they decide in their arbitrary fashion—skirts will be short and
waists will be height; zips are in and buttons are out. Next year the law (10) _____
is reversed and far from taking exception; however, no one is even mildly surprised.

政治经济类

【高分演练29】

Until the coming of the Industrial Revolution, science and
technology evolved for the most part independently of each other.
Then as industrialization became increasingly complicated, the craft
techniques of preindustrial society gradually gave to a technology (1) _____
based on the systematic application of scientific knowledge and
science methods. This changeover started slowly and progressed (2) _____
evenly. Until late in the nineteenth century, only a few industries (3) _____
could use scientific techniques or cared of using them. The list (4) _____
expanded noticeably after 1870, but even then much of what passed
for the application of science was "engineering science" rather than
basic science. Nevertheless, by the middle of the nineteenth century,
the rapid expansion of scientific knowledge and of public awareness—if

not understanding—it had created a belief that the advance of   (5) _____

science would in some unspecified manner automatically generate

economic benefits. The widespread and usual uncritical acceptance   (6) _____

of this thesis led in turn to the assumption that the application of

science with industrial purposes was a linear process, starting with   (7) _____

fundamental science, then proceeding to applying science or technology,   (8) _____

and through them to industrial use. This is probably the most common

pattern, but it is not invariable. New areas of science have opened   (9) _____

up and fundamental discoveries made as a result of attempts to solve

a specific technical or economic problem. In sum, the science-technology-

industry relationship may flow in several different way, and the   (10) _____

particular channel it will follow depends on the individual situation.

【高分演练30】

The digital revolution, as exemplified by the Internet and

electronic commerce, has shaken marketing practices in their core.   (1) _____

In a recent paper, Wharton's Jerry Wind, director of the SEI Center

for Advanced Studies in Management, and author Vijay Mahajan,   (2) _____

a marketing professor at the College of Business Administration of

the University of Texas at Austin, examines the impact of digital   (3) _____

marketing on concepts like pricing, when customers can propose their

own prices, or buyers and sellers can haggle independent in auctions.   (4) _____

The paper provides an overview of some of the emerging realties and

new rules of marketing in a digital world, and outlines the new   (5) _____

discipline of marketing may look like in the early part of the new century.

To begin with, say the authors, the rapid-fire growth of the Internet is

helping to drive changes. "It is not just our computers which are being   (6) _____

reprogrammed; it is customers themselves," says Wind. "These emerging

cyber consumers are like an alien race that have landed in the midst   (7) _____

of our markets. They have different expectations and different relationships

with companies from that they purchase products and services."   (8) _____

Cyber consumers expect to be able to customize everything—from the

products and services they buy and the information they seek, the price   (9) _____

they are willing to pay. And with digital technology open new channels   (10) _____

for gaining information, they are more knowledgeable and demanding than

previous consumers.

【高分演练31】

The largest stock market in the world is the New York Stock
Exchange. It is also the oldest financial market in the United States.
Its history dates to 1792. Today, two-thousand-eight hundred companies   (1)＿＿＿＿
trade their shares at the New York Stock Exchange. Together, the value   (2)＿＿＿＿
of those stocks is almost fifteen-million-million dollars. These
companies are all public traded. That means any investor can buy their   (3)＿＿＿＿
stock. A foreign company can trade on the New York Stock Exchange by
placing some of its shares in a bank. An American Depositary Receipt is
giving in place of the stock, and can be traded on the exchange. About   (4)＿＿＿＿
four-hundred-seventy companies from fifty-one other nations are
represented on the New York Stock Exchange.

Stock is share in the ownership of a company. Debt is also traded   (5)＿＿＿＿
on the exchange. Bonds are generally sold in amount of one-thousand   (6)＿＿＿＿
dollars or more. Companies and governments sell bonds as a way to
borrow money. Buyers earn interest as they wait for the bonds to reach
full value. Bonds can be resold or divided.   (7)＿＿＿＿

The New York Stock Exchange is owned by its members. It has
more than one-thousand-three-hundred members. It have the right   (8)＿＿＿＿
to buy and sell securities on the trading floor, for other investors or for
them. A membership is traditionally called a seat. These can   (9)＿＿＿＿
also be bought and sold. Memberships have sometime sold for more   (10)＿＿＿＿
than two-million dollars.

【高分演练32】

The fiscal year for the United States government starts on October
first and ends September thirtieth. Other fiscal years begin in April or July.
The American Institute of Certified Public Accountants begin its fiscal year   (1)＿＿＿＿
on August first. Accountants add earnings and losses at the end of a fiscal   (2)＿＿＿＿
year. These numbers are needed to know how much is owed for taxes, and
how much is left for the next budget. Congress is supposing to approve   (3)＿＿＿＿
federal spending for the coming fiscal year by October first. This does not
always happen. Both the House of Representatives or the Senate must   (4)＿＿＿＿
write and vote for their own budget resolution. This is a general plan for   (5)＿＿＿＿
spending. Then, a conference committee meet. Members from both houses   (6)＿＿＿＿
are on this committee. They approve a final budget resolution which goes to

242

a vote in both houses. But this is not the end of the process. Committees in
both houses must also approve the exact number of money for each program.　(7) _____
This is called appropriations. Below the committees are subcommittees that　(8) _____
make decisions about areas alike education and defense. Bills to permit　(9) _____
spending then go to the full House and Senate for a vote. The appropriations
process often takes place at the same time if the budget resolution process.　(10) _____

【高分演练33】

　　Could the bad old days of economic decline be about to return?
Since OPEC agreed to supply-cuts in March, the price of crude oil　(1) _____
jumped to almost $26 a barrel, up from less than $10 last December.
This near-tripling of oil prices calls for scary memories of the 1973　(2) _____
oil shock, when prices quadrupled, and 1979~80, when they also
almost tripled. All previous shocks resulted in double-digitinflation　(3) _____
and global economic decline. So where the headlines warning of　(4) _____
gloom and doom this time?

　　The oil price was given another push up this week when Iraq
suspended oil exports. Strengthen economic growth, at the same　(5) _____
time as winter grips the northern hemisphere, could push the price
higher still at the short term.　(6) _____

　　Yet there are good reasons to expect the economic consequences
now to be less severe than in the 1970s. In most countries the cost of
crude oil now accounts for a small share of the price of petrol than it　(7) _____
did in the 1970s. In Europe, taxes account for to four-fifths of the　(8) _____
retail price, as even quite big changes in the price of crude have a　(9) _____
more muted effect on pump prices than in the past. Rich economies
are also more dependent on oil than they were, and so less sensitive to　(10) _____
swings in the oil price.

【高分演练34】

　　The entrepreneur, according to French economist J.B. Say, "is
a person who shifts economic resources out of an area of lower and
from an area of higher productivity and yield." But Say's definition　(1) _____
does not tell us who this entrepreneur is. Some define the entrepreneur
simple as one who starts his or her own new and small business. For　(2) _____
our purposes, we will define the entrepreneur as a person who takes the

necessary risks to organize and manage a business and receives the
financial profits and nonmonetary reward. (3) _____

    The man who opens a small pizza restaurant is of business, but (4) _____
is he an entrepreneur? He took a risk and did something, but did he
shift resources or started the business? If the answer is yes, then he is (5) _____
considered an entrepreneur. Ray Kroc is an example of an entrepreneur
because he founded and established McDonald's. His hamburgers
were not a new idea, and he applied new techniques, resource allocations, (6) _____
and organizational methods in his venture. Ray Kroc upgraded the
productivity and yield from the resources applying to create his fast-food (7) _____
chain. This is what entrepreneurs do; this is what entrepreneurship
means.

    Entrepreneurs exhibit similar behaviors; searching for a (8) _____
specific personality pattern is very difficult. Some entrepreneurs are
quiet, introverted, and analytical. At the other hand, some are brash, (9) _____
extroverted, and very emotional. Many of them share some qualities.
Viewing change as the norm, entrepreneurs usually search for it, respond
to it, and treat it as opportunity. (10) _____

【高分演练35】

    The ways of history are so intricate and the motivations of human actions
so complex that it is always hazardous to attempt to represent events cover (1) _____
a number of years, a multiplicity of persons, and distant localities as the
expression of one intellectual and social movement; yet the historical process (2) _____
which culminates in the ascent of Thomas Jefferson to the presidency (3) _____
can be regarded as the outstanding example not only of the birth of a new
way of life but also nationalism as a new way of life. The American Revolution (4) _____
represents the link between the seventeenth century, in which modern England
became conscious of itself, and the awakening of modern Europe in the (5) _____
end of the eighteenth century. It may seem strange that the march of history
should have to cross the Atlantic Ocean, but only in the North American (6) ____
colonies a struggle for civic liberty lead also to the foundation of a new (7) ____
nation. Here, in the popular rising for a "tyrannical" government, the fruits (8) _____
were more than the securing of a free constitution. They included the growth (9) _____
of a nation born in liberty by the will of the people, not from the roots
of common descent, a geographic entity, or the ambitions of king or dynasty.

With the American nation, in the first time, a nation was born, not in the (10) _____
dim past of history but before the eyes of the whole world.

科普类

【高分演练36】

The second most important constituent of the biosphere is
liquid water. This can only exist in a very narrow range of
temperatures, since water freezes at 0℃ and boils at 100℃. This is
only a tiny range compared with the low temperatures of some other
planets and the hot interior of the earth, let the temperature of the sun. (1) _____
As we know, life would only be possible on the face of a planet (2) _____
had temperatures somewhere within this range. The earth's supply (3) _____
of water probably remains quite fairly constant in quantity. A certain (4) _____
number of hydrogen atoms, which are one of the main constituents
of water, are lost by escaping from the atmosphere to out space, (5) _____
but they are probably just about replaced by new water rising away (6) _____
from the depths of the earth during volcanic action. The total quantity
of water is not known, and it is about enough to cover the surface of (7) _____
the globe to a depth of about two and three-quarter kms.

Most of it—97%—is in the form of the salt waters of the oceans.
The rest is fresh, but three quarter of this is in the form of ice at the (8) _____
Poles and on mountains, and cannot be used by living systems
when melted. Of the remaining fraction, which is somewhat (9) _____
fewer than 1% of the whole, there is 10-20 times as much stored as (10) _____
underground water as is actually on the surface. There is also a minor,
but extremely important, fraction of the water supply which is present
as water vapor in the atmosphere.

【高分演练37】

Vitamins, like minerals, are chemicals. There is absolutely not (1) _____
difference in the chemical structure of the (2) _____
nature vitamin C and the chemical structure of the synthetic (3) _____
vitamin C. Also, while most substances are harmless
at very low level of intake, all substance—even the elements (4) _____

that are essential to life—can be dangerous if you overdo
them. Take water for example. Six or eight glasses a day
will keep your body in good fluid balance. But you can also
be drown in it. Some people argue that individuals vary greatly
in their need for nutrients, it cannot necessarily be stated any   (5) _____
given amount is too much; that is all relative. But since
there is little solid information on what is the optimal intake
of any essential nutrient in healthy individuals, it would   (6) _____
be impossible to give guidelines that take these proportional
needs into the account. Just as with other drugs, the   (7) _____
relation to different vitamin dosages varies, with some people
better able than others to tolerate large amounts. While we do   (8) _____
know that very specifically what the toxic level is for   (9) _____
vitamins A and D, we are far less sure about vitamin E, even
though it, too, is fat-soluble, and we still don't understand the
water-soluble vitamin, the C and the B groups, which the body   (10) _____
can't store.

【高分演练38】

　　Because the air in the country is really clean, we ought to live
there much as possible. Since, however, a great deal of the world's   (1) _____
work must be done indoor in cities, it is important that we take every   (2) _____
precaution to ventilate our houses properly. Some people have
thought that night air is injurious. But careful study shows that night
air is identical with which we breath during the day. In fact the   (3) _____
proper ventilation of a bedroom is one of the first necessity for good   (4) _____
health. Since the exhaled air is usually warmer and lighter than the
inhaled air, it rises to the top of the room. Therefore it is better to
open a window both at the top to let the warm up air out and also at   (5) _____
the bottom to admit the fresh air in. Of course, this does not mean   (6) _____
that one should sleep in a strong draft. In many places it is feasible to
sleep out-of-the-doors on a sleeping porch and so to secure perfect   (7) _____
ventilation.

　　In recent years we have seen steady progress made in the development
of equipments to supply proper conditioned air not only in large   (8) _____
auditoriums, class-rooms, and factories, but also in railroad trains
and in private homes. This equipment cleans the air off dust, keeps   (9) _____

the temperature comfortable, holds the humidity at the right point,
and keeps the air in the motion. Such a condition is conductive to   (10) _____
efficiency as well as good health.

【高分演练39】

Fear and its companion pain are two of the most useful thing that   (1) _____
men and animals possess, if they are properly used. If fire did not hurt
when it burn, children would play with it until their hands were burnt away. (2) _____
Similarly, if pain existed but fear did not, a child would burn itself again
and again, because fear would not warn it to keep away the fire   (3) _____
that had burnt it before. A really fearless soldier—and some do exist—is
not a good soldier so he is soon killed, and a dead soldier is of no   (4) _____
use to his army. Fear and pain are therefore two guards with which   (5) _____
men and animals might soon die out. In our first sentence we suggested
that fear ought to be properly used. If, for example, you never go out of
your house because the danger of being knocked down and killed in   (6) _____
the street by a car, you are letting fear rule you too much. Even in your
house you are not absolute safe: an airplane may crash on your house,   (7) _____
or ants may eat away some of the beams in your roof so that the later falls (8) _____
on you, or you may get cancer! The important thing is not let fear rule   (9) _____
you, but instead to use fear as your servant and guide. Fear will warn
you of dangers; then you have to decide what action to make.   (10) _____

【高分演练40】

Chemistry is the study of the behavior and composition
of matter. All foods are made up of chemical substance which
undergoes chemical changes when cooking in an oven or   (1) _____
digested within the body. The cooking of meat and vegetables
induce chemical changes, making it more delicious; similarly   (2) _____
the leaving action of baking powder is a straightforward
chemical change, as is the conversion of starch into sweet
sugars by digestion. Cookery is a science requiring   (3) _____
for knowledge of chemistry. This is evident from the variety   (4) _____
of cooking products and food additives available as cooking   (5) _____
oils, fats, colorings, sweeteners, tenderizers, flavorings,
screaming agents, preservatives, etc. Each is carefully

prepared before painstaking research. It is therefore essential   (6) _____

for trained cookers to understand chemical science in order to   (7) _____

appreciate the chemistry nature of foods and the changes   (8) _____

achieving on cooking. Homeworkers should also know   (9) _____

cleansing agents and textiles used in the home and how   (10) _____

the latter responds to the effects of heat, light, water, and

chemical cleansing agents.

第二节 答案精析

语言类

【高分演练1】

文章精要

　　文章指出，语言学者通过研究文字的起源来确定人类的祖先。在几种不同的语言中，意为"父亲"的单词发音相近，这很可能意味着那几个单词起源于同一种语言。

答案精析

1. ［答案］whole → all
   ［精析］原文想要表达的是"所有人种"，因此应将意为"整体的"的whole改成意为"所有的"的all。

2. ［答案］第二个by → in
   ［精析］原文想要表达的是"研究掩藏在文字中的线索"，因此将介词by改为in。

3. ［答案］去掉such
   ［精析］原文想要表达的是"语言学者是人们对语言侦探的称呼"，其中并不包含"例如"（such as）的概念，因此去掉such。

4. ［答案］去掉back
   ［精析］原文想要表达的是"从欧洲、印度……太平洋诸岛的民族追溯文字的踪迹"，因此去掉back。

5. ［答案］in → to
   ［精析］trace...to sth.为固定搭配，意为"找出……的根源"，与原文相符，因此将名词短语a tiny...tribe之前的介词in改为to。

6. ［答案］writing → written
   ［精析］written history为固定搭配，意为"有文字记载的历史"，与原文相符，因此将writing改为written。

7. ［答案］Since → For
   ［精析］用于引导一段时间的应该是介词for而非since，since后面经常接一个时间点。

8. ［答案］likely → alike
　　［精析］原文想要表达的是"所有这些单词发音都很像"，因此将意为"很可能"的likely改成意为"相似地"的alike。

9. ［答案］在baffled之前加has
　　［精析］原文想要表达的是"这个问题已经困扰了语言学家很多年"，应该采用现在完成时，因此在动词baffled之前加上助动词has。

10. ［答案］Towards → At
　　［精析］原文想要表达的应该是一个时间点，即"18世纪末"，因此将表示倾向的towards改为at。

【高分演练2】

（文章精要）

　　文章指出，语言发音是一门技巧，需要通过学习而获得，因此想要学会英语发音，就需要教师花时间来教授发音的技巧。

（答案精析）

1. ［答案］with → in
　　［精析］be expert in sth.为固定搭配，意为"擅长某事物"，因此将介词with改为in。

2. ［答案］在reasons之后加for
　　［精析］名词reason常与介词for搭配，表示"……的原因"，因此此处要加上介词for。

3. ［答案］which → why
　　［精析］以名词reason为先行词的定语从句通常用关系副词why来引导，因此将which改为why。

4. ［答案］are → is
　　［精析］原文想要表达的是"人们说不好外语的根本原因是……"，该部分的主语是单数名词reason，因此系动词要用is，而非are。

5. ［答案］在fail之后加to
　　［精析］动词fail通常接动词不定式作宾语，因此要在两个动词fail和grasp之间加上to。

6. ［答案］在set后加about
　　［精析］set about为固定搭配，意为"开始，着手"，与原文刚好相符。

7. ［答案］careless → careful

［精析］原文想要表达的是"许多人没有意识到外语发音是一种技巧，需要进行特殊的仔细训练"，因此应将意为"粗心的"的careless改成意为"仔细的"的careful。

8. ［答案］concerning → concerned

［精析］be concerned with为固定搭配，意为"关于"，be作名词的后置定语时相当于（which is）concerned with，因此此处将concerning改为concerned。

9. ［答案］which → that

［精析］先行词中如果出现序数词first，定语从句的关系代词就要用that而非which。

10. ［答案］在worthy之后加of

［精析］worthy of为固定搭配，意为"值得的，应得的"，与原文相符。

【高分演练3】

文章精要

文章指出，语言教师大多不注意句子的构成，但实际上句子是语言教学的语言学对象，与句子构成有关的知识有助于学生更好地在实际中运用语言。

答案精析

1. ［答案］saying → say

［精析］此处的to为不定式的标志词，因此后面应该接动词原形，故将saying改为say。

2. ［答案］disconnected → connected

［精析］原文想要表达的是"句子组合构成连贯的表达"，因此将意为"不连贯的"的disconnected改成意为"有联系的"的connected。

3. ［答案］to → on

［精析］concentrate on为固定搭配，意为"集中，全神贯注于"，与原文相符。

4. ［答案］setting → set

［精析］set与these应为被动关系，因此将setting改为set。

5. ［答案］brain → mind

［精析］原文想要表达的是抽象的"思维"概念，而非具体的"大脑"概念，因此将brain改为mind。

6. ［答案］drill → drills

［精析］并列连词and连接的应该是形式并列的两个部分，因此可数名词drill应该

和之后的exercises一样采用复数形式。

7. ［答案］去掉that

［精析］原文想要表达的是"语言教师对构成语言知识的内容的看法"，其中what可以理解为all that，因此去掉表意重复的that。

8. ［答案］去掉a

［精析］原文想要表达的是"乔姆斯基有关句子的句法结构的知识"，因此应去掉表泛指的不定冠词a。

9. ［答案］在language之后加teacher

［精析］原文想要表达的是"语言教师想要提出的假设是一旦学生们被提供该基础，那么他们在语言的实际应用上就不会有困难"，因此在language之后加上teacher。

10. ［答案］去掉dealing之前的the

［精析］have difficulty in doing sth.为固定搭配，意为"做某事有困难"，因此去掉现在分词dealing之前的定冠词the。

【高分演练4】

文章精要

文章指出，语言总是在改变。研究表明，19世纪80年代夏威夷地区夏威夷克利奥尔语的出现是不同语言融合的结果。

答案精析

1. ［答案］在sure之前加for

［精析］原文想要表达的是"没有人确切知道是谁做出的改变"，因此在sure之前加上for构成固定搭配for sure，表示"确定地；确切地"。

2. ［答案］linguistic → linguistics

［精析］原文想要表达的是"语言学教授"，因此将形容词linguistic改成意为"语言学"的名词linguistics。

3. ［答案］Sometimes → Sometime

［精析］原文想要表达的是"19世纪80年代的某一时期"，因此将意为"有时"的sometimes改成意为"在某一时间"的sometime。

4. ［答案］emigrant → immigrant

［精析］原文想要表达的是"数千名被带到岛上的外来工人"，因此将意为"移居外国者"的emigrant改成意为"（从外国）移民来的"的immigrant。

5. ［答案］去掉spoke之后的in
   ［精析］speak在表示说某种语言时为及物动词，因此去掉后面的介词in。

6. ［答案］and → but
   ［精析］原文中的"它更像是一系列用于称呼物品的口头信号"和"没有表达想法所需的语法规则"应为转折关系，因此将表并列的and改为表转折的but。

7. ［答案］people → peoples
   ［精析］people在意为"民族，人种"时为可数名词，因此此处应该用复数形式peoples。

8. ［答案］去掉was
   ［精析］speech和contain之间应为主动关系，因此去掉两者之间的系动词was。

9. ［答案］beared → bore
   ［精析］bear是不规则动词，其过去式为bore，而非beared。

10. ［答案］在as之后加a
    ［精析］language为可数名词，因此应在as之后加上不定冠词a，用来限定夏威夷克里奥尔语(Hawaiian Creole)这种原始的语言。

【高分演练5】

文章精要

文章指出，英语是国际性语言，但现在以英语为外语的人，大多只了解并擅长使用特定领域范围内的英语，那些以英语为母语的人甚至也是如此。

答案精析

1. ［答案］在even之后加such
   ［精析］原文想要表达的是"像俄罗斯这样大的国家"，因此应该用such...as...来表示。

2. ［答案］because → so
   ［精析］原文中的"丹麦、波兰或俄罗斯的学者常用英语写作或发表作品"和"他的作品将会有更广泛的受众"之间应该是因果关系，前者是因，后者是果，因此将because改为so。

3. ［答案］去掉for
   ［精析］短语reach for意为"够到某事物"，而原文想要表达的是"到达更广泛的公众那里"，因此直接用reach即可。

4. ［答案］does → done

［精析］原文想要表达的是"某人已经修改或检查过英语，甚至是做了很多翻译"，其中corrected, checked和does应该是并列关系，因此将does改为过去分词形式done，和之前的助动词has一起表示现在完成时。

5. ［答案］any → other

［精析］other...than...为固定搭配，意为"与……不同的……, ……之外的……"，与原文相符，因此将any改为other。

6. ［答案］that → what

［精析］该句是表语从句，因此关系代词应该是有实际意义的what而非只具有指代功能的that。

7. ［答案］increasingly → gradually

［精析］原文想要表达的是"我们已经逐渐意识到"，因此将通常用于修饰形容词的increasingly改为通常用于限定动词的gradually。

8. ［答案］去掉the

［精析］原文想要表达的是"大量地实际应用该语言"，因此去掉多余的定冠词the。

9. ［答案］amount → number

［精析］amount通常与不可数名词连用表示"数量"，因此将其改为number用于表示可数名词fields的数量。

10. ［答案］where → which

［精析］该句是以fields of discourse为先行词的定语从句，由介词in可知，此处应该用关系代词which，而非关系副词where。

【高分演练6】

文章精要

　　文章指出，语言是人类交流的有效工具，但也可能给人与人之间的理解造成障碍，因为人们总是倾向于用一个词来表示多个含义。

答案精析

1. ［答案］Therefore → However

［精析］原文中的"人类语言是交流的极好工具"和"它可能造成误导"之间应该是轻微的转折关系，因此将表因果关系的therefore改为however。

2. ［答案］在a之前加and

［精析］原文想要表达的是"人类语言可能极易让人误解，可能是人与人之间相互

理解的障碍"，因此应该在a之前加上并列连词and，将二者连接为并列的表语。

3. ［答案］for → to
   ［精析］give sth. to sth.意为"将某事物用于某事物"，与原文相符，因此将介词for改为to。

4. ［答案］colour → colours
   ［精析］原文想要表达的是"我们只是在谈论肤色"，而上文提到了白人和有色人种，因此此处的colour要采取复数形式colours。

5. ［答案］little → less
   ［精析］由than可知，原文想要表示比较的概念，因此采用little的比较级less。

6. ［答案］raises → arises
   ［精析］raise通常用作及物动词，意为"提高，升起"，而原文想要表达的是"发生危险"，因此将其改成意为"出现，发生"的不及物动词arise。

7. ［答案］在then之后加that
   ［精析］原文采用的应该是强调句型it is...that...，其中that是不可以省略的，因此在被强调词then之后加上that。

8. ［答案］to → with
   ［精析］动词link常与介词with搭配表示"与……有关"，因此将介词to改为with。

9. ［答案］去掉that
   ［精析］so that意为"以便"，而原文想要表达的是"因此我们在谈论白人或有色人种时倾向于认为……"，故去掉that，直接用so表示"因此"。

10. ［答案］去掉question之前的the
    ［精析］in question为固定搭配，意为"正被考虑或讨论的"，与原文相符，因此去掉多余的定冠词the。

【高分演练7】

文章精要

　　文章指出，文字的起源是一个谜，但可以确定的是，人类发明了特定的声音和文字来表达思想和感情，以便相互交流。文章还指出，由于文字的含义具有多样性，在使用时需小心选择。

答案精析

1. ［答案］thought → thoughts
   ［精析］原文中的thought, feelings, actions和things应该是并列的名词，因此可数名

词thought也应采用复数形式，故将thought改为thoughts。

2. ［答案］calling → called
   ［精析］插入语calling letters修饰的应该是certain signs，其中signs和call之间应该是被动关系，因此将calling改为过去分词形式called。

3. ［答案］在第一个written之后加down
   ［精析］write down为固定搭配，意为"写下"，与原文刚好相符，因此在第一个written之后加上down，表示这些字母不仅代表某些发音，还能被写下来。

4. ［答案］take → bring
   ［精析］bring up为固定搭配，意为"提出；产生"，原文想要表达的是"词汇组合在我们的意识反应过来之前就产生了"，因此将take改为bring。

5. ［答案］better → longer
   ［精析］原文想要表达的是"我们活得越久，就有越多的文字……"，因此将意为"更好"的better改成意为"更久"的longer。

6. ［答案］increase → increases
   ［精析］句子的主语是number，因此将谓语动词increase改为increases。

7. ［答案］for → to
   ［精析］appeal to为固定搭配，意为"吸引"，与原文刚好相符，因此将介词for改为to。

8. ［答案］After → Above
   ［精析］above all为固定搭配，意为"尤其是"，与原文想要表达的"尤其是，真正的诗人是文字方面的大师"相符，因此将after改为above。

9. ［答案］with → to
   ［精析］原文想要表达的是"联想可以将人感动得落泪"，而常用于表示达到某种程度的介词是to，因此将with改为to。

10. ［答案］dully → dull
    ［精析］原文想要表达的是"它们将使我们的话变得愚蠢而又无聊"，其中silly和dully都应该为形容词，因此将副词dully改为形容词dull。

【高分演练8】

文章精要

　　文章指出，许多语言学家认为世界上超过一半的语言已经灭绝，可能再经过两代人，世界上的大部分语言就会消失。有人认为这会促进各民族之间的沟通，但有人认为语言是文化传播的载体，语言的无法延续意味着文化的消失。

答案精析

1. ［答案］在situation之后加that
　　［精析］此处over half of the world's languages are moribund(世界上过半的语言都灭绝了)是situation的同位语从句，同位语从句用that连接，不能省略。

2. ［答案］在effectively前加not
　　［精析］i.e.意为"也就是说"，是对前文的解释，前文提到，许多语言学家认为世界上超过一半的语言已经灭绝，分析文意可知这里说的是"这些语言已不能有效地流传给下一代"，故要加上not。

3. ［答案］第一个in → at
　　［精析］at the point意为"时刻，现在"，其中的at不能用in代替，本句意为"我们和我们的子孙目前正处在人类历史中的……"。

4. ［答案］immediate → immediately
　　［精析］此处的词要修饰形容词life-threatening(威胁生命的)，故要用副词immediately。

5. ［答案］helps → help
　　［精析］由and连接的两个成分的语法形式要保持一致，此处的ease communication和helps build nations由and连接，紧跟前面的助动词will，动词都要用原形，故改为help。

6. ［答案］there → it
　　［精析］此处it作形式主语，it be pointed out...句型意为"有人指出……"，类似于it be said..."据说……"这个句型。

7. ［答案］suit → suited
　　［精析］分析句子结构可知suit for survival in a variety of environments作后置定语修饰前面的cultures，culture和suit构成动宾关系，故应用过去分词形式，将suit改为suited。

8. ［答案］在transmitted前加been

［精析］分析句子结构可知，句子的主语是These cultures，与transmit是动宾关系，故此处应用被动语态，意为"这些文化通过语言被传播到世界各地……"。

9. ［答案］latter → latterly

［精析］latter是形容词，意为"后面的"；而latterly是副词，意为"后来"，此处表达的是"这些文化通过口头传统传播，后来通过书面文字传播"，故用时间副词latterly。

10. ［答案］but → and

［精析］此处that knowledge is lost(语言消失)和humanity is the poorer(人类变得"贫穷")是顺承关系，并非转折关系，故用and。

【高分演练9】

文章精要

文章指出，英语的流行有其外在和内在的原因。外在的原因包括英国殖民者推动了英语的传播、20世纪科学技术的发展和美国的战后重建更加促进了英语的传播；内在的原因是英语本身是杂交语言，它发展更灵活并趋于简单化。

答案精析

1. ［答案］effects → efforts

［精析］effect意为"影响，作用"，effort意为"努力的结果，成就"，此处要表达的是"美国战后的重建工作促进了英语的传播"，是指为重建而做出的努力，故此处应为efforts。

2. ［答案］去掉reinforced前的were

［精析］此处要表达"文化、科学和艺术加强了英语的推广"，reinforce意为"加强"，并没有被动含义，故去掉were。

3. ［答案］high → highly

［精析］此处修饰形容词deliberate"故意的"要用程度副词highly"高度地，非常地"。

4. ［答案］challenged → unchallenged

［精析］此处要表达"现在英语已经毫无异议地成为国际语言"，unchallenged意为"毫无异议的"，challenged意为"受到挑战的，受到质疑的"，故改为unchallenged。

5. ［答案］far → further

［精析］此处要表达"英语内在的一些特点也使英语的传播更进一步"，要用比较级，故改为further。

258

6. ［答案］在allowed后面加it

［精析］此处要表达"这使得英语能快速、灵活、有效地发展"，it指代"英语"，allow sth. to...是固定用法，意为"使……做……"。

7. ［答案］so → and

［精析］分析句子含义可知，It has developed spontaneously与it has intended towards a simplification是承接递进关系，而不是因果关系，故改为and。

8. ［答案］intended → tended

［精析］intend意为"计划，打算"，tend意为"趋向"，常与towards连用，此处要表达"英语发展趋于简单化"，故改为tended。

9. ［答案］Therefore → Meanwhile

［精析］此段继续说明英语通用的另一个原因，与上文不构成因果关系。

10. ［答案］在essential前加an

［精析］此处要表达的是"无论在哪里，都没有人不把英语看作科学、艺术和商业等教育的一部分"，双重否定表达肯定含义，即"无论在哪里，人们都把英语看作科学、艺术和商业等教育的一部分"。表达"……的一部分"用a part of，冠词不可省，essential前用冠词an。

【高分演练10】

文章精要

　　文章指出，男人和女人的说话方式有所不同：男人说话时总是直奔主题，谈论话题经常转换，并且谈话中常常有一个主导人物；而女人总是先建立与说话者的亲密关系，然后再进入主题，在谈话中常涉及她们的个人生活，很少转换话题，并争取让每个人都参与到谈话中。

答案精析

1. ［答案］used → use

［精析］分析句子结构可知that men and women used to communicate(男人和女人用来交流的方式)是定语从句，修饰the styles，此处表示男人和女人对交流方式的主动采用，且文章整体时态为一般现在时，故改为use。

2. ［答案］with → to

［精析］solution to..."……的解决方法"是固定搭配。

3. ［答案］therefore → whereas

［精析］分析上下文语义，前文描述的是男人的说话方式，后文描述的是女人的说

话方式, 二者之间是转折关系, 而不是因果关系, 故用whereas替换therefore。

4. ［**答案**］show → showing

   ［**精析**］分析句子结构可知, 此处show与discussing problems由并列连词and连接, 故show应与discussing形式一致, 同为动名词形式作by的宾语。

5. ［**答案**］在found后加when

   ［**精析**］分析句子结构women talk to each other they reveal a lot about their private lives是found的宾语从句, 此处省略了连词that, 再分析从句可知, women talk to each other在从句中作状语, 故应在found后加when。

6. ［**答案**］去掉stick后的on

   ［**精析**］此处要表达女人谈话时总是坚持一个话题很长时间, stick to意为"坚持", stick on意为"粘在……上", 没有stick on to这种搭配。

7. ［**答案**］merely → rarely

   ［**精析**］前文说到女人在谈话时总是谈论私人生活, 接着用on the other hand转折, 说明男士相比之下则很少谈论个人关系和情感, merely意为"只, 仅仅", 不合文意, 应改为rarely, 意为"很少"。

8. ［**答案**］compete → competed

   ［**精析**］本句意为"男士们往往竞相证明自己更加了解当今的时事……", 本句的整体时态是过去时, 故此处compete也要用过去时。

9. ［**答案**］them → themselves

   ［**精析**］此处要表达的是"男士们往往竞相证明自己对当下时事更加了解……", 应该用反身代词, 故改为themselves。

10. ［**答案**］去掉others前的the

    ［**精析**］此处只是泛指除主导话题的男士外的"其他人", 不定指某一群体中的其他人, 故不用定冠词。

【高分演练11】

（文章精要）

文章分别叙述了非语言交流的三个主要部分: 人际距离学、肢体语言学和副语言。人际距离学研究的是人们在交流时彼此之间所保持的距离; 肢体语言学研究的是人类各种肢体语言的含义; 副语言则指的是人类用于表达情感和思想的一些语音信号, 如语调的高低、声音的大小和语气的轻重等。

1. [答案] 在which前加in
   [精析] 此处是一个定语从句，先行词是a process，此处要表达"在这个过程中，交流者……"，故加上in。

2. [答案] instinctive → instinctively
   [精析] 此处需要修饰动词词组deliver information and express specific meaning，故要用instinctive的副词形式instinctively，意为"本能地"。

3. [答案] 第一个and → or
   [精析] 从后文可以得知Kinesics也就是Body Language，此处是同一件事物的不同说法，应该用or连接。

4. [答案] 去掉certain前的a
   [精析] space意为"空间"，为不可数名词，故去掉冠词a。

5. [答案] fun → funny
   [精析] 本句中不定式短语to see they are in conversation作句子的真正主语，it作形式主语，形容词funny作表语，意为"有趣的"。

6. [答案] 在far后面加away
   [精析] 此处要表达"当他们结束对话的时候，他们已经离他们原来站的位置很远了"，"离……远"用far away from...表示。

7. [答案] that → which
   [精析] 本句为非限制性定语从句修饰先行词Kinesics，that不能引导非限制性定语从句，故用which。

8. [答案] like → as
   [精析] such as为固定搭配，意为"例如"，没有such like的用法，但有suchlike这个词，意为"诸如此类的事物；诸如此类的"。

9. [答案] signs → signals
   [精析] sign意为"记号，符号"，signal意为"信号"，这里应该是sound signals，意为"声音信号"。

10. [答案] Except → Besides
    [精析] besides和except都表示"除……以外"的意思，但besides表示"除……以外（还有）"，包含其后所说的内容，例如：Besides these honors he received a sum of money.（除了荣誉以外，他还得了一笔钱。）；而except表示"除了"，不包括其后所说的内容，例如：We all agreed except him.（我们都同意，只有他不同意。）

【高分演练12】

文章精要

　　文章首先指出，语言变化不可避免地会产生变体，"好的变体"通常被认为或者是有逻辑的，或者是历史悠久的，或者二者兼有，而"坏的变体"通常被认为是没有逻辑的，而且/或者是最近一些庸俗的人发明的。但作者认为逻辑性和历史悠久性都不能用来划分变体的好坏，如ain't，它有逻辑，也经历了长久的历史发展，但还是被学者们鄙视。作者最后指出评估语言变体的"好"、"坏"具有任意性。

答案精析

1. ［答案］在characterized后加by
　　［精析］此处要表达"好的变体通常被认为具有以下特点：或者有逻辑性，或者历史悠久……"，be characterized by为固定搭配，意为"具有……的特点"。

2. ［答案］either → both
　　［精析］此处要表达"好的变体通常被认为具有以下特点：或者有逻辑性，或者历史悠久，或者二者兼有"，either指的是"两者中选其一"，both指的是"两者都有"，故改为both。

3. ［答案］play → plays
　　［精析］neither...nor...结构的谓语形式要使用就近原则，great age作主语，谓语动词要用单数，故将play改为plays。

4. ［答案］去掉despised前的is
　　［精析］分析句子结构，本句是which引导的非限制性定语从句，despised by schoolteachers and pundits在定语从句中作后置定语修饰English word，English word与despise构成动宾关系，故用过去分词作定语，去掉is。

5. ［答案］logical → illogical
　　［精析］根据上下文，此处要表达ain't由am not变化而来，它既有逻辑又经历了很长时间，Far from being illogical or recent...应译为"不是没有逻辑，也不是最近才出现的"，双重否定表肯定，即为"既有逻辑又经历了很长时间"。

6. ［答案］in → into
　　［精析］fall into disrepute为固定搭配，意为"声名狼藉，声誉扫地"，disrepute意为"不光彩，坏名声"。

7. ［答案］sure → surely
　　［精析］sure作副词用时常用于口语中，意为"没问题；确实，的确，没错；不客气，

262

应该的"; 而surely作副词时常用于正式用语, 意为: 想必; 无疑, 必定"。此处应该用surely, 意为"想必没有人会说I'm going, am I not?"。

8. [答案] 去掉part前的the
   [精析] in part为固定搭配, 意为"部分地, 有些, 有几分", 这里in part because...意为"部分原因是……"。

9. [答案] possible → impossible
   [精析] 根据上下文可知此处要表达"母语是英语的人不会说I are going", 故改为impossible。

10. [答案] illustrating → illustrate
    [精析] 在not to...but to... 的结构中, to是不定式标志, 后面要接动词原形, 这里是不定式作表语。

【高分演练13】

文章精要

在本段文章中作者提到他做这次研究的目的是研究1840年到1898年间语言现象的特点, 证明现代汉语词汇是传统词汇基础和19世纪词汇发明的共同结果。作者还指出他的研究主要关注外国作家或中外作家合著的中文著作中汉字的特点。西方语言对汉字的影响可能是间接的, 而日语对汉语则影响较大, 因为汉语和日语在字形上很相似。

答案精析

1. [答案] much → little
   [精析] 此处要表达"虽然中国有古老的词典编纂的传统, 但我们对近代的汉字的词源却了解得很少", although表示的是转折关系, 暗示此处应该用little。

2. [答案] characteristic → characteristics
   [精析] characteristic作可数名词, 意为"特征, 特点", 根据后文出现的lexical events判断此处应该用复数形式。

3. [答案] simple → simply
   [精析] 分析句子结构可知, 此处simple修饰的是be动词is, 修饰动词应用副词, 故改为simply。

4. [答案] 在context前加the
   [精析] in the context of为固定搭配, 意为"在……的情况下, 在……的背景下", 其中the不能省略。

5. ［答案］在react后加to

［精析］根据上下文，此处要表达的是"语言对于外界刺激会产生反应"，react常用作不及物动词，与to搭配，意为"对……产生反应"。

6. ［答案］drew → paid

［精析］此处要表达"我特别关注了……"，表达"某人关注……"，用的是短语pay attention to，它的主语是人；而draw attention to意为"吸引对……的关注"，主语是被关注的事物。

7. ［答案］第一个by → in

［精析］分析句子结构，此处要表达的是"用汉语写的作品"，表达"用某种语言写作"应该用介词in，不用by，如：write in Japanese 用日语写作。

8. ［答案］direct → indirect

［精析］根据后文中的since Chinese has great difficulty absorb phonemic loans（因为汉语很难吸收借用其他语言的发音），可以判断西方语言对汉字的影响应该是间接的，故改为indirect。

9. ［答案］absorb → absorbing

［精析］have difficulty（in）doing sth.为固定用法，意为"在……方面有困难，做某事有困难"。

10. ［答案］Because → Although

［精析］本句话前半句说的是"汉语和日语在字的结构上有所不同"，后半句说的是"在某些程度上，日语和汉语在字形上很相似"，两个分句是在论述不同方面，表述的是转折关系，而不是因果关系，故改为although。

【高分演练14】

文章精要

文章指出因为信息的密度、速度和误解等因素，将来人类语言可能不足以编码信息，这个时候，人类语言将可能被数字语言取代。作者指出，人类语言数字化虽然可以解决密度、速度和误解的问题，但也有很多弊端，如人类的文化遗产消失。但最大的弊端是简化人类语言。

答案精析

1. ［答案］for → to

［精析］suffice意为"使满足，足够……用"，后面要接动词不定式作宾语，此处意

为"如果将来人类语言不足以编码信息……"。suffice for意为"满足……的需要"，后常接名词，故此处应改为to。

2. **［答案］away → way**
   ［精析］make way for为固定搭配，意为"给……让路，为……开路"，此处意为"数字语言将可能取代我们现在使用的语言"。

3. **［答案］去掉mean后的to**
   ［精析］mean to do sth. 意为"打算做某事"，mean doing sth. 意为"意味着，意思是"，此处意为"当然，我的意思不是……"，mean后应接动名词形式，故去掉to。

4. **［答案］在replaced后加by**
   ［精析］此处要表达的是"一旦人类语言被数字化或被数字语言所取代……"，表示"被……取代"的是be replaced by，故replaced后加上by。

5. **［答案］definite → definitely**
   ［精析］分析句子结构可知，此处definite要修饰的是be动词，而修饰动词应用副词，故应改为definitely。

6. **［答案］so → but**
   ［精析］根据上下文，前半分句说的是"这意味着有绝对的密度、速度和清晰度优势"，后半句说的是"我担心我所提到的不利因素将会随之而来"，很明显，两者之间的关系不是因果关系，而是转折关系，故将so改为but。

7. **［答案］that → those**
   ［精析］分析句子结构，此处代词指代上文的disadvantages，故that应改为those。

8. **［答案］Furthermore → Thus**
   ［精析］前文提到"压缩后的语言就意味着丢失了人们无法理解的那部分信息"，后文叙述的是"数字化意味着将人类语言简化为两种模式"，因此前文是后文产生的原因，两者间是因果关系，故将furthermore改为thus。

9. **［答案］Although → If**
   ［精析］此处要表达的是"如果我花两个小时在家看书，我就会失去两个小时与朋友交流的时间"，表述的是条件假设关系，故将although改为if。

10. **［答案］在make后加a或decision → decisions**
    ［精析］make a decision为固定搭配，意为"做决定"，也可以用复数形式make decisions。

社会类

【高分演练15】

文章精要

　　文章指出，在现代社会之中，繁忙的公司管理人员总是忘我地工作，却忽视了适当休息和放松的重要性，并对他们就如何放松提出了建议。

答案精析

1. ［答案］engrossing → engrossed
   ［精析］be engrossed in...为固定搭配，意为"全神贯注于……"，符合文意。

2. ［答案］to → of
   ［精析］原文想要表达的是"有在公司中获得更好的职位或更多的加薪的想法"，因此将介词to改为of。

3. ［答案］big → bigger
   ［精析］原文想要表达的是"获得更好的位置或更多的加薪"，因此将big改为比较级形式bigger与上文的greater构成并列。

4. ［答案］去掉over
   ［精析］exceed为及物动词，因此去掉后面多余的over。

5. ［答案］在run之后加out
   ［精析］run out of为固定搭配，意为"用完，耗尽"，符合原文意思。

6. ［答案］去掉have
   ［精析］devote oneself to sb. / sth.为固定搭配，意为"为某人 / 某事物付出（时间、精力等）"，因此去掉to之后的动词have。

7. ［答案］在even之后加if / though
   ［精析］原文中"放松的关键在于……每天至少花一些时间娱乐"和"只有半个小时"之间应该是转折让步关系，因此应该用意为"即使"的even if或even though来衔接。

8. ［答案］require → requiring
   ［精析］原文想要表达的是 "那些需要与其他人进行大量沟通的工作"，动宾短语require...others应该作jobs的后置定语，因此将require改为现在分词形式requiring。

9. ［答案］在engage之后加them
   ［精析］原文想要表达的是"那些……工作可以让他们（公司管理人员）从事安静、平和的活动"，因此要在engage之后加上宾语them。

266

10. ［答案］client → clients

［精析］由表并列关系的连词and可知，可数名词client应该和之后的associates一样采用复数形式。

【高分演练16】

文章精要

文章指出，网上购物发展迅速，随着信息产业的发展，网上购物吸引了越来越多的人。网上购物尽管存在一些问题，但发展前景广阔。

答案精析

1. ［答案］在never之前加had

［精析］原文想要表达的是"我从未想过这么快就能拿到我的书"，是对过去事实的假设，因此应使用虚拟语气，在never之前加had。

2. ［答案］retailer → retail

［精析］"零售商店"应该用retail store来表示，而非retailer store。

3. ［答案］giving → given

［精析］原文想要表达的是"考虑到众多的人口，在线购物有巨大的市场潜力"，因此应将giving改成意为"考虑到"的介词given。

4. ［答案］necessity → necessities

［精析］necessity在此意为"必需品"，为可数名词，因此应使用复数形式necessities。

5. ［答案］multiple → multiply

［精析］原文想要表达的是"这一数字很可能会增加"，因此将常用作形容词的multiple改为动词multiply。

6. ［答案］去掉up

［精析］mark意为"标记，表明"时，为及物动词，而短语mark up意为"提高价格"，与原文不符，因此去掉up。

7. ［答案］pot → pool

［精析］原文想要表达的是"有限的上网人数"，而pot表示容器，想要表示人的集合体应用名词pool。

8. ［答案］on → for

［精析］通常用介词for引出征收费用的对象，因此此处将on改为for。

9. ［答案］on → in

［精析］invest...in为固定搭配，意为"投资于……"，符合原文意思。

10. ［答案］extend → expand

［精析］extend意为"延伸、伸长或扩展(某物)到较大程度或最大长度"，而原文想要表达的是"拓展在线产品的种类"，因此将extend改成意为"扩大，增加"的expand。

【高分演练17】

文章精要

文章指出，电视和收音机剥夺了人们自我娱乐的机会，但作者还是喜欢自我娱乐的方式。作者认为，卡拉OK现在是唯一一种可以让人们尽情歌唱、自我娱乐的电子产品。

答案精析

1. ［答案］it → they

   ［精析］it指代的是television and radio，因此应将其改为表示复数概念的they。

2. ［答案］去掉hundred之后的of

   ［精析］hundred在表示具体数字时后面应直接接限定的名词，因此去掉多余的of。

3. ［答案］by → with

   ［精析］entertain sb. with sth.为固定搭配，意为"利用某事物娱乐某人"，符合原文意思，因此将介词by改为with。

4. ［答案］在turn之后加on

   ［精析］原文想要表达的是"打开收音机或电视"，因此在turn之后应加上on，用短语turn on来表示"打开"。

5. ［答案］so → and

   ［精析］原文中的"我们在他们五岁左右前给他们读简单的书"和"一旦他们学会自己读书，我们就变成聋子了"之间应该是递进关系，因此将表因果关系的so改为and。

6. ［答案］with → to

   ［精析］be alive to sth.为固定搭配，意为"注意到某事物，对某事物敏感"，与原文意思相符，因此将with改为to。

7. ［答案］number → deal

   ［精析］a number of在表示"许多，大量"时通常用于限定复数可数名词，而singing为不可数名词，因此应将number改为deal，即用a good deal of来限定singing。

8. ［答案］is → was

   ［精析］整句话中其他分句采用的都是一般过去时，因此将此处的is改为was，使该分句的时态统一为一般过去时。

9. ［答案］liberated → liberating

［精析］liberated一般用作定语，表示"解放的，不受传统思想束缚的"，而原文想要表达的是"人们发现卡拉OK很放松"，因此将liberated改为现在分词形式的liberating。

10. ［答案］在Even之后加if / though

［精析］原文中的"他们的声音走调"和"至少它是有意义的自我娱乐"之间应该是转折让步关系，因此在even之后加上if或though来表示"尽管"。

【高分演练18】

文章精要

文章指出，办公室工作受到了电脑应用的严重冲击，许多秘书类工作会因为电脑的应用而消失，但从业者可通过培训和学习重新获得上岗的机会。

答案精析

1. ［答案］在the之前加over

［精析］原文想要表达的是"文字处理人员和打字人员在未来几年将失去九万三千份工作"，因此应该在the next few years之前加上介词over，用来引导时间状语。

2. ［答案］anyone → everyone

［精析］原文想要表达的是"不是每个失去工作的人都会最终失业"，因此此处应将意为"任何人"的anyone改成意为"每个人"的everyone。

3. ［答案］grown → growing

［精析］原文想要表达的是"公司内部增加的职位"，故此处不存在被动关系，因此将grown改为现在分词形式growing作positions的定语。

4. ［答案］在now之后加a

［精析］technician为可数名词，想要表示"她现在是一位通信技术人员"，就要在now之后加上不定冠词a。

5. ［答案］problem → problems

［精析］原文想要表达的是"处理复杂的问题"，其中问题应该不止一个，因此将problem改为复数形式problems。

6. ［答案］demands → demand

［精析］分析句子结构可知，句子的主语应该是all而非one，因此谓语动词demands应为动词原形demand。

269

7. ［答案］less → fewer

　　［精析］less是用于限定不可数名词，因此应将其改为fewer用于限定可数名词jobs。

8. ［答案］在care之后加for

　　［精析］动词短语care for sb.意为"照顾某人"，与原文意思相符。

9. ［答案］means → meaning

　　［精析］原文想要表达的是"工资将会非常低，这意味着电脑的应用会加大贫富差距"，因此将means改为meaning用于引导伴随状语。

10. ［答案］在keep之后加up

　　［精析］keep up with为固定搭配，意为"跟上，同步前进"，与原文意思相符。

【高分演练19】

文章精要

　　文章指出，在美国，老年人数量增长得很快，有一个特殊组织专门了解老年人的问题，它在寻找途径帮助老年人解决问题，并帮助老年人保持年轻的心态。

答案精析

1. ［答案］health → healthy

　　［精析］用于修饰名词citizens的health、busy和productive应该是并列的形容词，因此将名词health改为形容词healthy。

2. ［答案］of → in

　　［精析］原文想要表达的是"五分之一的美国人"，因此将介词of改为in。

3. ［答案］majority → minority

　　［精析］原文想要表达的是"老年人是国家里快速增长的少数人群的成员"，因此将意为"多数"的majority改成意为"少数"的minority。

4. ［答案］在made之后加up

　　［精析］be made up of为固定搭配，意为"由……构成"，与原文想要表达的"该组织由青年公民和老年公民构成"相符，因此在made之后加上up。

5. ［答案］treat → deal

　　［精析］deal with为固定搭配，意为"处理"，与原文意思相符。

6. ［答案］healthy → health

　　［精析］表示"健康问题"应该用名词health，而非形容词healthy。

7. ［答案］在fast之前加so

［精析］固定句型so...that...意为"太……以至于……"，与原文想要表达的"物价上涨非常快，使得老年人无法负担所需食物、衣服和住房的费用"相符，因此在fast之前加上so。

8. ［答案］and → or

［精析］原文想要表达的是"许多老年人由于丈夫或妻子的去世而感到孤单"，因此将表示并列关系的and改为表选择的or。

9. ［答案］at → for

［精析］look for为固定搭配，意为"寻找"，与原文意思相符，因此将at改为for。

10. ［答案］youthfully → young

［精析］stay此处为连系动词，后面可直接接形容词，因此将youthfully改为形容词young，表示"保持年轻"。

【高分演练20】

文章精要

文章指出，现在家庭中男女角色的划分已不再明显，女性的活动场所不再限于家庭，而幸福家庭的打造需要男女双方的共同努力。

答案精析

1. ［答案］in → to

［精析］常与名词extent搭配的是介词to，表示"在某种程度上"，因此将in改为to。

2. ［答案］make → makes

［精析］句子的主语是pattern，句子使用的是一般现在时，因此谓语动词make应该改为makes。

3. ［答案］less → further

［精析］原文想要表达的是"这反过来会导致进一步的分享"，因此将意为"较少"的less改成意为"更进一步的"的further。

4. ［答案］case → cases

［精析］原文想要表达的是"在某些情形下"，因此可数名词case应该采用复数形式cases。

5. ［答案］That → What

［精析］原文想要表达的是"我们需要的是认识到……"，因此将that改为what。

6. ［答案］of → on

［精析］原文想要表达的是"家庭方面的专家"，因此将表示所属关系的of改为on。

7. ［答案］在they之前加that

［精析］psychiatrists...play和they...blame都是signs的同位语从句，而同位语从句中关系词that不可省略，因此在they之前应加上关系词that。

8. ［答案］therefore → however

［精析］原文中的"我们开始分析男性在家庭中的地位"和上文之间应该是轻微转折关系，而非因果关系，因此将therefore改为however。

9. ［答案］up → down

［精析］lay down为固定搭配，意为"制定（规则、原则等）"，与原文意思相符，故将up改为down。

10. ［答案］在work之后加out

［精析］work out为固定搭配，意为"找出处理某事物的方法"，与原文相符，因此在work之后加out。

【高分演练21】

文章精要

文章指出，与男孩相比，女孩不太喜欢使用电脑，女孩大多将电脑当做文字处理的工具，而非解决问题的有效工具。

答案精析

1. ［答案］with → as

［精析］the same...as...为固定搭配，意为"和……一样的……"，与原文意思相符，因此将介词with改为as。

2. ［答案］在major之前加a

［精析］gap为可数名词，因此在原文中应该用不定冠词a加以限定。

3. ［答案］more → less

［精析］原文想要表达的是"和男孩相比，女孩更不习惯使用电脑"，因此将more改为less。

4. ［答案］在which之前加in

［精析］which引导的应该是以ways为先行词的定语从句，而定语从句想要表达的是"以新的方式来了解信息"，因此应该在关系代词which之前加上介词in。

5. [答案] consistent → consistently
[精析] 用于限定谓语动词rate的应该是副词, 因此将形容词consistent改为副词consistently。

6. [答案] 在often之前加less
[精析] 原文想要表达的是"和男孩相比, 她们在教室之外更少利用电脑", 由其中表示比较的than可知, 应该在often之前加上比较级less。

7. [答案] what → that
[精析] 原文想要表达的是"男孩不太担心他们可能做一些会损害电脑的事", 其中what...computer应该是修饰something的定语从句, 因此将what改为关系代词that, 且该关系代词在从句中作主语。

8. [答案] anyhow → somehow
[精析] 原文想要表达的是"女孩担心自己可能不知何故就弄坏了电脑", 因此将意为"总之"的anyhow改成意为"不知何故"的somehow。

9. [答案] after → behind
[精析] fall behind为固定搭配, 意为"落后", 与原文意思相符, 因此将after改为behind。

10. [答案] incredible → incredibly
[精析] 用于修饰形容词boring的应该是副词, 因此将incredible改为副词incredibly。

文化教育类

【高分演练22】

文章精要

　　文章指出, 一家教育中心开设了教授婴幼儿外语的课程。中心负责人指出, 孩子有同时学习几种语言的能力, 而且孩子学习外语最好的时间是从出生到三岁之间。

答案精析

1. [答案] and → but
[精析] 原文中的"它可能看起来像是另一个幼儿游戏组"和"曼哈顿一个独特的教育中心确实在给予婴儿可说的东西"之间应该是转折关系, 因此将表示并列关系的and改为but。

2. [答案] by → with
[精析] 原文想要表达的是"它是一所通过游戏、歌曲教婴幼儿语言的学校", 因此将介词by改为with。

3. ［答案］在place之后加where

［精析］原文想要表达的是"一个婴幼儿变得会说两种语言的地方"，其中babies become bilingual应该是place的定语从句，其关系副词where不可省略，因此在place之后加上where。

4. ［答案］after → before

［精析］原文想要表达的是"几个月大的孩子在他们还不能说英语之前就接触法语和西班牙语"，因此将意为"在……之后"的after改为before。

5. ［答案］talking → talk

［精析］be ready to do sth.为固定搭配，意为"准备做某事"，与原文相符，因此将动词现在分词talking改为动词原形talk。

6. ［答案］say → tell

［精析］原文想要表达的是"分辨……之间的差别"，因此将意为"说"的say改成可表示"分辨"的tell。

7. ［答案］在never之前加has

［精析］由并列连词and可知，前后两个分句应该使用相同的时态，即现在完成时，因此在never之前加上助动词has。

8. ［答案］to → with

［精析］combine...with...为固定搭配，意为"将……与……相结合"，与原文意思相符，因此将to改为with。

9. ［答案］continue → continues

［精析］the learning...at home是make sure的宾语从句，应使用正常时态，因此将continue改为continues。

10. ［答案］including → included

［精析］原文想要表达的是"磁带和书被包含在内"，其中include和tapes and books之间应该是被动关系，因此将including改为过去分词included。

【高分演练23】

文章精要

　　文章指出所有的艺术在本质上是独立的，但它们彼此之间也存在着某种联系。比如我们在谈论一部交响曲时会用到"架构"一词，而建筑又被称作"凝固的音乐"。这些说法大多运用了比喻的修辞手法，关注的是艺术作品对我们的影响；还有一些运用了类比的手法，更关注作品的创作意图和创作工艺。

答案精析

1. [答案] 去掉employ后的with
   [精析] 根据上下文，此处employ意为"使用，采用"，是及物动词，后面直接接宾语，不用加介词。

2. [答案] return → turn
   [精析] in turn为固定搭配，意为"反过来"，符合文意，in return意为"作为回报"，不合文意。

3. [答案] sometime → sometimes
   [精析] 根据上下文，此处要表达"有时我们将一件雕刻品描述为'石头上的诗'"，sometime意为"（在过去或将来）的某个具体时间"，不合文意，故改为sometimes。

4. [答案] traffic → traffics
   [精析] 分析句子结构，traffic是作定语从句中的谓语动词，意为"来来往往"，其先行词是much of the phraseology，故谓语动词traffic应为第三人称单数形式。

5. [答案] pure → purely
   [精析] 根据上下文，此处pure要修饰形容词metaphorical，形容词不能修饰形容词，故改为副词purely。

6. [答案] 在is后面加of
   [精析] 分析句子结构，在indicate的宾语从句中，its effect on us为主语，is为系动词，that impalpable kind为表语，we normally receive from poetry为省略that的定语从句修饰kind。原文意在表达"……是那种难以理解的类型"，应该用"of...kind"来表示，故加上of。

7. [答案] 在useful后加for
   [精析] 根据上下文，此处要表达"这种比喻，虽然对于描述的目的来说很有用，但不能帮助更深层次地理解作品"，此处表达的是"对描述的目的来说有用"，而不是"有用的描述目的"，故在useful后加for。

8. [答案] cannot → can
   [精析] 前文提到，用比喻的方法描述作品不能帮助我们理解作品，但此段以表示转折的on the other hand开头，表明接下来要讲的是"类推的方式可以帮助我们更好地理解艺术品"，help towards this end意为"达到这个目的"，故cannot应改为can。

9. [答案] taking → making
   [精析] 此处意为"我们在做一种客观的论述……"，表示"做论述"用的是make a statement，故改为making。

10. ［答案］governing → governed

［精析］此处governed作form的后置定语，govern与form为动宾关系，故应该用过去分词表被动。

【高分演练24】

文章精要

文章指出跑酷是一种比较难分类的活动，它既不是体育运动也不是极限运动，有些跑酷爱好者说它更接近于武术。因为当面对敌人的时候，可以说话、动手，或者逃跑，而跑酷就是训练逃跑的一种方式。跑酷自身的一个特点是效率。

答案精析

1. ［答案］and → or

［精析］and表示的是并列或顺承关系，而or表示的是选择关系。这里要表达的是"跑酷经常被错误地归类为体育运动类或极限运动类"，应表选择关系，故改为or。

2. ［答案］在parkour后加as

［精析］此处要表达"大多数有经验的跑酷运动者把跑酷看作一种更接近于武术的训练运动"，think of...as意为"把……看作是"，故应加上as。

3. ［答案］going → getting

［精析］根据上下文，此处要表达"跑酷就是要克服道路上的所有障碍……"，go over意为"复习，审查"，而get over意为"克服"，故改为getting。

4. ［答案］emergence → emergency

［精析］根据上下文，此处要表达"……就好像你处在紧急状态中一样"。emergence意为"浮现，出现"，而emergency意为"突发事件，紧急状况"，in an emergency意为"处于紧急状态中"，故改为emergency。

5. ［答案］去掉As后的if

［精析］as if意为"好像"，引导的是方式状语从句，常表示叙述的情况不是事实，此处想表达的是"和武术是训练'打'的一种方式一样，跑酷是训练'逃跑'的一种方式"，表达"和……一样"，应该用as。

6. ［答案］uniquely → unique

［精析］nature是名词，修饰名词要用形容词unique，意为"独特的，独一无二的"。

7. ［答案］effective → efficient

［精析］effective意为"有效的，产生效果的"，efficient意为"效率高的"，前文提到跑酷的一个特点就是效率，由此可知，effective应改为efficient。

8. ［答案］在distinguishes后加it

［精析］此处要表达的是"一个能将跑酷和其他类似的自由跑训练区分开来的特点"，表达"将……和……分开"要用distinguish sth. from sth.，故加上代词it。

9. ［答案］in → on

［精析］place emphasis on为固定搭配，意为"强调，重视"，介词on不能用其他词替换。

10. ［答案］avoid → avoiding

［精析］本句谓语involve意为"包含，牵涉"，它要直接接动名词作宾语，故将avoid改为avoiding。

【高分演练25】

文章精要

文章指出"抓扶手"是一个意向性动作，并给予了具体的场景进行解释。主人和客人已经谈了许久，主人因约会想离开，但出于对客人的礼貌，他还是继续坐在椅子上。把手撑在扶手上是他要离开时的第一个动作，这表明他要准备离开了。

答案精析

1. ［答案］can → must

［精析］根据上下文，短文第一句指出"'抓扶手'是典型的意向性动作"。第二句就来解释这个动作发生的情景"主人和客人已经谈了许久，主人有个约会，必须离开去赴约"，这里要表达主人"必须"去做这件事，而不是能去做，故将can改为must。

2. ［答案］在not后加to

［精析］此处意为"他不愿对客人不礼貌……"one's desire not to do sth.意为"不愿去做……"，not to do sth.是动词不定式的否定形式作定语，故加上to。

3. ［答案］of → about

［精析］此处要表达"如果他不在乎客人的感受，他就会从座位上站起来，说他要离开"，care about意为"对……在意，在乎"，而care of一般和take一起构成take care of，意为"关心，照顾"。

4. ［答案］去掉to

［精析］本句中的get up out of his chair（从椅子上站起来）和announce his departure（说他要离开）由and连接，在形式上要保持一致，根据前文出现的助动词would可知，动词要用原形，故去掉to。

277

5. ［答案］therefore → but

　　［精析］根据上下文，前文说到"他身体表达的是他想走"，后文说的是"他的礼貌让他坐在椅子上"，两者之间不存在因果关系，而是转折关系，故改为but。

6. ［答案］raise → rise

　　［精析］raise为及物动词，意为"使升高，提升；抚养，养育"，其后必须接宾语。而本句中的动词raise后无宾语，所以应改为rise。rise为不及物动词，意为"起身"。

7. ［答案］在as后加if或though

　　［精析］本句意为"他身体向前，抓住椅子的扶手，就好像要把自己支撑起来一样"。而连词as不能表达"仿佛，好像"的意思，故用as if / though。

8. ［答案］make → perform或do

　　［精析］文中要表达的意思是"如果他要走，这是他首先要做出的动作"，表达"做动作"并与act连用的动词只有perform和do，而没有make an act这一表达。

9. ［答案］第二个the → a

　　［精析］定冠词the表特指，不定冠词a / an表泛指。这里是说"如果他不迟疑，动作只会花不到一秒的时间"，是泛指任何一秒，而不是特指某一秒，故second之前用不定冠词。

10. ［答案］post → posture

　　［精析］post意为"柱杆；邮件；职位，岗位"等；posture意为"姿势，举止；态度"。这里是说"他保持着'随时起身'的姿势"，故用posture。

【高分演练26】

文章精要

　　文章指出不同地区有不同的商务礼仪，比如在中东，谈生意时咖啡或茶最多只能喝三杯，在谈话的过程中有人闯入也不被视为不礼貌的行为，然而英国人认为说话时有人闯入是极其不礼貌的。

答案精析

1. ［答案］adhere后加to

　　［精析］adhere只作不及物动词，要与to连用，意为"坚持；遵守；黏附"。

2. ［答案］them → themselves

　　［精析］此处意为"在中东，爱喝咖啡的人要控制住自己"，由于主语和宾语指的是同一群人，故要用反身代词themselves。

3. ［答案］counsel → counsels

［精析］counsel意为"忠告"，是句子的谓语，主语是"Travel Pak"，而且文章通篇用的都是一般现在时，故改为counsels。

4. ［答案］And → But

［精析］根据上下文，前文说到"在商务会面时最多喝三杯咖啡或茶是礼貌的行为"，此处说到"如果主人一直喝，你也要一直喝"，前后文有转折关系，故改为but。

5. ［答案］在should后加not

［精析］根据下文"阿拉伯礼仪提倡'开放的办公室'"，显然此处要表达"当你们在办公室里聊天时有人闯入，你也不要吃惊"，故要加上not。

6. ［答案］去掉interrupt后的into

［精析］interrupt意为"打扰"，为及物动词，不需要介词，故去掉into。

7. ［答案］sensible → sensitive

［精析］根据上下文，此处要表达"商务来访者要对这一点（打扰别人谈话）十分敏感，知道什么时候离开……"，sensible意为"合理的，明智的"，而sensitive意为"敏感的"。

8. ［答案］with → without

［精析］根据上下文，后文提到"在聚会上，日本人认为正式的告别可能会打扰到其他客人"，故此处要表达"他们（日本人）允许不正式的告别就离开"，故改为without。

9. ［答案］remain → remaining

［精析］此处要表达的是"留下来的客人"，现在分词remaining修饰guests。注意此处to为介词，意为"对……"。

10. ［答案］On → In

［精析］In contrast意为"相反"，为固定搭配。

【高分演练27】

文章精要

本文介绍了美国大学教育的基本制度。学生一般须经过四年八个学期的学习，得到足够的学分方可毕业，但是也可能会延长学制；转学也会发生，但是不多。学生所学的每一门课程都有成绩记录在案，如果考试作弊的话，会被学生法庭审判。

1. **[答案]** 去掉attends后的and

   [精析] 此处如果有and，那么就证明gives和attends是并列关系，都是定语从句的谓语。可是这样一来，主句就缺少谓语动词了。根据上下文，此处的gives应该是主句的谓语动词，句意为"……他上的每一门课程都会让他获得一个学分……"。

2. **[答案]** lasts → lasting

   [精析] 如果此处使用lasts，则此句在没有连词的情况下出现了两个谓语动词；显然，此处应当使用lasting，现在分词短语作定语修饰前面的courses。

3. **[答案]** 第一个attend → attending

   [精析] 此从句没有主语，连词为while，可以视为状语从句省略句。当状语从句的主语和主句相同时，如果状语从句中是主动语态则要把谓语动词变为现在分词。本句未省略前应该是while he attend，省略了主语后变成while attending。

4. **[答案]** long → longer

   [精析] 上句提到一般情况下一个学生要上四年共八个学期。此句说"但是也可能会上_____的时间"。很显然是和前一句在进行比较，所以应该用longer而不是long。

5. **[答案]** for → as

   [精析] 此处意为"作为常规"，所以使用介词as。

6. **[答案]** 第二个and → but

   [精析] 此句的前半个分句说所有的这些都增加了工作压力，后半个分句说尽管如此，还是有些学生有时间参加社团活动。显然，两个分句间是转折关系，所以用but。

7. **[答案]** arise → arouse

   [精析] arise是不及物动词，意为"出现"，如problems arise, phenomena arise，而arouse才是及物动词，意为"唤醒，激起"。

8. **[答案]** efficient → effective

   [精析] efficient意为"效率高的"，一般用来指人，如an efficient secretary；而effective意为"产生效果的"，一般用来指物或事，如an effective medicine。

9. **[答案]** 第二个have → has

   [精析] 此句的主语为any student，是单数，主语和谓语动词被定语从句和插入语分隔开了；此句时态为一般现在时，所以谓语动词应该用have的单数第三人称形式。

10. **[答案]** activity → activities

   [精析] a number of意为"许多"，修饰可数名词复数，故后面应该用activities。

【高分演练28】

文章精要

   文章指出，通过看电影就会发现女人的穿着打扮总是受到时尚的影响，而男人却与此相反。女人总是喜欢遵循所谓顶尖设计师制定的时尚法则。

答案精析

1. **[答案]** the → an

   [精析] 原文想要表达的是"每当你看老电影时"，其中老电影(old film)应该是泛指，因此将定冠词the改为不定冠词an。

2. **[答案]** be → being

   [精析] can't help doing sth.为固定用法。

3. **[答案]** nor → or

   [精析] either...or...为固定搭配，意为"不是……就是……"，与原文刚好相符。

4. **[答案]** something → nothing

   [精析] 原文想要表达的是电影中男演员的形象看起来不可笑，没有时尚的痕迹，无法表明他们属于另一个年代，因此应将something改为nothing。

5. **[答案]** changed → changing

   [精析] 原文想要表达的是"变化的时尚"，强调的是处于不断变化的状态，因此将过去分词changed改为现在分词changing。

6. **[答案]** has → have

   [精析] 由句子的主语the great majority of men可知，主语是复数，因此应将谓语部分的has改为have。

7. **[答案]** 去掉them后的to

   [精析] make为使役动词，其后接不带to的不定式，构成make sb. do sth.，因此要去掉宾语them之后的to。

8. **[答案]** so-call → so-called

   [精析] so-called意为"所谓的"，与原文刚好相符。

9. **[答案]** 去掉on

   [精析] lay down the law为固定搭配，意为"发号施令"，因此应去掉多余的介词on。

10. [答案] height → high

[精析] 原文想要表达的是"裙子要短,腰线要高",因此应该将名词height改为形容词high,作表语。

政治经济类

【高分演练29】

文章精要

文章指出,工业革命之后,科学和技术紧密结合,技术的发展不再与科学相脱离,推动了产业的发展。

答案精析

1. [答案] 在gave之后加way

[精析] give way to为固定搭配,意为"让步,让路",与原文刚好相符。

2. [答案] science → scientific

[精析] 修饰名词methods的应该是形容词,因此将science改为scientific,和and之前的scientific相呼应。

3. [答案] evenly → unevenly

[精析] 原文想要表达的是"这种转变开始得很缓慢,进展得不算顺利",因此将evenly(平坦地;平衡地)改为unevenly(不平坦地;不平衡地)。

4. [答案] of → about

[精析] care about为固定搭配,意为"关心",与原文想要表达的"只有少数行业能运用科学技术或关心使用它们"相符,因此将of改为about。

5. [答案] 在it之前加of

[精析] 原文想要表达的是"科学知识的快速发展和公众对科学知识认识的快速提高",其中it指代的就是scientific knowledge,因此应该在it之前加上of,构成短语public awareness of it。

6. [答案] usual → usually

[精析] 修饰形容词uncritical的应该是副词,因此将形容词usual改为副词usually。

7. [答案] 第一个with → to

[精析] 原文想要表达的是"将科学用于产业目的",因此将介词with改为用于引导对象的介词to。

8. ［答案］applying → applied

［精析］原文想要表达的是"应用科学或技术"，因此将applying改为过去分词形式applied。

9. ［答案］在have之后加been

［精析］原文想要表达的是"新的科学领域已经被开放"，其中"领域"（areas）和"开放"（open up）之间应该是被动关系，因此在过去分词opened之前加上been。

10. ［答案］way → ways

［精析］由修饰复数名词的several可知，可数名词way应该采用复数形式ways。

【高分演练30】

(文章精要)

文章指出，数字革命改变了市场营销的方式。数字营销不仅影响了商家的销售模式，也影响了消费者的购物模式。

(答案精析)

1. ［答案］in → to

［精析］原文想要表达的是"数字革命彻底撼动了营销"，固定搭配to one's/the core表示"彻底；直至核心"。

2. ［答案］author → co-author

［精析］原文想要表达的是"在近期的一份论文中，Wharton's Jerry Wind……和合著者Vijay Mahajan……"，因此将意为"作者"的author改成意为"合著者"的co-author。

3. ［答案］examines → examine

［精析］句子的主语是Wharton's Jerry Wind...and...Vijay Mahajan，因此将谓语动词examines改为examine。

4. ［答案］independent → independently

［精析］用作状语的应该是副词，因此将形容词independent改为副词independently，用于限定动词haggle。

5. ［答案］在the之前加what

［精析］原文想要表达的是"简略描述营销的新方法在新世纪之初可能是什么样的"，因此在the之前加上what用以引导宾语从句。

6. ［答案］which → that

［精析］本句应该是强调句型it is...that...，因此将which改为that。

7. ［答案］have → has
［精析］关系代词that指代的是先行词race，因此将助动词have改为has。

8. ［答案］that → which
［精析］如果定语从句的关系代词之前出现了介词，关系代词就只能用which，因此将that改为which。

9. ［答案］在the price之前加to
［精析］原文想要表达的是"从他们购买的产品和服务以及他们寻找的信息，到他们想要支付的价格"，因此在the price之前加to，和前面的from构成短语from...to...。

10. ［答案］open → opening
［精析］with后面不能接句子，只能够成with+n.+doing的结构，因此将状语部分中的open改为现在分词形式opening。

【高分演练31】

文章精要

　　文章指出，世界上规模最大的股票交易市场是纽约证券交易所。文章简要介绍了纽约证券交易所的历史发展及其现状。

答案精析

1. ［答案］在to之前加back
［精析］date back to为固定搭配，意为"追溯到……"，与原文刚好相符，因此在to之前加上back。

2. ［答案］at → on
［精析］表示在证券交易所应该用介词on，由下文也可知，纽约证券交易所之前的介词应该是on。

3. ［答案］public → publicly
［精析］用于限定动词过去分词traded的应该是副词，因此将public改为副词publicly。

4. ［答案］giving → given
［精析］原文想要表达的是"给出一张美国受托收据来代替股票"，其中receipt和give之间应该是被动关系，因此将giving改为过去分词形式given。

5. ［答案］在share之前加a
［精析］share在表示"股份"时为可数名词，因此应该在之前用不定冠词a加以限定。

6. ［答案］amount → amounts

［精析］原文想要表达的是"债券通常以一千美元或更高的价格出售"，因此可数名词amount应采用复数形式amounts。

7. ［答案］在be之前加also

［精析］原文中的"债权可以被再次出售或分割"与上文应该是递进关系，因此在系动词be之前加上意为"也，同样"的also。

8. ［答案］It → They

［精析］it用于指代的应该是上文中的members，因此将其改为复数形式they。

9. ［答案］them → themselves

［精析］原文想要表达的是"为其他投资者或为他们自己……"，因此将them改为反身代词themselves。

10. ［答案］sometime → sometimes

［精析］原文想要表达的是"成员资格有时能卖到超过两百万美元"，因此将sometime改成sometimes。

【高分演练32】

文章精要

文章指出，美国政府的财政年度开始于10月1日，结束于次年9月30日。文章还介绍了其他财政年度的起止时间，以及美国国会批准政府开销的程序。

答案精析

1. ［答案］begin → begins

［精析］句子的主语是institute，因此将谓语动词begin改为begins。

2. ［答案］在add之后加up

［精析］add up为固定搭配，意为"加算，合计"，与原文刚好相符，因此在add之后加上up。

3. ［答案］supposing → supposed

［精析］be supposed to为固定搭配，意为"应该"，因此将supposing改为supposed。

4. ［答案］or → and

［精析］both...and...意为"……和……两者都"，与原文相符，因此将表选择的or改为and。

5. ［答案］第一个for → on

［精析］原文想要表达的是"就他们自己的预算决议投票表决"，vote on意为"就……表决"，而vote for意为"投票赞成"，因此将介词for改为on。

6. ［答案］meet → meets

［精析］原文想要表达的是"然后会议委员会碰面"，该句主语为单数的committee，因此将谓语动词meet改为meets。

7. ［答案］number → amount

［精析］常用来表示钱数的名词是amount，而非number。

8. ［答案］Below → Under

［精析］原文想要表达的是"在委员会之下的是小组委员会"，below一般用于表示位置位于下面、下方，而under可表示抽象概念"从属的"。

9. ［答案］alike → like

［精析］原文想要表达的是"做有关教育和国防领域的决议"，因此将意为"相似的"的alike改成意为"像，如同"的like。

10. ［答案］if → as

［精析］原文想要表达的是"拨款经常和预算决议同时进行"，因此将表示条件的if改为as。

【高分演练33】

文章精要

　　文章指出，自从石油输出国组织决定减少石油供应，原油价格就开始上涨，但由于现在原油成本仅是汽油价格的一小部分，因此原油价格的上涨不会给汽油价格带来很大的影响。

答案精析

1. ［答案］在oil之后加has

［精析］由时间状语从句since...可知，主句应该采取现在完成时，因此在oil之后加上助动词has。

2. ［答案］for → up

［精析］call up为固定搭配，意为"使想起"，与原文刚好相符，因此将for改为up。

3. ［答案］All → Both

［精析］上文只提到两次石油危机，因此应该用意为"两者"的both。

4. ［答案］在the之前加are

　［精析］该句为特殊疑问句，缺少谓语，由句意可知，应在where之后加系动词are，表示"……在哪里"。

5. ［答案］Strengthen → Strengthening

　［精析］动词原形不能作主语，而应该用非谓语动词，由于此处表示泛指的"加强经济增长"，因此将动词原形strengthen改为现在分词strengthening。

6. ［答案］at → in

　［精析］in the short term为固定搭配，意为"在短期之内"，与原文刚好相符，因此将at改为in。

7. ［答案］small → smaller

　［精析］由表示比较关系的than可知，small应改为比较级smaller。

8. ［答案］在to之前加up

　［精析］up to为固定搭配，意为"达到"，与原义相符，因此在to之前加上up。

9. ［答案］as → so

　［精析］原文中的"税款占到零售价格的五分之四"和"即使是价格的大幅变化对汽油价格的影响也没有过去明显"之间应该是因果关系，其中前者为因，后者为果，因此将as改为so。

10. ［答案］more → less

　［精析］原文想要表达的是"富有国家的经济对石油的依赖没有过去那么强烈"，因此将more改为less。

【高分演练34】

文章精要

　　文章指出，企业家是敢于承担风险、开创事业的人。企业家尽管行为方式和性格各有不同，但他们都将改变视为常规，敢于寻求改变，并将其视为机会。

答案精析

1. ［答案］from → into

　［精析］原文想要表达的是"将经济资源从生产力和收益较低的领域转移到生产力和收益较高的领域"，shift...into...意为"将……转移到……"，因此将from改为into。

2. ［答案］simple → simply

　［精析］原文想要表达的是"有些人将企业家简单定义为……"，其中simple修饰的应该是动词define，因此将simple改为副词simply。

3. ［答案］reward → rewards

　　［精析］由表示并列关系的and可知，可数名词reward应该和前面的profits一样用复数形式，即rewards。

4. ［答案］of → in

　　［精析］in business为固定搭配，意为"在做买卖"，与原文刚好相符，因此将of改为in。

5. ［答案］started → start

　　［精析］该句为一般疑问句，因此谓语动词shift和start都应该为原形形式，故将started改为start。

6. ［答案］and → but

　　［精析］原文中的"他的汉堡包不是个新主意"和"他采用了新的技术……"之间应该是转折关系，因此将and改为but。

7. ［答案］applying → applied

　　［精析］applying...应该是resources的后置定语，而resources和apply之间应该是被动关系，因此将applying改为applied。

8. ［答案］similar → different

　　［精析］由下文"很难找到一种特定的性格特点"可知，企业家表现出的行为方式应该是不同的，而不是相似的，故将similar改为different。

9. ［答案］At → On

　　［精析］on the other hand为固定搭配，意为"另一方面"，与原文刚好相符。

10. ［答案］在as之后加an

　　［精析］原文想要表达的是"将它视为一个机会"，因此在可数名词opportunity之前加上不定冠词an加以限定。

【高分演练35】

（文章精要）

　　文章简单探讨了Thomas Jefferson总统执政时期的美国历史。文章指出，美国的独立革命意义非常重大。18世纪末，欧洲已经开始觉醒，但是只有在北美洲这块土地上，民族革命才取得了胜利，一个新的国家脱离了英国的殖民统治诞生了。

（答案精析）

1. ［答案］cover → covering

　　［精析］如果使用动词原形cover，则that引导的结果状语从句内部在没有任何连词

的情况下出现了两个谓语动词is和cover（to attempt和to represent是非谓语动词），句子结构混乱。因此cover应使用非谓语动词形式，由于cover和它的逻辑主语events是主动关系，所以使用其现在分词covering。

2. [答案] and → or
   [精析] 此处intellectual 和social之间是选择关系，而非并列关系，否则前面就不会使用one了，所以用or。

3. [答案] culminates → culminated
   [精析] 这里讲的是Thomas Jefferson的时代，应该使用一般过去时，culminate意为"达到高潮，达到顶点"。

4. [答案] 在nationalism前加of
   [精析] not only...but also...并列的两个成分应该是对等的。not only 后是of the birth of a new way of life，那么but also后就应该是of nationalism as a new way of life。

5. [答案] in → at
   [精析] at the end of，意为"在……末"，没有in the end of这种说法。

6. [答案] 在to前加had
   [精析] 句子的主语是the march of history，指过去的事情，谓语部分应该使用"should have done"的形式，表示应该做却没有做某事。此处句意为"奇怪的是，历史征程应该早就越过大西洋，但是只有在北美的殖民地民族解放运动才最终导致了新国家的建立"。

7. [答案] 在colonies后加did
   [精析] 句首为only开头的介词短语作状语，那么句子应该部分倒装，就是在主语之前加上助动词，而实义动词的原形依然放在主语之后。

8. [答案] for → against
   [精析] 此处指"反对残暴的政府"，而非支持，所以应该使用介词against。

9. [答案] free → freer
   [精析] 根据上下文，constitution(宪法，国体)在反抗中有可能变得比以前更自由一些，而不可能是变得"自由"，因为只要是国家，就不会出现所谓的free constitution。此处应该使用freer，与前半句的tyrannical作对比。

10. [答案] 第一个in → for
    [精析] 表达"第一次"用for the first time，介词不可替换成in。

科普类

文章精要

　　文章指出，液态水是生物界第二大要素。文章具体介绍了液态水存在的温度范围、水的来源，以及水资源在地球上的分布。

答案精析

1. ［答案］在let之后加alone

　　［精析］let alone是固定搭配，意为"更不用说"，与原文想要表达的"与其他星球的低温和地球内部的高温相比，这只是一个很小的温度范围，更不用说和太阳的温度相比了"意思相符，因此在let后加alone。

2. ［答案］face → surface

　　［精析］原文想要表达的是"在星球的表面"，因此把face改成意为"表面"的surface。

3. ［答案］had → having或在had之前加that / which

　　［精析］分析句子结构可知，had temperatures...是用于修饰限定之前的planet的，因此应将had改成现在分词形式having作后置定语，或在had之前加that或which引导定语从句。

4. ［答案］去掉quite或fairly

　　［精析］quite和fairly都是副词，且均意为"很，非常"，二者同时出现表意重复，因此要删除其中一个。

5. ［答案］out → outer

　　［精析］out是副词，不能修饰名词space，而原文想要表达的是"太空，外层空间"，因此将out改为形容词outer，且outer space为固定搭配。

6. ［答案］去掉away

　　［精析］原文想要表达的是"它们可能会被从地球深处冒出来的新水所代替"，因此应删去away，用rise from表示"从……升上来"。

7. ［答案］and → but

　　［精析］原文"总水量还不知道"和"它足以覆盖整个地球表面"之间是转折关系，因此把表并列的and改为but。

8. ［答案］quarter → quarters

　　［精析］quarter为可数名词，当分子大于一时，分母就应该用复数形式，故此处用quarters。

9. ［答案］when → unless

［精析］原文想要表达的是"有四分之三的淡水以冰的形式存在于两极和山上，如果不被融化就不能被生物系统所利用"，因此应把when改成意为"除非"的unless。

10. ［答案］fewer → less

［精析］句中的fraction指代的是上文提到的fresh water，为不可数名词，而few不能用于修饰不可数名词，因此将fewer改成less。

【高分演练37】

文章精要

文章指出，维生素是化学物质，如果服用过量会对人体有害，但大多数维生素的理想摄入量还有待进一步确认。

答案精析

1. ［答案］not → no

［精析］用于否定名词difference的应该是形容词no，而非副词not。

2. ［答案］in → between

［精析］原文想要表达的是"天然维生素C的化学结构和人造维生素C的化学结构完全没有差别"，因此应将in改为between，与difference构成固定搭配difference between A and B，表示"A和B之间的差别"。

3. ［答案］nature → natural

［精析］用于修饰名词vitamin的应该是形容词，因此将名词nature改为形容词natural。

4. ［答案］substance → substances

［精析］substance为可数名词，结合之前的most substances和all可知，此处应用复数形式substances。

5. ［答案］在it前加so

［精析］原文的"个体对营养的需求相差很大"和"不能确切地说某个假定的量过多"之间应该是因果关系，因此应该用so连接。

6. ［答案］in → to

［精析］用于连接对象healthy individuals的介词应该是to，而非in。

7. ［答案］去掉account之前的the

［精析］take...into account为固定搭配，意为"把……考虑在内"。

8. ［答案］amounts → amount
   ［精析］amount在表示"数量"时通常为不可数名词，因此将amounts改为amount。

9. ［答案］去掉that
   ［精析］分析句子结构可知，know的宾语从句由what引导，very specifically在句中作状语修饰know，所以that在句中是多余的，因此去掉that。

10. ［答案］vitamin → vitamins
    ［精析］water-soluble vitamin（水溶性维生素）指代的是后面的the C and the B groups（维生素C和维生素B族），因此vitamin应采用复数形式vitamins。

【高分演练38】

文章精要

　　文章指出，应该特别注意房间的通风，这样有益于人体健康。目前已经开发出为房间通风的设备，创造对人体有益的环境。

答案精析

1. ［答案］在much之前加as
   ［精析］原文想要表达的是"我们应该尽可能住在那里"，因此应该在much之前加上as，用as much as possible来表示"尽可能"的含义。

2. ［答案］indoor → indoors
   ［精析］indoor为形容词，不能用于修饰动词done，因此应将其改为副词indoors。

3. ［答案］breath → breathe
   ［精析］名词breath无法充当谓语，因此要将其改为动词breathe。

4. ［答案］necessity → necessities
   ［精析］原文想要表达的是"首要条件之一"，因此意为"必需品，必要性"的necessity应采用复数形式。

5. ［答案］up → upper
   ［精析］原文想要表达的是"让上部暖和的空气出去"，其中"上部"指的是空气处于上部，因此将意为"向上的"的up改成意为"上部的"的upper。

6. ［答案］去掉in
   ［精析］admit本身意为"准许……进入"，可用于表示让新鲜的空气进入房间，因此应去掉表意重复的in。

7. ［答案］out-of-the-doors → out-of-doors

［精析］并没有out-of-the-doors这个复合词，而out-of-doors为合成副词，意为"户外地"，与原文刚好相符。

8. ［答案］equipments → equipment

［精析］equipment通常用作不可数名词，因此将equipments改为equipment。

9. ［答案］off改为of

［精析］原文想要表达的是"清除空气中的灰尘"，因此应将off改为of，构成短语clean...of...。

10. ［答案］去掉第二个the

［精析］原文想要表达的是"让空气流动"，而搭配keep...in motion即意为"让……运动"，与原文相符，因此去掉第二个the。

【高分演练39】

文章精要

文章指出，恐惧和痛苦如果被合理利用，就是人类和动物所拥有的最有用的东西，但需要注意的是，不能被恐惧感控制，而是要让恐惧和痛苦为你自己服务。

答案精析

1. ［答案］thing → things

［精析］原文想要表达的是"最有用的事物之中的两个"，因此可数名词thing要用复数形式things。

2. ［答案］burn → burnt

［精析］原文想要表达的是"如果火在燃烧时没有造成伤害"，其中时间状语从句中的burn应该和主句中的did一样采用一般过去时的形式，故将burn改为burnt。

3. ［答案］在away之后加from

［精析］keep away from为固定搭配，意为"远离（某事物）"，与原文相符，因此在away之后加上介词from。

4. ［答案］so → because

［精析］原文中的"真正无畏的士兵不是好士兵"和"他很快就被杀死了"之间应该是因果关系，其中前者是果，后者是因，因此将引导结果的so改为引导原因的because。

5. ［答案］with → without

［精析］原文想要表达的是"因此恐惧和痛苦是两个守卫，没有这两个守卫，人和动物可能很快就会灭绝"，因此应将with改成without。

6. ［答案］在because之后加of

［精析］because之后应该为完整的句子，而原文中是名词短语the danger of...，因此应该在because之后加上of，用于引导名词短语。

7. ［答案］absolute → absolutely

［精析］用于修饰形容词safe的应该是副词，因此将absolute改为副词absolutely。

8. ［答案］later → latter

［精析］原文想要表达的是"后者落到你身上"，因此将意为"晚的"的later改成具有指代功能的表示"后者"的latter。

9. ［答案］在not之后加to

［精析］此处作表语的应该是动词不定式，和下文中的动词不定式to use... 相对应，因此在not之后加上不定式的标志词to。

10. ［答案］make → take

［精析］与名词action相搭配的通常是动词take，因此将make改为take。

【高分演练40】

（文章精要）

　　文章指出，所有食物都是由化学物质构成的，因此会在烹饪时以及被人体吸收时发生化学反应。此外清洁用品也会发生化学反应。

（答案精析）

1. ［答案］cooking → cooked

［精析］foods和cook之间是被动关系，因此要采用过去分词形式cooked和之后的digested构成并列。

2. ［答案］it → them

［精析］原文想要表达的是"烹饪肉和蔬菜会发生化学反应，使它们变得更加美味"，其中it指代的应该是meat and vegetables，因此将it改为them。

3. ［答案］sugars → sugar

［精析］sugar意为"糖"时通常为不可数名词，因此将sugars改为sugar。

4. ［答案］去掉for

［精析］require为及物动词，意为"需要"，因此去掉多余的介词for。

5. ［答案］在as之前加such

［精析］原文中cooking oils...etc.是对cooking products and food additives的举例说明，

因此在as之前加上such，用such as来表示"例如"。

6. ［答案］before → after
   ［精析］原文想要表达的是"每一个都是经过认真研究之后才被精心准备好的"，因此将before改为after。

7. ［答案］cookers → cooks
   ［精析］cooker意为"炉具"，而原文想要表达的是"接受过训练的厨师"，因此将cookers改成意为"厨师"的cooks。

8. ［答案］chemistry → chemical
   ［精析］用于修饰名词nature的应该是形容词，因此将名词chemistry改为形容词chemical。

9. ［答案］achieving → achieved
   ［精析］changes和achieve之间应该是被动关系，因此将achieving改为过去分词形式achieved，作changes的后置定语。

10. ［答案］home → house
    ［精析］home一般表示抽象意义上的"家"，而原文想要表达的是"家里使用的清洁用品"，因此将其改为具体表示"家，房屋"的house。